The EU and the Proliferation of Integration Principles under the Lisbon Treaty

The entry into force of the Lisbon Treaty has brought about a proliferation of "integration principles". In addition to the environmental integration principle, which has been part of the EU legal framework for some time, the Lisbon Treaty introduced the principles of gender equality integration, social policy integration, non-discrimination integration, consumer protection integration as well as animal welfare integration. Furthermore, a general principle of integration policy objectives is contained in Article 7 TFEU, requiring that the Union must ensure consistency between its policies and activities, taking all relevant policy requirements listed under the TFEU into account in the adoption of any legislative measure. These integration principles must be pursued, or at least taken into account, when decisions are being taken in almost any area of EU policy-making. However, there is considerable uncertainty regarding the normative implications of the various integration principles as well as their legal value and practical relevance for EU policymaking.

This book addresses the implications of the proliferation of sectorial integration principles and the introduction of a universal requirement of policy consistency in terms of the division of competences between the Union and the Member States as well as the scope for judicial review of the EU legislative process. In particular, it explores whether the introduction of various integration principles has led to an extension of Union competences and whether it has limited the scope for judicial review by extending the discretionary power of the Union institutions.

Francesca Ippolito is Associate Professor of EU law at the University of Cagliari.

Maria Eugenia Bartoloni is Associate Professor of EU law at the University of Naples Vanvitelli.

Massimo Condinanzi is full Professor of EU law at the University of Milan Statale.

Routledge Research in EU Law

Available titles in this series include:

The Early Warning System for the Principle of Subsidiarity
Constitutional Theory and Empirical Reality
Philipp Kiiver

The European Constitution, Welfare States and Democracy
The Four Freedoms vs. National Administrative Discretion
Christoffer C. Eriksen

New Governance and the European Strategy for Employment
Samantha Velluti

Human Rights and Minority Rights in the European Union
Kirsten Shoraka

Centralized Enforcement, Legitimacy and Good Governance in the EU
Melanie Smith

EU External Relations and Systems of Governance
The CFSP, Euro-Mediterranean Partnership and migration
Paul James Cardwell

The EU Social Market Economy and the Law
Theoretical Perspectives and Practical Challenges for the EU
Delia Ferri and Fulvio Cortese

Gender and the Court of Justice of the EU
Jessica Guth and Sanna Elfving

The EU and the Proliferation of Integration Principles under the Lisbon Treaty
Francesca Ippolito, Maria Eugenia Bartoloni, Massimo Condinanzi

https://www.routledge.com/Routledge-Research-in-EU-Law/book-series/ROUTEULAW

The EU and the Proliferation of Integration Principles under the Lisbon Treaty

Edited by
Francesca Ippolito,
Maria Eugenia Bartoloni and
Massimo Condinanzi

Routledge
Taylor & Francis Group
LONDON AND NEW YORK

First published 2019
by Routledge
2 Park Square, Milton Park, Abingdon, Oxon OX14 4RN

and by Routledge
52 Vanderbilt Avenue, New York, NY 10017

First issued in paperback 2020

Routledge is an imprint of the Taylor & Francis Group, an informa business

British Library Cataloguing in Publication Data
A catalogue record for this book is available from the British Library

Library of Congress Cataloging in Publication Data
Names: Ippolito, Francesca, editor. | Bartoloni, Maria Eugenia, editor. | Condinanzi, Massimo, editor.
Title: The Proliferation of Integration Principles Under the Lisbon Treaty / edited by Francesca Ippolito, Maria Eugenia Bartoloni, Massimo Condinanzi.
Description: Abingdon, Oxon [UK] ; New York , NY : Routledge, 2018. | Series: Routledge research in EU law | Includes bibliographical references.
Identifiers: LCCN 2018026490 | ISBN 9780415789257 (hbk)
Subjects: LCSH: Treaty on European Union (1992 February 7). Protocols, etc. (2007 December 13) | European Union countries--Economic integration. | Civil rights--European Union countries. | Trade regulation--European Union countries. | Antitrust law--European Union countries.
Classification: LCC KJE4443.32007 .P76 2018 | DDC 341.242/2--dc23
LC record available at https://lccn.loc.gov/2018026490

ISBN 13: 978-0-36-758510-5 (pbk)
ISBN 13: 978-0-415-78925-7 (hbk)

Typeset in Galliard
by Taylor & Francis Books

Contents

List of contributors vi

1 Introduction: integration clauses – a prologue 1
FRANCESCA IPPOLITO, MARIA EUGENIA BARTOLONI AND MASSIMO CONDINANZI

2 Fundamental rights mainstreaming in the EU 14
VASILIKI KOSTA

3 The principle of gender mainstreaming: possibilities and challenges 45
EUGENIA CARACCIOLO DI TORELLA

4 Mainstreaming equality in the EU legal order: more than a Cinderella provision? 55
FRANCESCA IPPOLITO

5 The horizontal social clause in a legal dimension 83
MARIA EUGENIA BARTOLONI

6 The environmental integration principle: a necessary step towards policy coherence for sustainability 105
BEATE SJÅFJELL

7 On the current meaning and potential effects of the horizontal consumer clause of Article 12 of the TFEU 123
FRANCESCO SEATZU

8 Animal welfare 136
JULINDA BEQIRAJ

9 Deconstructing and reconstructing Article 7 TFEU 160
NIAMH NIC SHUIBHNE

10 Conclusions: integration clauses – a comparative epilogue 181
BRUNO DE WITTE

Index 189

Contributors

Julinda Beqiraj is senior research associate at the British Institute of International and Comparative Law, and lecturer and post-doc fellow at the Legal Sciences Department of the University of Trento (Italy). She is also teaching assistant in EU Law and International Organizations at the Free University of Bolzano, Italy. She holds a PhD from the School of European and International Studies (Trento).

Eugenia Caracciolo di Torella is currently associate professor of EU law and lecturer at the University of Leicester after being a Lecturer in Law at the University of Sussex (1998–2000), and completed her PhD (2000) at the University of Durham. Eugenia's main interest is the impact of the principle of gender equality on various aspects of law and policy at both domestic and EU level, where she publishes extensively.

Vasiliki Kosta is Assistant Professor at the Leiden School of Law. She studied law at King's College London, obtaining the LLB in 2006 and the LLM in European Law with 'Distinction' in 2007. Subsequently she pursued her PhD research at the European University Institute in Florence on 'Fundamental Rights in Internal Market Legislation'. From 2009–2011 she also worked as a research associate at the Academy of European Law, EUI Florence. In 2011 Kosta was a 'stagiaire' at the Court of Justice of the EU and she completed a traineeship at the EU Agency for Fundamental Rights in 2011/2012.

Niamh Nic Shuibhne is Professor of European Union Law at the School of Law, University of Edinburgh and Visiting Professor at the College of Europe (Bruges), where she teaches a course on EU citizenship law. She was Joint Editor of the European Law Review from 2009–2014, and remains a member of its Editorial Board. She acted as Joint General Rapporteur on 'Union Citizenship: Development, Impact and Challenges' at the FIDE Congress, May 2014 (with J. Shaw). She has published widely on the free movement of persons and the legal regulation of EU citizenship.

Francesco Seatzu is full Professor of International Law at the School of Law of the University of Cagliari. He completed his studies for a PhD at the University of Nottingham and was Visiting Scholar at Universitad Complutense de Madrid

(2001), at the University of Nottingham (2003), Visiting Fellow at the University of Glasgow (2006) and Visiting Professor of International Human Rights Law, Université de Bordeaux IV (2010). Professor Francesco Seatzu has been a Member of the Doctoral School of International and EU Law since 2007, the CIDOIE (CentroInteruniversitario sul Diritto delle Organizzazioni Internazionali Economiche), the Italian Society of International Law and the British Institute of International and Comparative Law. He has also been a member of the Board of Editors of the Journal of Private International Law and Revista Mexicana de derecho internacional privado y comparado.

Beate Sjåfjell is Professor Dr. Juris at the University of Oslo, Faculty of Law, Department of Private Law. She is the head of the Sustainable Companies project, and head of the Company Law Research Group and the European Law Network at the Faculty of Law in Oslo. Beate has published extensively on EU company and securities law and the integration of sustainable development.

Bruno De Witte is currently Professor of European Law and co-director of the Ceneter of EU law at Maastricht University (The Netherlands), and Part-time Professor of Law at the European University Institute, Florence. He is a member of the Board of Editors of the European Human Rights Law Review, the Revista Española de Derecho Europeo and the Revista de Llengua i Dret; and Member of the Advisory Board of the European Constitutional Law Review, the Maastricht Journal of European and Comparative Law, and the Zeitschrift für öffentliches Recht.

1 Introduction

Integration clauses – a prologue

Francesca Ippolito, Maria Eugenia Bartoloni and Massimo Condinanzi

Background of the book

The entry into force of the Lisbon Treaty has brought about a proliferation of 'integration principles',[1] realising the insertion of the 'provisions having general application' articulated in Articles 7–13 TFEU an expansion of the original policy integration instructions to be pursued, or at least taken into account, when decisions are being taken in almost any area of EU policy-making. In other words, should one assume that 'integration principles' are those principles that are 'overarching' and their purpose is to 'harmonize' or 'streamline' the EU's own actions in such a way that certain central values or objectives of the Union can be reached more effectively.

Balancing clauses were originally provided at the level of EU primary law regarding environmental protection,[2] consumer protection requirements[3] and gender equality.[4] Also a separate set of principles with distinct Treaty origins concerning: a '*universal* requirement of policy consistency' emerged first in the Single European Act and then in the Maastricht Treaty; the consideration that the Union pursue a range of different objectives at once; and the limit to any of its actions represented by the powers States conferred upon it by this Treaty and its objectives.[5] These latter principles have been collected together in current Article 7 TFEU stating that '[t]he Union shall ensure consistency between its policies and activities, taking all of its objectives into account and in accordance

1 The expression was used as to environmental clause in Article 11 TFEU by Jan Jans, 'Stop the integration principle?' (2011) 33 *Fordham International Law Journal* 1533, 1543, referring to Case C-341/95 *Bettati* EU:C:1998:353.
2 Article 130r(2) EEC (Single European Act), rephrased as 'must be integrated into the definition and implementation of other Community policies' at Maastricht and relocated to Article 6 EC of the Treaty at Amsterdam, and later Article 3c.
3 Article 129a of the Amsterdam Treaty provided that 'consumer protection requirements shall be taken into account in defining and implementing other Community policies and activities'.
4 Article 3(2) EC provided that 'the Community shall aim to eliminate inequalities, and to promote equality, between men and women' in the carrying out of the activities listed in Article 3(1).
5 Article 3b EC Treaty (Maastricht).

with the principle of conferral of powers'. It is so required that the Union must ensure consistency between its policies and activities, taking all relevant policy requirements listed under the TFEU into account in the adoption of any legislative measure.

Article 8 TFEU providing that '[i]n all its activities, the Union shall aim to eliminate inequalities, and to promote equality, between men and women' reworks the gender equality integration principle which dates back to the 1990s. There the innovative dimension of gender mainstreaming appeared as an 'innovative feature' of the 1991 Third Action Program on Equal Opportunities[6] with a following established structure for its implementation in a global strategy through the Platform for Action at the United Nations Fourth World Conference on Women in Beijing in September 1995. Then the European Commission that had actively participated at the preparation of the Conference accepted and endorsed the concept[7]; as well, in 1996 it expressly provided for the mobilisation of all Community policies for the purpose of promoting gender equality[8] and in 1997 gender mainstreaming was finally embedded in the Treaty of Amsterdam.

Article 11 TFEU sets out that environmental protection requirements *must be integrated* into the definition and implementation of the Union policies and activities, in particular with a view to promoting *sustainable development.* [9] But it dates back to the Declaration of the Council of European Communities and of the Representatives of the Governments of the Member States meeting in the Council of 22 November 1973 on the program of action of the European Communities on the environment, which first, as highlighted by Jans, integrated environmental protection requirements into economic development.[10] On another note, since

6 Commission of the European Communities, *Equal Opportunities for Women and Men: the Third Medium-Term Community Action Programme 1991–1995*, COM(90) 449.

7 European Commission, Beijing + 5: An Overview of the European Union Follow-up and Preparations, Brussels: Directorate General for Employment and Social Affairs.

8 Communication from the Commission of 21 February 1996 'Incorporating equal opportunities for women and men into all Community policies and activities' COM(96) 67 final available at http://eur-lex.europa.eu/legal-content/EN/TXT/HTML/?uri=LEGISSUM:c10921&from=EN.

9 Emphasis added. The Treaty on the functioning of the European Union, last amended by the Treaty of Lisbon, [2008] OJ C115 (consolidated version), abbreviated TFEU. See J. Nowaq, 'The Sky is the Limit: On the Drafting of Article 11 TFEU's integration obligations and its intended reach', in B. Sjåfjell, A. Wiesbrock (eds), *The Greening of European Business under EU Law: Taking Article 11 TFEU Seriously* (Routledge 2015), Ch. 2, gives an introduction to the enhancement of the environmental integration rule over time and also sets out the Member States' clear intention with the rule.

10 The Declaration stated '[w]hereas in particular, in accordance with Article 2 of the Treaty, the task of the European Economic Community is to promote throughout the Community a harmonious development of economic activities and a continuous and balanced expansion, which cannot be imagined in the absence of an effective campaign to combat pollution and nuisances or of an improvement in the quality of life and the protection of the environment.' See for further specification and analysis of the roots of environmental integration within the EU legal order Jan Jans, (n 1) 1534–1540.

Advocate General Slynn's famous opinion in the so-called 'Danish Bottles' case,[11] a judicial route for the integration of environmental considerations into the market freedoms of the European Community (later the European Union) had been enabled and facilitated.

Moving to Article 12 of the TFEU, it requires EU organs and institutions, since the date of the entry into force of the Lisbon Treaty (December 2009), to ensure that in all their activities and acts, namely the definition and implementation of any EU policies and other decision-making processes, certain consumer rights and general principles are embodied. Notwithstanding the fact that nine years ago some potential was recognised in this TFEU Article, looking retrospectively at the post-Lisbon EU Commission's official documents, EU developments and judgments of the EU Court of Justice (CJEU), it is evident that the horizontal consumer clause (HCC) in Article 12 has not transformed the European Union's approach to consumer protection and policy.

Complementary to these 'already consolidated' integration principles Article 9 TFEU and the principle of social policy integration, Article 10 TFEU on the non-discrimination integration, and Article 13 on the animal welfare integration represent an important addendum: the 'constitutionalisation' of mainstreaming duties as to these matters for the EU institutional framework. An expansion that has generated since the beginning at the level of academic writers is the quest for the need of stopping such integration principles in light of the consequent de-potentiating 'minestrone effect', at least on the most advanced and imperative integration principle, that is the environmental one.[12]

Article 9 provides that 'in defining and implementing its policies and activities, the Union *shall take into account* requirements linked to the promotion of a high level of employment, the guarantee of adequate social protection, the fight against social exclusion, and a high level of education, training and protection of human health'. According to Article 10 TFEU '[i]n defining and implementing its policies and activities, the Union *shall aim to combat* discrimination based on sex, racial or ethnic origin, religion or belief, disability, age or sexual orientation'; while Article 13 TFEU recognizes that animals are sentient beings and affirms that the Union and the Member States *shall pay full regard* to the welfare requirements of animals '*in formulating and implementing* the Union's agriculture, fisheries, transport, internal market, research and technological development and space policies'. However, this should be pursued while respecting the legislative or administrative provisions and customs of the Member States relating to, in particular, religious rites, cultural traditions and regional heritage.

11 Opinion of Advocate General Slynn, Case 302/86 *Commission v Denmark* [1988] ECR 4619. In that case the Court held that a system requiring manufacturers and importers to market beer and soft drinks only in reusable containers (which had to be approved by a National Agency for the Protection of the Environment) was subject to what is now article 34 of the Treaty on the Functioning of the European Union ('TFEU') since the Lisbon Treaty entered into force.

12 J. Jans (n 1).

A constitutionalisation of the 'harmonisation' of the EU's own actions in such a way that certain central values or objectives of the Union can be reached more effectively as a cross-cutting objective to be woven into all areas of law and policy[13] does not mean that a de facto institutionalised practice of the same principles was in place before the Lisbon Treaty. Concerns about animals' well-being were occasionally addressed under a number of explicit treaty objectives, such as the common agriculture policy (CAP), the internal market, and the common commercial policy. Article 9 TFEU catches up on Article 127(2) Treaty of Nice ('high level of employment'), and goes back to the European Convention's working group XI ('Social Europe') whose members discussed horizontal clauses on social values as well as on topics like social cohesion. Furthermore, Article 9 TFEU has to be considered in conjunction with the model of the 'social market economy' enshrined in Article 3(3) TEU. It is clear from the preparatory document for the European Constitutional Treaty that the aim of inserting the social market economy provision was to maintain the existing system of protection associated with the European social model throughout Member States. As such, it is suggested that the Court of Justice should continue in its tradition of giving a broad, Union-based interpretation of Treaty provisions. Such an approach would be consistent with the constitutional heritage of most of the Member States. It would also be consistent with the aim of promoting social justice which, as a result of the Lisbon Treaty, has now been added as a task of the Union under Article 2(3) TEU. Article 10 TFEU limits to extend mainstreaming principles across the equality spectrum that originally were confined to gender equality mainstreaming,[14] introducing it in EU primary law from a soft law engagement since 1996 when the Commission called for a disability non-discrimination mainstreaming,[15] subsequently reinforced in 2003 with the *European Year of People with Disabilities* [16]; and then with the Action Plan 2004–2010 that called for the 'reinforcement of the mainstreaming of the disability perspective into all relevant policies at the stages of policy formulation,

13 C. McCrudden, 'Equality' in C.J. Harvey, *Human Rights, Equality and Democratic Renewal in Northern Ireland* (Hart Publishing 2001) 75 indicates how this requires 'the principle that equality be seen as an integral part of all public policy-making and implementation, rather than something separated off in a policy or institutional ghetto'; and the Council of Europe 'Gender Mainstreaming: Conceptual Framework, Methodology and Presentation of Good Practices, Final Report of Activities of the Group of Specialists on Mainstreaming' EG-S-MS (98), (Strasbourg: Council of Europe 1998 May) indicates it in terms of 'the incorporation of a concern with achieving equality in all public sector policies at all levels and at all stages in policy making'.

14 On the principle of gender mainstreaming see E. Caracciolo di Torella, 'The Principle of Gender Mainstreaming: Possibilities and Challenges', in this Volume.

15 European Commission, Equality of Opportunity for People with Disabilities, A New European Community Disability Strategy, COM(1996) 406 final (Dec. 20, 1996).

16 'Non-Discrimination mainstreaming: Instruments, Case studies and the way forward' (2007) http://ec.europa.eu/employment_social/fundamental_rights/pdf/pubst/stud/mainstr07_en. pdf.

implementation, monitoring and evaluation'[17]; and in 1997, with the *European Year Against Racism* [18] and the relative Action Plan.[19] Moreover, Article 10 TFEU has spread the model of positive duties to all the discrimination grounds.

Indeed, the 'constitutional', not uniform formulation, also for the use of abstract or vague legal terms (high level, adequate, sustainable development), for the ambiguous purpose (shall take into account, shall pay full regard, shall aim to), for the ambiguous degree of obligation (binding or non-binding character of the provision) and for the unclear normative quality (whether the mainstreaming clauses entail the power and the legitimacy for legislation) ends in producing a considerable uncertainty regarding the normative implications of the various integration principles (which, by the way, is not less valid for the oldest integration principles).

Rationale and objectives of the book

In the light of the above considerations, a theory of integration principles at the legal level is very much needed. This could have the merit of clarifying still obscure elements of conceptualisation of the mainstreaming/balancing/integration clauses and will offer a first appraisal – ten years after their introduction – of their effective role and their evaluation in terms of improvements or not. The present collection aims precisely to achieve the answers to the following different issues so far neglected in the legal scholarship and at the core of a theorisation of the clauses of Articles 7–13 TFEU. The whole analysis presented in its compartmental chapter(s) and in the conclusive one will offer a comparative reading of the various contributions, and will therefore highlight the nature of such provisions, their legal effect and binding character; will clarify if they should be considered procedural rules or provisions of goals, as well as what is the material scope of each clause and what precisely has to be integrated and in what strength. On another note, the profile lying with the 'competences' will be the object of deep investigation both from the side of what is the allocation of competences between EU and its Member States in application of these integrated principles; as well as if the introduction of various integration principles led to an extension of Union competences. The latter question arises because according to *the principle of conferral*, 'the Union shall act only within the limits of the competences conferred upon it by the Member States in the Treaties to attain the objectives set out therein'. So, the competences not conferred upon the Union in the treaties remain with the Member States. But, the requirement to balance multiple blurry objectives, according to the multiplicity of integration principles, makes it more difficult to draw a clear line between Union and Member State competences.

17 Commission Communication 'Equal Opportunities for people with disabilities (A European Action Plan) 2004–10' (COM(2003) 650 final of 30 October 2003).

18 European Commission, Press Release Database, http://europa.eu/rapid/press-release_IP-96-1133_en.htm.

19 Communication from the Commission, 'An Action Plan Against Racism', COM (1998) 183, at 3.

Furthermore, the collection will highlight if the integration principles have broadened the objectives of the other competences laid down in the TFEU by extending the discretionary power of the Union institutions; have they consequently limited the scope for judicial review? Furthermore, from interpretative perspective each contribution will look at the issue of whether European law must be interpreted in the light of integration principles outside of the specific field concerned; and of what is the effectiveness, scope and binding effect of the clauses enshrined in articles 7–13 TFUE.

Last but not least, the issue of any hierarchy between these integration principles given that the TFEU does not prioritize a specific clause: could one policy or requirement override other policies? Or instead, the silence of the Treaty should be interpreted as the 'integration clauses' considerations might be equally balanced by the EU institutions without any sort of legal priority compared to other genuine policy objectives and considerations, making the task of the European legislator to balance sometimes conflicting interests even more complex. This is important also in order to acknowledge if eventually some standards become diluted against other interests and policy considerations.

The need of such a study derives from the absence at present of any systematic and comprehensive analysis of all these profiles. Legal scholarship which has focused on the integration aspects of the European Union has mainly combined perspectives from international relations, comparative politics and social and political theory, offering a complete overview of the many competing approaches that have sought to capture and explain the evolving European polity.[20] Moreover, in so doing this scholarship has dealt with single and specific principles[21] overlooking

20 D. N. Chryssochoou, *Theorizing European Integration* (SAGE Politics Texts series 2014).

21 See for the principle of gender equality integration, K. Sarikakis, E.T. Nguyen, *The Trouble with Gender: Media Policy and Gender Mainstreaming in the European Union* (2009) *Journal of European Integration* 201–216; E. Ellis and P. Watson, *EU Anti-Discrimination Law* (2nd ed OUP 2012), or Alexander Somek, *Engineering Equality. An Essay on European Anti-Discrimination Law* (OUP 2011); Lise Rolandsen Agustín, *Gender Equality, Intersectionality, and Diversity* (Palgrave Macmillan 2013); for the principle of social policy integration, see M.D. Ferrara, *The Horizontal Social Clause and Social and Economic Mainstreaming: A New Approach for Social Integration?* (2013) *European Journal of Social Law* 288–301; P. Vielle, 'How the Horizontal Social Clause can be made to work: the lessons of gender mainstreaming' in N. Bruun, K. Lörcher and I. Schömann (eds), *The Lisbon Treaty and Social Europe* (Hart Publishing 2012) 105. Note that legal literature mainly focuses in that case on the institutional efforts to coordinate economic policies with social policies based on the social and economic mainstreaming approach understood as a harmonious and coherent ensemble of competition policies. For the principle of animal health integration, see L. Rasso, R. O'Gorman, 'A Cock and Bull Story?: Problems with the protection of animal welfare in EU Law and some proposed solutions' (2008) *Journal of Environmental Law* 363–390, while a to Article 11 TFEU see, inter alia, N. de Sadeleer, *EU Environmental Law and the Internal Market* (OUP 2014) 21 ss. and B. Sjåfjell, A. Wiesbrock (eds), *Art 11 The Greening of European Business under EU Law Taking Article 11 TFEU Seriously* (Routledge 2015) proposing an overview of the role played

legal issues such as the question of the normative nature and the scope of the provisions contained in Title II.[22]

The added values of this book are to produce a unitary, systematic and all-encompassing approach to the legal issues arisen from the multifaceted integration principles: their normative and judicial implications as well as their legal value and practical relevance for EU policymaking. In so doing, the present collection has decided to include within the analysis also the 'horizontal underlying integration clause' that concerns 'fundamental rights mainstreaming', a term that does not appear as such in the Treaty but which is referred to in the EU Charter of Fundamental Rights (the 'Charter'), and in policy documents of the European Commission,[23] Parliament[24] and the Fundamental Rights Agency.[25] Also declaratory strategy for the incorporation of human rights into all EU external action was forewarned by the 2001 Council conclusions. At the multilateral level, the European Union consistently addresses human rights in international fora and within multilateral organisations, besides in bilateral policies ensuring that human rights are embedded in bilateral dialogues. It also carries out country-level reporting and elaborates human rights country strategies. In so doing, the European Union follows the Council's 2001 conclusions, which stressed how 'human rights and democratisation should systematically and at different levels be included in all EU political dialogues and bilateral relations with third countries',[26] and the 2001 Commission Communication on the European Union's role in promoting human rights and democratisation in third countries as,

> to be effective, respect for human rights and democracy should be an integral, or 'mainstream', consideration in all EU external policies. This means

by the environmental integration principle in EU law, both at the level of European legislation and at the level of Member State practice.

22 For example, most of the papers on integration principles focus on the so called 'Commission's Impact Assessment' (IA), a method used by the Commission in reconciling social, economic and environmental concerns in the development of the EU policy, highlighting that it is the main tool of implementation of these integration principles.

23 European Commission Communication, '2016 Report on the Application of the Charter of Fundamental Rights' {SWD(2017) 162 final}, COM(2017) 239 final, at p. 7, emphasis added.

24 E.g. in its Resolution of 8 September 2015 on the situation of fundamental rights in the European Union (2013–2014) (2014/2254(INI)), A8-0230/2015, the European Parliament, the European Parliament referred to mainstreaming in the context of children's rights and the right of migrants and applicants for international protection.

25 FRA also includes in its glossary the term 'human rights mainstreaming' and defines it with reference to a UN source as '[a]ssessing how any planned policy action[s], including legislation and policy-shaping instruments, in all sectors and levels may have an impact on human rights or have a human rights dimension.'

26 Council of the European Union (2001), 'Council conclusions on the European Union's role in promoting human rights and democratisation in third countries', para 13.

> including these issues in the planning, design, implementation, and monitoring of policies and programs, as well as the dialogue pursued with partners both by the Commission and the Council.[27]

With the Lisbon Treaty this de facto HR mainstreaming in EU external action has been made explicit within the treaty. It derives from the amended provisions of Article 3(5) in conjunction with Article 2 of the Treaty of the European Union:

> [i]n its relations with the wider world, the Union shall uphold and promote its values and interests and contribute to the protection of its citizens. It shall contribute to [...] the protection of human rights.

in combination with Article 21(1) of the TEU, according to which:

> [t]he Union's action on the international scene shall be guided by the principles which have inspired its own creation, development and enlargement, and which it seeks to advance in the wider world: democracy, the rule of law, the universality and indivisibility of human rights and fundamental freedoms, respect for human dignity, the principles of equality and solidarity, and respect for the principles of the United Nations Charter and international law.

and together with Article 21(2)(b) TEU which reads:

> [t]he Union shall define and pursue common policies and actions, and shall work for a high degree of cooperation in all fields of international relations, in order to: [...] consolidate and support [...] human rights.

By virtue of these provisions, the EU is under an obligation to ensure respect for human rights worldwide, in the sense that its action must tend to promote and protect human rights, without being restricted to a particular geographical or functional sphere. This will serve to complete horizontally the operationalising set of actions for mainstreaming clauses. In other words, should one assume that Articles 3(5) and 21 TEU establish the promotion, or even the protection, of human rights as a foreign policy directive? From this perspective, it is therefore clear that the principles and objectives set out in these Articles apply not just to EU policies, or even only to EU external policies, but they apply also to the external aspects of the EU's internal policies. These require the EU to 'uphold', 'contribute to', and be 'guided by' the principles and objectives described therein. As the EU Court of Justice has affirmed, these phrases are not devoid of normative force.[28]

27 European Commission (2001), 'Communication from the Commission to the Council and the European Parliament – The European Union's role in promoting human rights and democratisation in third countries', at 8.

28 Case C-366/10, *Air Transport Association of America* [2011] ECR I-13755, at para 101.

Structure of the book

The book follows the structure of the Treaty: each contribution explores one of the sectorial integration principles contained in the TFEU with a view to analysing to what extent it has affected EU decision-making and jurisprudence. It is preceded by Kosta's introductory chapter focusing on the deliberate incorporation of human rights considerations into processes not explicitly mandated to deal with human rights, methodologically operating in a way which fosters those norms, standards and principles. The aim of the analysis is to provide for a definition of this concept and inquire into the extent to which there is a legal obligation, resting on the EU institutions and the Member States when implementing EU law to conduct fundamental rights mainstreaming. In a second step, her chapter discusses the tools and mechanisms that have been put in place to mainstream fundamental rights, or which pre-existed. It will consider not only the legislature (European Commission, European Parliament and Council of the European Union), but also the two advisory bodies with a legislative role (Committee of the Regions and European Economic and Social Committee), which tend to be overlooked. Finally, it considers advisory bodies with a legislative role which have a fundamental rights specific mandate (EU Agency for Fundamental Rights and European Data Protection Supervisor).

Within this framework Caracciolo di Torella moves to examine the principle of gender equality integration (Article 8 TFEU), introduced in EU law by the Treaty of Amsterdam, requiring that 'in all its activities, the Union shall aim to eliminate inequalities and to promote equality, between men and women' and which represents the first legally-binding commitment to mainstreaming with the EU legal order since the ancient Art. 3(2) EC Treaty the European Union which promoted: 'the systematic integration of the respective situations, priorities and needs of women and men in all policies'. Although potentially very important, it remains relatively underexplored by the legal academic debate. This is probably because, rather than being a tangible legal goal in itself, it indicates a strategy to integrate gender concerns into all policies and programs of the European Union, institutions and Member States. At that regard, the aim of the chapter is to contribute to the growing debate on the principle of gender integration. On the one hand, it seeks to fully unveil its (admittedly underused) potential to challenge norms and achieve gender equality. On the other hand, it acknowledges that the 2008 recession and the austerity measures that several Member States have implemented in the aftermath have had serious consequences on gender equality measures. In this light, the principle of gender equality might be seen as a luxury that Governments cannot afford. But, if the analysis joins those voices that maintain that the principle has not achieved the success that was hoped for,[29] because of the difficult definition and appreciation of the concept as well as of the failed (adequate) incorporate

29 See also U. Behning and P. Amparo Serrano, *Gender Mainstreaming in the European Employment Strategy* (Brussels ETUI 2001).

of a feminist reading,[30] Caracciolo di Torella introduces us to a positive perspective where gender mainstreaming has achieved some success, namely that of work-life balances; an area where the European Pillar of Social Rights has the potential to inject new emphasis into it.

This chapter is complemented by Ippolito's one which more broadly turns to the principle of non-discrimination integration (Article 10 TFEU). It starts elucidating the concept and its roots before the entry into force of the Lisbon Treaty when non-discrimination mainstreaming was first inserted in the Community agenda: in soft law policy documents in its internal dimension but was equally present in EU external action and some of the agreements the EU concluded with third countries; and was finally inserted in the Draft Constitutional Treaty. After such elaboration of the prelude and current contitutionalisation of a general comprehensive equality mainstreaming duty for the EU institutions, the analysis will further examine the question of 'the effectiveness of the mainstreaming duty' that will heavily depend on its practical implementation. In that regard the chapter critically assesses whether and to what extent different equality strands covered by Article 19 TFEU are being taken into consideration in policy-making: first by the European Commission through various tools (particularly the one represented by the Impact Assessment), but also by the other EU institutions, namely the legislative ones, such as the European Parliament and the Council, and the monitoring ones, that are the European Ombudsman and the European Court of Justice.

Bartoloni's chapter is the first of those chapters that deal with more 'economic balancing' integration clauses that are the ones concerning social integration, environmental concerns, consumer protection and animal welfare. Bartoloni especially looks at the principle of social policy integration (Article 9 TFEU), an element that could help dissolve the perceived increasing tensions between the economic and social dimensions of European integration and the potential for conflict between national and EU levels of policy-making. Article 9 TFEU offers an important stepping stone for mainstreaming social objectives in all relevant EU policies. This Article requires the EU institutions to assess all their policies in the light of their implications for the achievement of social goals. In particular, Article 9 TFEU asks the EU to 'take into account' requirements linked to a number of social objectives, such as the guarantee of adequate social protection or the fight against social exclusion, in defining and implementing its policies. This chapter analyses how the 'horizontal social clause' works in infusing social values into other policies. Even at first reading, it is apparent that it is not a new competence but rather an attempt at regrouping and coordinating the exercise of a number of other autonomous policies, which therefore maintain their own nature and scope. The fact remains that, while the EU must take into account social objectives in the conduct of the other policies, it is more doubtful that it could adopt normative acts inspired by purely social aims, not adequately supported by the specific aims assigned by the ad hoc legal basis. In particular, this chapter intends to assess the

30 E. Lombardo, P. Mayer, 'Gender Mainstreaming in the EU: Incorporating a Feminist Reading?' (2006) *European Journal of Women's Studies* 151–166.

interaction between economic objectives and social aims enshrined in the pertinent normative acts. This purpose is fulfilled by using twofold criteria: first of all, the test balance used by the EU legislator; second, the one used by the ECJ. The outcome of this dual examination should permit us to better define the nature and the scope of the social clause encapsulated in Article 9.

The object of Sjåfjell's investigation is Article 11 TFEU, which sets out an all-encompassing legal duty to integrate environmental protection requirements in the policies and activities of the Union, in order to see what this entails for the EU institutions and for the Member States. The analysis will demonstrate how Article 11 TFEU connects sustainable development as an EU law objective, principle and rule. The argument is presented that particularly the codification of the sustainable development principle in Article 11 TFEU has significant legal implications for the institutions of the European Union, entailing direct obligations on all levels: law-making, administration, supervision and judicial control. The implications for the Member States are rather more indirect, but nevertheless highly relevant, influencing the interpretation, implementation and application of EU law; the justification of Member State initiatives that restrict free movement; entailing a possible duty to act to promote overarching objectives under certain circumstances, and perhaps also indicating a coming general principle of sustainable development on Member State level. The chapter thereby shows how EU Treaty law, taken seriously, may be used as a tool to ensure that EU law itself and the national laws of its Member States truly work towards a global, sustainable development, so overcoming the current inefficiency of the Court of Justice that has not taken upon itself clearly enough the role Article 11 TFEU bestows upon it: to be a guardian of the planetary boundaries; as well as even making contradictory statements in its case-law. But also overcoming the influence on policy-making, by the compartmentalisation that perpetuates the illusion that environmental protection can be left to environmental law, while other areas of law do not have to concern themselves with environmental protection.

Seatzu's chapter investigates in her turn Article 12 TFEU which provides that 'consumer protection requirements shall be taken into account in defining and implementing other Union policies and activities'. This article may be interpreted as requiring that the protection of the consumer's interest should be an integral part of any other Union policy. Even though consumer protection is not one of the objectives of the Union, it is an important principle to be taken into account when defining and implementing EU policies and activities. This applies in particular to the area of competition law, where consumer protection requirements must be taken into account and balanced with the need to protect effective competition. The chapter explores the Court's prevalent approach of integrating consumer protection requirements into a wider internal market framework and discusses the potential role to be played by Article 12 TFEU in this respect.

Beqiraj analyses the principle of animal welfare integration. After tracing the evolution of EC and EU animal welfare policy and against the background of a brief overview of the fragmentary and largely uncoordinated animal welfare legislation, the chapter will analyse the significance of the incorporation of animal welfare as an EU value in the post-Lisbon legal framework where Article 13 TFEU recognizes that animals are sentient beings and affirms that the Union and the Member States *shall pay full regard* to the welfare requirements of animals '*in formulating and implementing* the Union's agriculture, fisheries, transport, internal market, research and technological development and space policies'. This should be pursued while respecting the legislative or administrative provisions and customs of the Member States relating to, in particular, religious rites, cultural traditions and regional heritage. In particular, Beqiraj's chapter addresses the question of the significance and impact of the mainstreaming provision in Article 13 TFEU. From a legislation-making perspective, the chapter will analyse and discuss the scope of the powers of the Commission to set out policy directions and develop secondary legislation on animal welfare, whether by mainstreaming animal welfare considerations in pre-legislation impact assessments or by carefully drafting the rationales for new proposed legislation to accommodate animal welfare concerns. From the Member States' perspective, the chapter will also discuss their scope of action in promoting and protecting animal welfare through measures resulting in restrictions to trade, in light of the new Article 13 TFEU. From a judicial review perspective, the chapter will consider the role and powers of the Court of Justice of the EU in establishing the validity of EU secondary legislation related directly or indirectly to the promotion and protection of animal welfare, as well as in interpreting and applying EU law. Finally, the chapter will consider possible external implications relating to compliance with international trade obligations in the WTO framework. It will conclude with some general considerations on the significance of the protection of animal welfare within the overall architecture of the Treaty of Lisbon.

The analysis of the principle of policy integration and consistency follows, framing the series of sectoral integration principles above examined, and so being the ideal background and premise for the conclusive comparative analysis of the integration principles horizontally conceived. Nic Shuibhne will look at Article 7 TFEU, which first provides that '[t]he Union shall ensure consistency between its policies and activities, taking all of its objectives into account and in accordance with the principle of conferral of powers'. The value of this statement as a general instruction for good decision-making practice is self-evident. But what does Article 7 add beyond this? Notwithstanding the prescriptive tone of its wording, for example it is one of the few Lisbon amendments that has not even been mentioned in the case law of the Court of Justice to date. Also, was Article 7 intended merely to reflect the imprints of consistency as a general principle already developed in certain areas of EU law – for example, in the field of external relations – or to innovate novel responsibilities and expectations? Nic Shuibhne's chapter aims to interrogate the nature, scope, and implications of Article 7 TFEU as a substantive legal obligation on its own terms. It profiles the range of the principle in institutional terms and examines its usefulness as a tool with which to mediate the division of competences between the Union and the Member States, noting the explicit link in Article 7 between a consistency obligation and the principle of conferral of powers. Overall, the chapter therefore asks *what* this obligation actually is, *when* it applies, and *how* it might actually function.

The exercise conducted by each author exploring each of the sectoral integration principles contained in the TFEU, and its relevance in EU decision-making and jurisprudence are followed by De Witte's chapter which draws some conclusions assessing the legal and political impact of the various integration clauses since the time of their inclusion in the Treaties (which, for some of them, predates the Lisbon Treaty), but also discussing the lessons for the future that can be drawn from this state of play, including whether it is reasonable to expect the integration clauses to exercise a measurable impact on the EU's policy process.

2 Fundamental rights mainstreaming in the EU

Vasiliki Kosta

I. Introduction

The term 'fundamental rights mainstreaming' does not appear in the Treaties of the EU and seems, at first sight at least, to be an elusive concept with no clear (legal) definition. This chapter aims to provide a definition of mainstreaming in EU law and inquire into the extent to which there is a legal obligation, resting on the EU institutions and the Member States when implementing EU law to conduct fundamental rights mainstreaming (section II). In a second step (section III), this chapter will discuss existing tools and mechanisms for fundamental rights mainstreaming in the EU institutional landscape. It will consider not only the legislature (European Commission, European Parliament and Council of the European Union), but also the two advisory bodies with a legislative role (Committee of the Regions and European Economic and Social Committee), which tend to be overlooked in this discussion. Finally, it will also consider advisory bodies with a legislative role, which have a fundamental rights specific mandate (EU Agency for Fundamental Rights and European Data Protection Supervisor).

II. Defining 'fundamental rights mainstreaming' in the EU

1. Origins and meaning of fundamental rights mainstreaming

The term 'mainstreaming' is not as such expressly included in the Treaties of the EU, but is used expressly in policy contexts relating to the implementation of the EU Charter of Fundamental Rights ('Charter') today.

The concept can be traced to UN activities. The 1993 UN World Conference on Human Rights has been described as a milestone of 'human rights mainstreaming'. This conference established the Office of the UN High Commissioner for Human Rights (OHCHR), which 'gave an impetus for collaboration between the Office and other UN agencies.'[1] Today the OHCHR lists 'mainstreaming'

1 André Frankovits,'A Human Rights based approach and the United Nations System' (the United Nations Educational, Scientific and Cultural Organization, 2006) 15 <http://unesdoc.unesco.org/images/0014/001469/146999e.pdf> accessed 11 May 2017.

explicitly as one of its official tasks on its website, and defines it as 'injecting a human rights perspective in all United Nations Programmes.'[2] This idea was articulated in the 1997 United Nations Programme for Reform, launched by the United Nations Secretary General.[3] The Programme identified human rights as an issue cutting across each and every of the substantive fields of the Secretariat's work programme.

However, the (broader) concept of human rights mainstreaming followed and was inspired by a specific form of mainstreaming – one that could be construed as a sub-category of human rights mainstreaming today – namely, gender mainstreaming. Gender mainstreaming was already expressly introduced as an important strategy in international gender equality policy at the fourth UN World Conference on Women in Beijing in 1995.[4]

Similarly, at EU level, gender mainstreaming clearly preceded the broader concept of fundamental rights mainstreaming. The first EU Commission Communication on the matter followed one year after the Beijing Conference and positioned its commitment to gender equality as a 'logical extension' of the central position that the Union had taken in that Conference and in the drafting of the final Declaration and the action platform.[5] Interestingly, the Council of Europe seems to have been a frontrunner in this regard. In 1992, the Council of Europe held a conference on 'Equality between Women and Men in a Changing Europe'. The General Rapporteur spoke in her conclusions of 'mainstreaming' as one limb of a two-fold strategy[6] to promote gender equality. 'Mainstreaming' was defined here as 'integrat[ing] women's concerns in all fields of politics'.[7]

The European Commission's Communication provides for the following, more elaborate, definition of gender mainstreaming:

> mobilising all general policies and measures specifically for the purpose of achieving equality by actively and openly taking into account at the planning stage their possible effects on the respective situations of men and women

2 'What we do' <www.ohchr.org/EN/AboutUs/Pages/WhatWeDo.aspx> accessed 11 May 2017.

3 United Nations Report of the Secretary General, 'Renewing the United Nations: A Programme for Reform', A/51/950, paras 78 et seq <www.securitycouncilreport.org/atf/cf/%7B65BFCF9B-6D27-4E9C-8CD3-CF6E4FF96FF9%7D/SGE%20A-1997-51-950.PDF> accessed 11 May 2017 (as cited in DS Olawuyi, 'Mainstreaming Human Rights Under National and International Law: Legal And Epistemic Questions' (2013) 3 Indonesia Law Review 213.

4 United Nations, 'Report of the Fourth World Conference on Women' (Beijing, A/CONF.177/20/Rev.1, 14–15 September 1995).

5 Commission, 'Incorporating Equal Opportunities For Women and Men Into All Community Policies and Activities' (Communication) COM (96) 67 final 2.

6 The second limb is to 'overcome discrimination by specific positive actions'. Steering Committee for Equality between Women and Men, *Conference on equality between women and men – proceedings Poznań (Poland) 31 March-2 April 1992* (Council of Europe 1994) 196, para 23.

7 Ibid.

> (gender perspective). This means systematically examining measures and policies and taking into account such possible effects when defining and implementing them.[8]

When it comes to the broader term 'fundamental rights mainstreaming' at EU level, the European Parliament[9] and most prominently the European Commission ('Commission') and the EU Agency for Fundamental Rights ('FRA') have used that term in policy documents related to the EU Charter of Fundamental Rights ('Charter').

The European Commission stated that 'it puts a lot of effort into mainstreaming fundamental rights, *i.e. ensuring that they are fully respected in all its legislative and policy proposals*.'[10]

The FRA noted in its 'Focus' section of the 2017 Annual Report that '[a]n increasing focus on mainstreaming fundamental rights led the European Commission to promote a "culture of fundamental rights" from 2005 onwards.'[11] Apart from more generic references to fundamental rights mainstreaming, the FRA titled its 'Focus' section of its 2014 Annual Report 'Mainstreaming Fundamental Rights: turning words into action'.[12] This section provides no concise and sharp definition of mainstreaming. A textbox dedicated to the concept mentions however the following: an 'increasing commitment (…) to *protect and promote* human rights – fundamental rights – within the EU system itself more *systematically and effectively*'.[13] It also notes 'fundamental rights are at the very heart of EU affairs'[14] so that the Charter 'is becoming an essential element in the normative core of all EU action.'[15] The FRA also includes in its glossary the term 'human rights mainstreaming' and defines it with reference to a UN source[16] as '[a] ssessing how any planned policy action, including legislation and policy-shaping

8 Commission Communication 1996 (n 5) 2.
9 E.g. The European Parliament referred in European Parliament, Resolution of 8 September 2015 on the situation of fundamental rights in the European Union (2013–2014) (2014/2254(INI)), A8–0230/2015 to mainstreaming in the context of children's rights and the right of migrants and applicants for international protection.
10 Commission, '2016 Report on the Application of the Charter of Fundamental Rights' (Communication) SWD (2017) 162 final, COM (2017) 239 final 7, emphasis added.
11 European Union Agency for Fundamental Rights, 'Focus – Between promise and delivery: 10 years of fundamental rights in the EU' 8 <http://fra.europa.eu/en/publication/2017/fundamental-rights-report-2017> accessed 11 May 2017.
12 European Union Agency for Fundamental Rights, 'Annual Report 2014 – Fundamental Rights: challenges and achievements in 2014' 12, http://fra.europa.eu/en/publication/2015/fundamental-rights-challenges-and-achievements-2014 accessed 11 May 2017.
13 Ibid, emphasis added.
14 Ibid.
15 Ibid.
16 Namely, the UN Practitioner's Portal on Human Rights Based Approaches to Programming <http://fra.europa.eu/de/joinedup/about/glossary?title=m>, accessed 11 May 2017.

instruments, in all sectors and levels may have an impact on human rights or have a human rights dimension.'[17]

Several features characterising mainstreaming follow from the various definitions cited above. The first one relates to timing: mainstreaming is triggered *at the very outset* of the law and policy-making process. Mainstreaming is thus anticipatory[18] in nature and relates to *ex ante* fundamental rights protection as opposed to fundamental rights violations being remedied *post hoc* by courts. This links to the second feature, which relates to the actors: policy and law-makers, as opposed to courts, are responsible for mainstreaming; and one may add they should do so in a participatory manner.[19] That is, they should involve all relevant stakeholders. Finally, when it comes to what mainstreaming is actually supposed to do, it results both from the FRA definitions and the Commission's gender mainstreaming definition provided above[20] that fundamental rights considerations should be taken into account in a *proactive, systematic and effective way across all policy* fields. The word 'systematic' is key to understanding the process: it means that law and policy-makers have to consider the fundamental rights implications of any and all laws/policies they produce, and not just of those whose subject matter is evidently one of fundamental rights or impacts on these. That in turn implies a proactive approach because the question of fundamental rights has to be considered even if it does not obviously arise.

Two questions need to be clarified at this point however: first, how – if at all – is mainstreaming different from meeting classic fundamental rights obligations. The Commission's and the FRA's explanations on mainstreaming above are not clear on this and, when read together, appear to obscure the point further: the Commission speaks of 'respecting' fundamental rights whereas the FRA speaks of 'protecting' and 'promoting' them. Second, to the extent that mainstreaming is different from classic fundamental rights obligations, is there a legal obligation to mainstream fundamental rights under EU law, and if so, what is its source?

17 European Union Agency for Fundamental Rights, 'Mainstreaming Human Rights' <http://fra.europa.eu/en/joinedup/about/glossary/mainstreaming-human-rights> accessed 11 May 2017.

18 C. McCrudden, 'Mainstreaming Human Rights' in C. Harvey, *Human Rights in the Community: Rights as Agents for Change* (Hart, 2004), available as University of Michigan School of Law, *Public Law & Legal Theory*, Research Paper Series, Research Paper No. 47, 1, at 7.

19 Ibid.

20 See also, De Schutter's definition of fundamental rights mainstreaming, that is based on the Commission's gender mainstreaming definition:

'the systematic integration of [fundamental rights] in all policies [...] with a view to promoting [fundamental rights] and mobilising all general policies and measures specifically for the purpose of [realising them] by actively and openly taking into account, at the planning stage, their [impact on fundamental rights].' O. De Schutter, 'Mainstreaming Human Rights in the European Union', in P. Alston and O. de Schutter (eds), *Monitoring Fundamental Rights in the EU – The Contribution of the Fundamental Rights Agency* (Oxford, Hart Publishing, 2005) 37, 43.

2. *The nature of fundamental rights mainstreaming*

In order to answer these two questions, we shall firstly clarify the meaning of 'classic fundamental rights obligations' as employed here. Subsequently, we will recall the obligations flowing from the wording of the Charter in order to assess whether mainstreaming, as defined above and as further elaborated on in this section, entails something beyond those obligations. In a final step we shall assess the question of mainstreaming as a legal obligation.

Turning to the first question. The concept 'classic fundamental rights obligations' is employed here to mean obligations that under international human rights law have been categorised as the obligations to respect, protect and fulfill.[21] We shall briefly recall this distinction based on observations made by McCrudden on this topic. The obligation to respect means, 'states [have to] refrain from infringing a human right directly through its own actions'.[22] The obligation to protect 'places the state under a duty to prevent a right from being infringed by actors other than the state'[23] and the state must take active steps in this regard. Finally, the obligation to fulfill human rights 'requires states to facilitate access to these rights, or to provide these rights directly through the use of state power.'[24] Socio-economic rights (that require progressive realisation and thus expenditure of resources) are frequently associated with this obligation (e.g. the right to social security and social protection, the right to an adequate standard of living etc.), but the obligation to fulfill may be equally applicable to rights that are traditionally categorised as 'civil and political'. For example, the right to an effective remedy and to a fair trial includes an obligation to make legal aid 'available to those who lack sufficient resources in so far as such aid is necessary to ensure effective access to justice' (Art. 47 of the Charter). It should also be noted that one and the same right can have both: a dimension that requires the state to refrain from unduly interfering with it and a dimension that requires the state to act positively in order to realise it.[25]

Under EU law, the fundamental rights obligations imposed on EU institutions – whenever they are acting, and to the Member States when acting within the scope of EU law,[26] are defined in Art. 51(1) of the Charter.[27] Based on this

21 Shue, *Basic Rights: Subsistence, Affluence, and US Foreign Policy* (2nd ed, Princeton University Press, 1996) as cited in McCrudden (n 18) 4.
22 McCrudden, *ibid.*
23 Ibid 5.
24 Ibid.
25 An example under international human rights law would be the right to adequate housing. This grants to all persons 'a degree of legal security of tenure which guarantees a legal right against forced evictions by the state', but it also imposes an obligation on states to take steps to make housing affordable. See General Comment No. 7 on the right to adequate housing under art 11(1) of the International Covenant on Economic, Social and Cultural Rights (ICESCR), contained in Document E/1992//23.
26 The Charter speaks of 'implementing' EU law, but this has been interpreted by the Court to mean acting 'within the scope of EU law'. See Case C-617/10 *Åklagaren v Hans Åkerberg Fransson*, ECLI:EU:C:2013:280.
27 There remains of course also a 'parallel' obligation on EU institutions and Member States when acting within the scope of EU law, to act in compliance with fundamental rights protected as general principles of EU law, according to Art 6(3) TEU.

provision, the addressees of the Charter '*shall*...respect the rights, observe the principles and promote the application thereof'. It is immediately obvious that the Charter does not use the wording of the tripartite typology 'respect, protect, fulfil' mentioned above, and we cannot simply assume that 'respect the rights' in Art. 51 (1) of the Charter is meant in the sense of the wording under that tripartite typology. Instead we have to look closer at the Charter in order to understand the different obligations that may flow from it.

The Charter makes a distinction between rights, which have to be respected, and principles, which have to be observed. The Explanations Relating to the Charter ('Explanations') make clear that by 'rights that have to be respected' what is meant is 'subjective rights'.[28] This is commonly known as legally protected interests, which entitle the individual to enforce them in front of courts. Hence, 'rights' under the Charter are those (elements of) provisions, which are 'justiciable'. Subjective rights may contain both negative and positive obligations resting on public authorities in the sense of 'respect' and 'protect' under the tripartite typology originating in international human rights law. Furthermore, as Koch has explained, a right can be 'both justiciable *and* subject to progressive realisation at the same time' (e.g. the right to education).[29] So, it can be concluded that 'respecting rights' under the Charter can mean complying with the obligations to protect, respect and fulfil as the case may be.

Art. 52(5) of the Charter explains the nature of principles: principles 'may be implemented by legislative and executive acts' and crucially '*shall* be judicially cognisable only in the interpretation of such acts and in the ruling on their legality.' So, principles, unlike rights, are not per se justiciable; they do not 'give rise *to direct claims for positive action* by the Union's institutions or Member States authorities' – hence the wording '*may be* implemented'.[30] But it is clear that all provisions – those containing 'rights' and those containing 'principles' are substantively binding the EU institutions and Member States when acting within the scope of EU law, irrespective of the question of justiciability. The Charter does not make it unequivocally clear which (elements of) provisions contain rights and which principles, but the Explanations do point to the fact that a Charter Article may contain both, elements of a right and of a principle.[31]

Art. 51(1) of the Charter also speaks of an obligation 'to promote the application thereof'. It is worth noting that on the face of the text of Art. 51(1) CFR it is

28 Explanations Relating to the Charter of Fundamental Rights (Charter) [2007] OJ C303/17, on Art. 52(5) CFR.

29 Koch explains this by reference to the right to primary education under art 13(2)(a) of the ICESCR, which is 'capable of immediate implementation (justiciable)' but the content of that right is supposed to change and improve over time depending on available resources. Ida Elisabeth Koch, 'The Justiciability of Indivisible Rights' (2003) 72 Nordic Journal of International Law 3, 21.

30 Explanations Relating to the Charter of Fundamental Rights (n 28), hence the wording 'may be implemented'.

31 Ibid, the following examples are given: arts 23 (Equality between women and men), 33 (Family and professional life) and 34 (Social security and social assistance) of the Charter.

not clear what the word 'thereof' refers to, i.e. whether the obligation to promote relates only to principles or whether that also includes rights and thus relates to the Charter in its entirety. The Explanations[32] are equally ambiguous on this point.[33] A more concrete understanding of the phrase 'promote the application' may allow us to resolve this point.

We have established above that 'respecting rights' refers to justiciable (elements of) Charter provisions and can mean to involve any of the obligations to respect, protect and fulfil under the tripartite typology of human rights obligations, as we know it from international human rights law. We have also noted that 'principles' are binding on EU institutions and Member States implementing EU law ('shall be observed'), but they are not justiciable. Thus, the obligation 'to promote' must mean something else.

The 'obligation to promote' or 'facilitate' has been put forward by some international human rights law scholars as a fourth obligation, to be added to the tripartite typology described above. It can also be found under international human rights law and national constitutional law.[34]

'Promote' can mean two things in these contexts, both of which directly relate to the concept of mainstreaming, as explained above: first, 'promoting compliance with fundamental rights', in the sense of advancing awareness and acceptance thereof (fundamental rights education) and promoting a culture of fundamental rights.[35]

32 Explanations Relating to the Charter of Fundamental Rights (n 28).

33 The only reference to 'promoting' in the Explanations relating to art 51(1) is to be found in this sentence: 'an obligation (…) for the Union's institutions to promote principles laid down in the Charter may arise only within the limits of these same powers.' This sentence does not reveal however whether the obligation relates *only* to 'principles', as opposed to *both* 'principles' and 'rights'. The Explanations prepared by the Convention drafting the Charter are entirely silent on this point, Draft Charter of Fundamental Rights of the European Union [2000] CHARTE 4473/00, CONVENT 49.

34 Koch (n 29) 10. Koch points to the Committee on Economic Social and Cultural Rights, which points sometimes to an obligation to facilitate, and to art 7(2) of the South African Constitutions, which enshrines an obligation to 'respect, protect, *promote* and fulfil rights in the Bill of Rights.'

35 See International Network for Economic, Social and Cultural Rights, 'The Obligation to Promote' <www.escr-net.org/resources/obligation-promote> accessed 11 May 2017; see also House of Lords, House of Commons; Joint Committee on Human Rights, 'The Case for a Human Rights Commission', HL Paper 67-I; HC 489-I, 19–20, <https://publications.parliament.uk/pa/jt200203/jtselect/jtrights/67/67.pdf> accessed 11 May 2017:

'The Head of the Civil Service has suggested that so far as it applies to Whitehall and the wider world of public authorities, this idea of mainstreaming of human rights involves—

- developed awareness at all levels of the [ECHR] rights *and the associated balances and limitations*, as an integral part of public administration and policy-making;

- frequent practical expression of the positive difference the [ECHR] can and does make, by voluntary good practice as well as by court decision;

- clear and public demonstration of commitment to the [ECHR] values and principles at the highest levels of government and public authorities;

The latter can be understood to include, but not be limited to, the establishment of *ex ante* fundamental rights protection mechanisms in public organs.

Second, and this seems closer to the European Commission's gender mainstreaming definition provided above, 'promote' can mean 'promoting fundamental rights in the sense of further realising them' and going above and beyond compliance. De Schutter has put forward this understanding of mainstreaming in the following terms. Mainstreaming requires:

> that we take into account, in the policy choices we make, the impact the different policy options we have at our disposal will produce on our capacity to further realise those rights. The realisation of rights is however an objective which, it is submitted, is better understood as a process than as an outcome, as a general direction in which to move, than as a target we either hit or miss.[36]

Importantly, in De Schutter's definition, mainstreaming goes beyond making a fundamental rights compatibility assessment. He gives the following examples:

> [A] proposal made in the field of competition fails to contribute to the realisation of pluralism in the media as it does not offer safeguards against certain forms of concentration in that sector ... yet the same proposal may still be compatible with the requirements of freedom of expression, and even with the obligation imposed by the Charter that the pluralism of the media be 'respected'.
>
> Or we may note that a new information technology has not been designed in such a way as to minimise the impact on privacy and to facilitate the exercise by the individual concerned of the rights which safeguard from abuse in the processing of personal data (right of information, access and rectification, objection and appeal) ... and yet, find at the same time that such technology does not violate the requirements of Article 8 of the Charter of Fundamental Rights or the applicable legislation which develops its requirements.[37]

To have such obligation, as described in the quote, follow from the word 'promote' in the Charter would seem illogical: promotion is clearly an obligation ('shall promote'); so it is not possible to have a legal obligation in place, which has to be met in order to achieve compatibility with the Charter, but at the same time requires more than compatibility.

However, to the extent that a (element of a) provision is at stake, which requires progressive realisation in order to achieve compliance, 'promoting' in the sense of 'further realising' as resulting from De Schutter's mainstreaming definition above, will actually lead to meeting the fundamental rights obligation.[38] But

- public recognition of the [ECHR] values and principles in delivering quality public services'

36 Ibid 55–56.

37 Ibid.

38 See V. Kosta, *Fundamental Rights in EU Internal Market Legislation* (Hart Publishing, 2015) ch 3, 43 et seq. This may be the reason why some scholars view the main

in the Charter context, that obligation of 'fulfilment' can be already derived from the words 'respecting rights' and, to the extent that such obligation may not be justiciable, from the words 'observe the principles.'

It therefore results from the above that 'promoting the application thereof' most logically refers to an obligation to 'promote fundamental rights compliance'. If this is true, we can then also draw the conclusion that this refers to the Charter in its entirety, and not just to principles. It would not make sense for the Charter to impose an obligation of promoting compliance only for some of the Charter's provisions.

This leads us to answering the final question on whether there is a legal obligation to mainstream fundamental rights under EU law. To the extent that mainstreaming is understood to mean a public sector duty to promote compliance with fundamental rights obligations as derived from the Charter, this is a duty that expressly results from the Charter. To be sure, the EU concept of mainstreaming fundamental rights can encompass more than that and include De Schutter's definition of going above and beyond compliance, but that dimension would not arise as a *legal obligation* under the Charter.

III. Mechanisms to implement the fundamental rights mainstreaming obligation at EU level

This section will consider the tools that have been put in place to mainstream fundamental rights at EU level. It will do so by focusing on the legislature, advisory bodies with a legislative role, and expert bodies with an advisory role. I have dealt with the tools employed by the legislature in detail elsewhere,[39] and will provide on that point (at section 1. below) only a summarised account of that work here.

1. The legislature

1.1 The European Commission

Ex ante fundamental rights scrutiny of EU legislation during its drafting stage has been systematically applied after adoption of the Charter and the European Commission ('Commission') has been the initiator and driving force for creating a 'methodology' that shall lock in a culture of fundamental rights in the EU institutional landscape.

After the Charter's proclamation, the then Commission President, Romano Prodi, and the Justice and Home Affairs Commissioner, António Vitorino,

added value of 'mainstreaming' in meeting the obligation of 'fulfilling' and 'further realising' rights. See McCrudden, (n 18) 7.

39 V. Kosta, ibid., ch 3. See also, O. De Schutter, 'The Implementation of the Charter by the Institutions of the European Union' in S. Peers et al., *The EU Charter of Fundamental Rights: A Commentary* (Hart Publishing, 2014).

declared in an 'internal' and not widely known[40] Decision of 13 March 2001[41] that all legislative proposals would be first scrutinised for compatibility with the Charter 'as part of the normal decision-making process'.[42]

A Commission Communication replaced this Decision in 2005.[43] The 2005 Communication did not introduce any fundamental changes. Its aim was to build on existing mechanisms and raise awareness by 'lock[ing] in *a culture of fundamental rights* in EU legislation'[44] among all actors in the law-making process. The Commission's 'methodology' to achieve this end consists of three components: First, Charter compatibility assessments (CCAs) with recitals affirming this process. This was introduced in 2002. Second, impact assessments (IAs) – a practice that was equally introduced in 2002.[45] Third, Explanatory Memoranda accompanying the Commission proposals and recitals in the Preamble, which are supposed to explain why and that the proposal is in line with the Charter. At the early stages of the introduction of 'the methodology' these tools were not operating well. In various instances recitals containing fundamental rights compatibility affirmations were included in proposals that did not seem to implicate fundamental rights; in others recitals were included but the accompanying Explanatory Memoranda was not explaining the fundamental rights relevance.[46]

After the Charter became legally binding, a further Commission Communication (of September 2010) adopted a strategy for the effective implementation of the Charter by the EU in the new post-Lisbon legal environment.[47]

Since the first 2001 Decision, none of the following Communications have introduced any important change in the 'methodology', except for one novelty in the 2010 Communication, namely, the introduction of the Commission's Annual Report on the application of the Charter.[48]

The difference between IAs and CCAs is worth recalling here. CCAs are conducted after an IA has been drawn up and is based on an actual draft legislative proposal. Once the lead department responsible for the proposal considers that it is sufficiently advanced it launches an 'Interservice Consultation'(CIS). This mechanism involves all the Directorate Generals and Services that have a legitimate interest are being asked for their

40 House of Lords, Select Committee on European Union, 'Human Rights Proofing EU Legislation', 16th Report (2005–06), 11, 12.

41 Commission, 'Application of the Charter of Fundamental Rights of the European Union' SEC (2001) 380/3.

42 Ibid. See also House of Lords 16th Report (n 40), at 11, para 10.

43 Commission, 'Compliance with the Charter of Fundamental Rights in Commission Legislative Proposals – Methodology for Systematic and Rigorous Monitoring' (Communication) COM (2005) 0172 final (hereinafter the '2005 Commission Communication').

44 President Barroso cited in Commission Press Releases IP/05/494, emphasis added.

45 Commission, 'Communication from the Commission on Impact Assessment' COM (2002) 276 final (hereinafter the 'COM IA Communication 2002').

46 Kosta (n 39).

47 Commission Communication, 'Strategy for the effective implementation of the Charter of Fundamental Rights by the European Union' (19 October 2010), 2.

48 Ibid 12–13.

opinion. Consultation of the Legal Service is mandatory at this stage. The role of the Legal Service is crucial here. It thoroughly examines the draft for fundamental rights compliance, based on the text, the accompanying Explanatory Memorandum, the draft IA report together with the preparatory documents. This is the mechanism at the Commission level that provides for the formal and decisive fundamental rights scrutiny of legislation and it plays a key role in the Commission's 'methodology.'

Assessing the degree to which this mechanism is or is not operating well (e.g. the degree to which Commission Legal Service Opinions may be ignored due to political pressure) is not an easy task because Legal Service Advice is confidential.

IA precedes the CCA and is 'a process that prepares evidence for political decision-makers on the advantages and disadvantages of possible policy options by assessing their potential [economic, social and environmental] impacts'.[49] Notably, there is no separate category for assessing fundamental rights impacts; instead they are dealt with within the three named categories and most of the fundamental rights impacts are assessed within the 'social impacts' table. According to the Commission the reason for not having a separate category is that fundamental rights 'cut across all sectors'[50] and a distinct category would lead to 'needless repetition.'[51] This state of affairs has been repeatedly criticised also beyond academic writing,[52] but it has remained unchanged.

Smismans and Minto[53] investigated whether the EU's system of integrated IA[54] is a useful tool for mainstreaming more generally. They noted that since

49 See Commission, 'Impact Assessment Guidelines' SEC (2009) 92 (hereinafter the '2009 IA Guidelines') 4, and also the Commission's 'operational guidance' for taking account specifically of fundamental rights in IAs. Commission Staff Working Paper, Operational Guidance on taking account of Fundamental Rights in Commission Impact Assessments SEC (2011) 567 (hereinafter the '2011 Guidance'). See also Tool #28 of the Commission's Better Regulation 'Toolbox', which provides an 'overview of the most salient points to consider when assessing fundamental rights in impact assessments.' Commission, 'Tool #28: Fundamental Rights & Human Rights' (2017) <https://ec.europa.eu/info/sites/info/files/file_import/better-regulation-toolbox-28_en_0.pdf> accessed 6 May 2018.

50 2005 Commission Communication, (n 43), 5, para 19.

51 2005 Commission Communication, (n 43), 5, para 19.

52 House of Lords, 16th Report, (n 40), 20–21, para 50; European Parliament, Report on compliance with the Charter of Fundamental Rights in the Commission's legislative proposals: methodology for systematic and rigorous monitoring, Committee on Civil Liberties, Justice and Home Affairs, Rapporteur: Johannes Vogenhuber (12 February 2017), 8, para 11; H Toner, 'Impact Assessment and Fundamental Rights in EU Law' (2006) 31 *European Law Review* 316, 325 ('the impression is that fundamental rights were and still remain tagged onto the impact assessment framework as a subsidiary concern'); ACM Meuwese, *Impact Assessment in EU Lawmaking* (The Hague, Kluwer Law International 2008) 86.

53 S. Smismans and R. Minto, 'Are integrated impact assessments the way forward for mainstreaming in the European Union?' (2016) Regulation & Governance, doi:10.1111/rego.12119. This study has also been discussed by O. De Schutter in his study for the European Parliament, AFCO Committee, 'The Implementation of the EU Charter of Fundamental Rights in the EU institutional framework' [2016], <http://www.europarl.europa.eu/RegData/etudes/STUD/2016/571397/IPOL_STU(2016)571397_EN.pdf> accessed 6 May 2018.

54 The EU employs an *integrated* Impact Assessments approach, which includes cost-benefit analysis, cost effectiveness analysis and multi-criteria analysis.

the introduction of IAs has oftentimes occurred within the broader framework of a policy agenda concerned with reducing regulatory burdens, 'mainstreaming may not be the primary objective of IA.'[55] On the other hand, since IAs always involve some element of scrutiny *across* policy fields it seems particularly apt as a mainstreaming tool.[56] More specifically, Smismans and Minto note:

> If mainstreaming is taken seriously, IAs systematically assess new policy initiatives on their potential impacts upon the realization of mainstreaming goals. A proactive approach to mainstreaming would take into account the mainstreaming objectives both at the level of defining objectives of a new policy initiative and of assessing its impacts.[57]

One important conclusion reached by the authors based on their empirical analysis[58] is that the six 'constitutional mainstreaming objectives', which they have identified based on the Treaties and the Charter[59] are not systematically taken into account in IAs. Specifically regarding fundamental rights they find that this constitutes 'a more ad hoc horizontal category',[60] and in any case fundamental rights do not really feature at the stage of the IA where the definition of objectives takes place. Smits and Minto,[61] as well as De Schutter[62] attribute this to fundamental rights being more perceived as a guarantee not to be negatively impacted upon rather than as a positive requirement to be proactively promoted through IAs, and they consider that the operational guidelines on IAs are steered towards that. However, the Commission's '2011 Guidance' does make clear that fundamental rights may be of relevance at the problem definition stage not only 'where the Union intends to act in order to protect individuals against interferences with their fundamental rights' but also 'where an act is designed to promote specific fundamental rights.'[63] So, the point is being formally acknowledged in fact, even if it does not materialise in practice.

A separate interesting, although maybe not surprising finding is that 'the assessment of economic impacts and of regulatory burdens are predominant in the set-up of the integrated IA system, although neither of these are set out in the treaties as constitutional horizontal objectives.'[64]

55 Smismans and Minto (n 53) 4.
56 Ibid 4.
57 Ibid.
58 Which is based on 35 IAs conducted between 2011–2014.
59 The six mainstreaming objectives derived from arts 7–12 TFEU and the Charter are: fundamental rights, gender, horizontal social clause, discrimination, environment, and consumers, Treaty on the Functioning of the European Union (TFEU) arts 7–12.
60 Smismans and Minto, (n 53), at 2.
61 Ibid., at 13.
62 O. De Schutter (n 53) 20.
63 2011 Guidance, *supra* (n 49), at 13.
64 Smismans and Minto, (n 53), at 2.

1.2 European Parliament

Traditionally the European Parliament, as a political institution, has been the most active one in pushing the EU's fundamental rights agenda. However, when it comes to systematic fundamental rights proofing of all EU legislation, it has only played a secondary role. Fundamental rights compliance will only be assessed when raised in the committee dealing with the legislative proposal and is therefore reactive in nature. This can happen via two routes: first, when the committee requests an Opinion from the European Parliament Legal Service, which, unlike the Commission Legal Service, does not conduct systematic fundamental rights compatibility assessments of all legislation. Second, when Rule 36[65] of the Parliament's Rules of Procedure is invoked, which states:

> Where the committee responsible for the subject matter, a political group or at least 40 Members are of the opinion that a proposal for a legislative act or parts of it do not comply with rights enshrined in the Charter (…), the matter shall, at their request, be referred to the committee responsible for the interpretation of the Charter. The opinion of that committee shall be annexed to the report of the committee responsible for the subject-matter.[66]

The 'committee responsible for the interpretation of the Charter' is the LIBE Committee (Committee on Civil Liberties, Justice and Home Affairs). The fact that this political committee (and not say the Committee on Constitutional Affairs (JURI))[67] is entrusted with fundamental rights proofing of legislation will certainly reflect upon the type of scrutiny conducted. LIBE is more likely to provide for an examination that is thoroughly legally informed if it is to request an opinion from the Legal Service or from the FRA, and it is not obvious to what extent that would happen systematically.

Another separate factor worth noting, which 'curtails the possibility for public deliberation about the content of legislation',[68] including fundamental rights,

65 European Parliament, 'Rules of Procedure', 7th parliamentary term (2010), rule 36.

66 European Parliament, 'Rules of Procedure', 7th parliamentary term (2010), rule 36, para 2.

67 According to rule 36 of the European Parliamentary Rules of Procedure, the role of JURI includes 'the interpretation and application of Union law and compliance of Union acts with primary law, notably the choice of legal bases and respect for the principles of subsidiarity and proportionality'. Fundamental rights are not expressly mentioned, but the Charter clearly constituted primary law, so that the check of legislation for compliance with the Charter could have fallen within this Committee's responsibilities. See European Parliament, Rules of Procedure (n 65), Annex XVI.

68 B. de Witte, A. Trechsel, D. Damjanović, E. Hellquist, J. Hien and P. Ponzano, 'Legislating after Lisbon: New Opportunities for the European Parliament' (Florence, EUDO study, European Union Democracy Observatory 2010) 27 <www.eui.eu/Projects/EUDO/Documents/EUDO-LegislatingafterLisbon(SD).pdf≥ accessed 6 May 2018.

more generally, is the practice of 'trialogues', i.e. informal meetings involving key actors and intended to achieve compromise solutions, which are then submitted to the respective official institutional settings.

In sum, the European Parliament does not assume a very *systematic* role in fundamental rights proofing of all draft legislation. However, some positive institutional developments have occurred post-Lisbon, which, albeit not fundamental rights specific, have the potential to improve the state of affairs also in respect of fundamental rights.

One such mechanism is the European Parliament's 'Directorate General for Impact Assessment and European Added Value' established in 2012.[69] Its creation had a dual aim: to 'strengthen the Parliament's capacity for scrutiny and oversight of the executive' and to 'contribute [...] to the quality of law-making itself.'[70] It consists of seven units in total which deal with the Policy Cycle as a Whole, *Ex-Ante* Evaluation (which deal both with added value of legislation and the quality of IAs), *Ex-Post* Evaluation (conducting implementation assessments of existing EU laws and policies as well as European Council oversight work) and Foresight (analysing emerging policy issues and trends as well as medium and long-term global trends).

If fundamental rights reflexes are operating properly at this level they could provide added value for mainstreaming. Another means to improve fundamental rights mainstreaming is a systematic cooperation with the FRA, and indeed this seems to be increasingly occurring.[71]

Arguably, such improvement is not optional: with the rise in the EP's power in the law making process post-Lisbon, it also has a responsibility to ensure that mechanisms are in place capable of guaranteeing a high level of fundamental rights protection.

1.3 Council of the European Union

In contrast to the Commission and the European Parliament, the Council of the European Union, as it itself acknowledged in a discussion document of 2011, did not have 'standing procedures and a structural framework to guarantee that all

69 See European Parliament, The Secretary General, 'Meeting with the team of the new Directorate for Impact Assessment and European Added Value' (1 October 2012) <www.europarl.europa.eu/the-secretary-general/en/activities-multimedia/meeting-with-the-team-of-the-new-directorate-for-impact-assessment-and-european-added-value> accessed 11 May 2017, and explanation of the set-up of the Directorate: European Parliament, European Parliamentary Research Service, 'Impact Assessment and European Added Value' (February 2018) <www.europarl.europa.eu/EPRS/EPRS-Impact-Assessment-European-Added-Value-presentation.pdf> accessed 11 May 2017.

70 Ibid.

71 The European Parliament increasingly requests Opinions from the FRA. All FRA Opinions are available here <http://fra.europa.eu/en/publications-and-resources/opinions>, accessed 6 May 2018.

fundamental rights are respected in all draft proposals'[72] when the Charter became legally binding. But it identified two measures that were already in place and could be used for fundamental rights scrutiny: first, as it is the case with the European Parliament, the possibility of requesting an opinion from its Legal Service when the question of compatibility with fundamental rights arises. Second, relying on Member State expertise: since 'Member States are the first check point where compliance with obligations resulting from the Charter as well as the constitutional traditions and international obligations common to the Member States is usually scrutinized',[73] each Member State should check a proposal against compatibility with the Charter before submitting it to a Council working group.[74]

Later in 2011 the Council adopted Guidelines for checking fundamental rights compatibility of draft legislation at the Council's preparatory bodies.[75] Framed as 'non-binding advice', the aim is awareness-raising in the preparatory bodies.[76] The guidelines stipulate that they should be used at the beginning of the first reading of any proposal,[77] leaving the possibility open for taking a fundamental rights perspective even on proposals that do not blatantly raise these issues or which would not be subject to amendments by the Council (other than on the ground of fundamental rights compliance). The need for further checks on any compromise proposal is also recognised, but what is even more interesting to note is that such a need is also expressed with regard to those that result from a trialogue with the European Parliament.[78] As noted above this is the stage where fundamental rights are more susceptible to being compromised or to not being given adequate attention in view of the informal nature of the negotiation and the pressing objective of reaching agreement. This is therefore a surprising but all the more welcome development conceded by the Council. It is also worth noting that the Council has expressly communicated its willingness to involve the FRA in the compatibility-check process.[79]

72 Council discussion document, 'The Role of the Council in Ensuring the Effective Implementation of the Charter of Fundamental Rights in the Legislative Process' (Informal meeting of the Justice and Home Affairs Ministers, 20–21 January 2011). This came as a response to both the Commission's Communication strategy on an effective implementation of the Charter, and the European Parliament's Resolution on the situation of fundamental rights in the EU (2009–2010).
73 Ibid 2–3.
74 Ibid 2.
75 Council of the European Union, 'Guidelines on Methodological Steps to be taken to check fundamental rights compatibility at the Council's preparatory bodies' 10140/11 [2011]. On a discussion of these Guidelines, see J. Morijn, 'The EU Fundamental Rights Charter, the European Commission and the Council of Ministers: Checking the "Charter Checklists" <https://eutopialaw.com/2011/09/30/the-eu-fundamental-rights-charter-the-european-commission-and-the-council-of-ministers-checking-the-charter-checklists'-part-2/> accessed 6 May 2018.
76 Ibid 2.
77 Ibid 4.
78 Ibid.
79 See also Council of the European Union, 'Council Conclusions on the Council's actions and initiatives for the implementation of the Charter of Fundamental Rights of the European Union, 3092nd General Affairs Council meeting' [2011] paras 36–37.

As to the substantive guidance provided for conducting the fundamental rights check, this document does not provide for great novelties when viewed against the various Commission Communications. Rather, it is a summarised version of the Commission's Fundamental Rights 'checklist'. What is specific to the Council Guidelines is that in case of doubt, they advise consulting the Council Legal Service, making use of the national experts' expertise in the Member State and consulting the Working Party on Fundamental Rights, Citizenship and Free Movement of Persons (hereinafter the 'FREMP Working Party') or another preparatory body specialising in a specific fundamental right.

In December 2014, the Council adopted a new set of revised Guidelines.[80] These include practical changes relating to enhancing awareness and changes to the wording of the fundamental rights checklist. As regards the former, two small yet useful insertions are worth noting: first, the Council Secretariat is to include the revised guidelines in the general training of incoming Presidencies[81]; and, second, the FREMP Working Party should be kept informed of all Council Legal Service legal assessments and advice on fundamental rights matters through the insertion of its acronym in the relevant documentation.[82]

As regards the wording of the checklist, three changes have to be pointed out. First, when checking the content of fundamental rights at issue in order to assess the compatibility of the proposal with the Charter (step 1), ECHR law has been expressly included in the checklist as a source for understanding the Charter rather than being merely listed in the Annex. Second, when assessing whether there is a limitation to fundamental rights and, if so, whether it is in compliance with the Charter, an additional element has been included, which requires asking whether the essence of the right(s) is respected. Finally, Article 52(1) of the Charter concerning legitimate limitations of fundamental rights is expressly spelled out in the checklist with reference to the applicable case law.

The 2014 Guidelines do not include any ground-breaking changes from the first Guidelines adopted in 2011. The revised version includes some improvements and the fact that they constitute a recurring item on the Council's agenda is to be welcomed, even if it is certain that it is the Court's recent case law that has drawn attention to this matter. The fact that the Council is reacting by aiming to improve its framework for *ex ante* fundamental rights assessments is a positive development.

A final novelty in the practices of the Council to be noted is the Hungarian presidency's introduction of a new 'tradition',[83] namely, 'adopting an evaluation of the application of the Charter of Fundamental Rights at Council level', which will become 'a compulsory component of the EU's annual work'.[84] In view of its

80 Council of the European Union, Guidelines on Methodological Steps to be taken to check fundamental rights compatibility at the Council's preparatory bodies, 16957/14 (16 December 2014).
81 Ibid 2.
82 Ibid 11.
83 Introduced in the General Affair's Council during the Hungarian Presidency in 2011.
84 See Council Conclusions, (n 79).

retrospective character, this practice does not contribute much to ensuring that concrete policies and legislation are fundamental rights-compliant. However, it can still provide for added value in terms of institutional learning, as it forces the Council to think about its actions in fundamental rights terms and as it also places a certain burden on it to actually take action in furtherance of the Charter rights in view of the upcoming evaluation.

2. Advisory bodies with a legislative role: EESC and CoR

The EESC and the CoR exercise advisory functions in a big number of policy areas and issue opinions on legislative and policy files, which can have as their subject matter fundamental rights or impact on these.

2.1. Legal framework within which the bodies operate

The European Economic and Social Committee (EESC) and the Committee of the Regions (CoR) are the Union's Advisory Bodies.[85] They are to assist the European Parliament, the Council and the Commission by exercising advisory functions and they are to be completely independent in performing their duties, in the Union's general interest.[86]

The composition of the two bodies is markedly different. The EESC consists of representatives of organisations of employers, of the employed, and of other parties representative of civil society, notably in socio-economic, civic, professional and cultural areas. The CoR is composed of representatives of regional and local bodies who either hold a regional or local authority electoral mandate or are politically accountable to an elected assembly.[87] Thus, the former committee is representative of special interests and experts; the latter has a political outlook.

The two bodies must be consulted where the Treaty so provides (mandatory consultation).[88] They can also be consulted where one of the institutions considers it appropriate,[89] and they can issue opinions on their own initiative.[90] In cases where the European Parliament, the Council or the Commission requests an Opinion from the EESC pursuant to Art. 304 TFEU, the Committee of the Regions must be informed and may issue an Opinion on the matter if it considers that specific regional interests are at stake.[91] The Opinions of these bodies are not binding.

The seeking of Opinions is mandatory in a large number of policy areas, notably those concerned with market-making and market-correction. Opinions can be

85 TFEU art 300.
86 TFEU arts 300(1) and (4).
87 See TFEU arts 300(2) and (3) respectively.
88 TFEU arts 304 and 307 respectively.
89 In the case of the CoR, cases concerning cross-border cooperation are singled out in the Treaties.
90 TFEU art 304 first para and art 307 fourth para.
91 TFEU art 307 third para.

sought within the ordinary legislative procedure as well as the special legislative procedure. The EESC has to be consulted in more areas than the CoR. According to empirical research, the two Committees 'are formally involved in more than 50 per cent of all EU legislative acts by giving opinions during the first reading of the ordinary legislative procedure and the consultation procedure.'[92]

Where consultation is mandatory, the Commission forwards its proposal simultaneously to the European Parliament, the Council and the Committee(s). When involved, the Committees need to issue their Opinions before the Parliament and the Council complete the first reading of a proposal.[93]

2.2. Institutional mechanisms for taking the Charter into account

The CoR is divided in six 'commissions',[94] whereas the EESC has six 'sections'.[95] CoR has one commission – on Citizenship, Governance, Institutional and External Affairs (CIVEX) – that has the Charter as one of the 'areas' it is expressly required to coordinate.[96] The EESC does not have a section, which expressly has the Charter of Fundamental Rights as a core area of activity, although it seems that it would fall on the section on Employment, Social Affairs and Citizenship (SOC) to deal with the majority of files implicating fundamental rights.[97]

The EESC and CoR can be and are confronted with fundamental rights issues irrespective of the type of Opinion in question: be it a mandatory, requested or own-initiative Opinion – and be it on a legislative proposal or an exploratory Opinion on a policy issue. It is also important to note that it is not only the

92 Christoph Hönnige and Diana Panke, 'Is anybody listening? The Committee of the Regions and the European Economic and Social Committee and their quest for awareness', (2016) 23 *Journal of European Public Policy* 624.

93 For a detailed account of the formal role and the *de facto* output of the CoR and the EESC see Diana Panke, Christoph Hönnige and Julia Gollub, *Consultative Committees in the European Union, no vote – no influence?* (Colchester: ECPR Press, 2015) ch 2 Consultative Commitees in the EU.

94 Citizenship, Governance, Institutional and External Affairs (CIVEX); Territorial Cohesion Policy and EU Budget (COTER); Economic Policy (ECON); Environment, Climate Change and Energy (ENVE); Natural Resources (NAT); Social Policy, Education, Employment, Research and Culture (SEDEC).

95 Agriculture, Rural Development and the Environment (NAT); Economic and Monetary Union and Economic and Social Cohesion (ECO); Employment, Social Affairs and Citizenship (SOC); External Relations (REX); The Single Market, Production and Consumption (INT); Transport, Energy, Infrastructure and the Information Society (TEN).

96 Out of many however, see: 'CoR Commissions' <http://cor.europa.eu/en/activities/commissions/Pages/cor-commissions.aspx?comm=CIVEX> accessed 11 May 2017.

97 SOC has the following list of policy areas: employment and working conditions, social policy and poverty, education and training, justice and home affairs (including immigration and asylum), health, gender equality, disability issues, demography, family, culture, sport, citizenship, volunteering and the Roma.

CIVEX commission and the SOC section respectively that are confronted or raise fundamental rights questions.[98]

There is no mechanism in place in either of the Committees that allows for taking the Charter *systematically* into account in all of their opinions. When considering the working cycle of an opinion in both Committees, it becomes evident that the whole process is member-driven. The preparatory work of draft Opinions is conducted in the designated commission in the case of CoR and in the designated section in the case of the EESC, and the rapporteur sets the tone for each Opinion. Thus, the question whether fundamental rights considerations will be identified and whether certain matters will be seen through the fundamental rights lens will depend on the expertise/profile of that person, the composition/outlook of the members of the commission/section tabling amendments, debating and voting on the draft within that, and subsequently in the Plenary which is attended by all members. This is similar to the European Parliament, where the profile of rapporteur, committee and members in plenary will be a determinant.

2.3. Towards achieving greater impact on fundamental rights questions?

It is not easy to find (an) example(s) of a CoR opinion or an EESC Opinion influencing a legislative file so as to provide for enhanced fundamental rights protection, which can be unequivocally and directly attributed to that opinion.[99]

However, a more in-depth *systematic* analysis combining quantitative and qualitative methods would be necessary in order to pronounce definite conclusions on this point and to subsequently make recommendations as to how to improve such impact.

The degree of influence/impact that these two advisory Committees have more generally has been questioned. Lack of influence/impact more generally has obviously also repercussions on the impact of advice provided by either or both Committees in the field of fundamental rights. There has been criticism concerning underperformance of these Committees and even some calls for their abolition.[100] However, recent academic research seems to provide for a more varied

98 For example, it was the EESC's Section for Transport, Energy and Infrastructure, which produced a legislative Opinion on the Commission's Proposal for a Data Retention Directive. This is not the most obvious Section where one would expect fundamental rights expertise, and yet the Committee was very outspoken about the fundamental rights implications of this proposal. See Opinion of the European Economic and Social Committee on the Proposal for a Directive of the European Parliament and of the Council on the retention of data processed in connection with the provision of public electronic communication services and amending Directive 2002/58/EC (COM(2005) 438 final – 2005/0182 (COD)) [2006] OJ C69/16.

99 Upon inquiry with staff of the respective secretariats of the CoR CIVEX Committee and the EESC SOC Section for such opinions, I was not able identify obvious 'success stories' based on the information received.

100 P. Craig and G. De Búrca, *EU Law – Text, Cases and Materials* (5th edn, Oxford University Press, 2011) 68; European Convention, Contribution by M. Helle Thorning Schmidt, alternate member of the Convention, 'Four good reasons to

picture.[101] The study of Panke, Hönnige and Gollub points out that '[t]he EU decision-making procedure has a timing-based, built-in disadvantage for the CoR and the EESC because they must deliver their recommendations well before the internal decision-making processes of the EP and the Council are completed [in order to be influential], although the CoR and the EESC receive the Commission's proposals at the very same time' and even though they have less resources at their disposal.[102] The fact that both Committees are consensus-driven in their decision-making is said to increase the problem of timely reaction even further and the wide mandate of the two Committees (based on the Treaty) only exacerbates the problem of workload.[103] The authors thus propose that the influence of the Committees might increase if they become more selective (in view of the workload), focusing on a limited number of high-quality opinions, in areas which are pre-defined for each legislative period (so that the work can start early), thus hopefully ensuring that targeted and concrete proposals can be delivered in a timely fashion.[104] The authors also suggest adopting additional channels of communication, in addition to those presently prescribed by the institutional framework, in order to disseminate information more proactively/earlier.[105] Moreover, given that both Committees are closer to 'information on the ground', they should be more involved in Commission impact assessments.

However, even if the two Committees' impact can thus be increased overall, the question remains whether fundamental rights would receive priority in their work. As discussed above, based on Art. 51(1) of the Charter, they have a legal duty not only to respect the rights and observe the principles contained therein, but also to promote the application thereof within their respective powers. Therefore, there is a constitutional duty resting also on these two Committees to place the question

abolish the European Economic and Social Committee', CONV 739/03, CONTRIB 234, Brussels 15 May 2003; European Parliament, 'Written Declaration pursuant to Rule 116 of the Rules of Procedure by Nils Lundgreen and Hélène Goudin on the Abolition of the Economic and Social Committee' [2007]; European Parliament, Motion for a Resolution pursuant to Rule 133 of the Rules of Procedure by Marine Le Pen, Matteo Salvini, Marcel de Graaff, Harald Vilimsky, Gerolf Annemans on the Abolition of the European Economic and Social Committee [17.12.2004]; European Parliament, Motion for a Resolution pursuant to Rule 133 of the Rules of Procedure by Marine Le Pen, Marcel de Graaff, Harald Vilimsky, Gerolf Annemans on the Abolition of the Committee of the Regions [17.12.2004].

101 See e.g. Milena I. Neshkova, 'The Impact of subnational interests on supranational regulation' (2010) 17 *Journal of European Public Policy* 1193, who examines the relationship between CoR and the European Commission. See also D. Panke, C. Hönnige and J. Gollub (n 93), who have examined CoR's and EESC's relationship vis-à-vis the European Parliament and Council, and Christoph Hönnige and Diana Panke, 'Is anybody listening? The Committee of the Regions and the European Economic and Social Committee and their quest for awareness', (2016) 23 *Journal of European Public Policy* 624.

102 D. Panke, C. Hönnige and J. Gollub, above (n 93), at 170–174.

103 Ibid.

104 Ibid.

105 Ibid.

of how to implement the Charter through their own advisory role, high on their agenda of priorities.

Within the area of fundamental rights, one could imagine a more strategic collaboration between the two Committees and the EU Fundamental Rights Agency[106] with a view to flagging important legislative initiatives with fundamental rights implications for each legislative period. The bodies would be complementary in this respect. FRA can offer the necessary expertise while the Committees can make use of their power to issue opinions on their own initiative.

There remains the question whether, from the perspective of the FRA, this investment would be worth making. Given its own limited resources it would also have to be selective in terms of which institution to engage with in order to provide advice. It may find it more sensible to target the law-makers directly, even though no formal Opinion has been requested, and provide informal advice, for example. Yet, at least with respect to files that are worth targeting, the FRA would not have to engage in any additional work; it would just be sharing the information with another body and could thereby target the same legislative (or policy) initiative at different institutional venues.

3. Expert bodies/agencies with an advisory role

3.1 FRA

The FRA[107] is the first and only EU body whose tasks are explicitly linked to all areas of EU fundamental rights protection. The FRA's tasks can be divided into three areas: first, data collection and analysis; second, providing assistance and expertise to EU institutions and bodies, and to Member States when acting within the scope of EU law[108]; third, the development of a communication strategy to increase fundamental rights awareness in civil society.[109]

The FRA can act either upon its own motion or upon request from one of the EU institutions, which can take the form of an opinion, conclusion or report. In the latter case, it can act on any of the Charter rights. In the former case however, when it acts *ex officio*, it is confined to its areas of activity as set out in its Multiannual Framework (MAF), which is adopted by the Council, after consulting the European Parliament, on the basis of a Commission proposal. Furthermore, the

106 The CoR engages already in an Annual Fundamental Rights Dialogue with the FRA. Further information is available here: European Union Agency for Fundamental Rights, 'European Committee of the Regions' <http://fra.europa.eu/en/cooperation/eu-partners/committee-of-the-regions> accessed 11 May 2017. For information on FRA – EESC cooperation see here: European Union Agency for Fundamental Rights, 'European Economic and Social Committee' <http://fra.europa.eu/en/cooperation/eu-partners/eesc> accessed 11 May 2017.

107 Established by Council Regulation EC No 168/2007 establishing a European Union Agency for Fundamental Rights [2007] OJ L53/1 (hereinafter the 'FRA Founding Regulation').

108 Ibid art 1.

109 Ibid art 4.

current FRA Founding Regulation, being adopted pre-Lisbon, defines the scope of the Agency's work as falling 'within the competences of the Community' as laid down in the EC Treaty. This leads to an argument that under the current Regulation the FRA cannot conduct work on its own initiative (and under the MAF) that falls within former third pillar matters (police and judicial cooperation).[110]

It is worth pointing to two especially important points regarding the FRA's current work structure that need to be improved in order to facilitate the fulfilment of its tasks.

The first one concerns the MAF. Toggenburg has argued for the abolition of the MAF altogether. This seems a sensible proposal for two reasons. First, the MAF is drafted in an inconsistent way so as to obscure what a 'thematic area' is, within which the FRA has to work: the MAF singles out certain fundamental rights but it also lists certain policy areas.[111] The result is that it puts an emphasis on only parts of the Charter and may give the misleading impression that the FRA can only act within these rights (whereas it can work on any fundamental right(s) that can be linked to the listed policy areas). Secondly, and what seems more important, is the argument that the FRA should decide itself on its own MAF, albeit in close cooperation with the EU institutions so as to be in line with the requirement that it is in line with the Union's priorities as required by Art. 5 of the FRA Founding Regulation. It is 'unclear why this prioritisation should be outsourced to a political institution like the Council of the European Union.'[112]

A second point that arguably needs to be changed concerns the fact that the FRA is denied the possibility to conduct legislative scrutiny of draft proposals out of its own motion. Dissatisfaction with this state of affairs has been expressed in academic literature[113] and in a UK House of Lords Report of 2005.[114] The FRA's Management Board also made this point as one of the recommendations issued to the Commission based on the results of an external independent evaluation of the FRA.[115]

110 The MAF adopted for the period 2013–2017 does not include the area of police and judicial cooperation as the Council could not agree on it. See G. Toggenburg, 'Fundamental Rights and the European Union: how does and how should the EU Agency for Fundamental Rights relate to the EU Charter of Fundamental Rights?' [2013] EUI Working Paper LAW 2013/13, 13.

111 Toggenburg, ibid 7.

112 Ibid 13. See also other references therein pointing to academic work making the same argument.

113 G.N. Toggenburg, 'The EU Fundamental Rights Agency: Satellite or Guiding Star?' (2007) 5 SWP Comments 1; Toggenburg (n 110); Kosta, (n 38), at 77 et seq.

114 House of Lords 16th Report (n 40), at 32–33. In particular, the NGO Justice and the Law Society saw a legislative scrutiny role for the FRA. Interestingly, the expert witness for the Commission, Dr Clemens Ladenburger, expressed the view that 'the possibility of the Agency scrutinising proposals and draft legislation was something to be considered'.

115 The recommendations to the Commission were issued in accordance with art 31(1) of the FRA Founding Regulation, see European Union Agency for Fundamental Rights (4 June 2013) <https://fra.europa.eu/sites/default/files/fra-management-board-recommendations-external-evaluation_0.pdf> accessed 11 May 2017.

The denial of such an *ex officio* legislative scrutiny competence is regretful. It would have provided for enhanced fundamental rights protection without depriving the Commission of its role as the guardian of the Treaties and fundamental rights because it would not have any legal effects for a draft proposal; nor would it 'have represented the competence to establish non-compliance within the framework of infringement proceedings, but merely the possibility of examining relevant proposals and opinions at all stages of the legislative process from the perspective of a human rights expert'.[116]

The possibility of *ex officio* legislative scrutiny would have arguably granted the FRA real teeth to contribute towards a fundamental rights culture within the law-making process.

*3.2 EDPS – specialised (supervisory) body with an advisory role (*inter alia*)*

3.2.1. LEGAL FRAMEWORK WITHIN WHICH THE EDPS OPERATES

The European Data Protection Supervisor (EDPS) is an independent supervisory authority for the protection of personal data. The EPDS itself describes its work as resting broadly on three pillars: first, supervision and enforcement; second, consultation (or advisory), which formally takes the form of opinions, comments or letters; third, cooperation (e.g. with national data protection authorities through the 'Art. 29 Working Party').[117] Importantly, the EDPS's advisory function is only one out of several others it performs, albeit one that turned out to become central to the EDPS. This was not immediately obvious when the legal framework establishing this body was put into place. It also differs most obviously from the advisory bodies described above in that its very mandate relates to protection of specific fundamental rights as enshrined in the Charter, namely protection of personal data (Art. 8 of the Charter) and privacy (Art. 7 of the Charter).

The EDPS was set up by Regulation 45/2001 relating to the processing of personal data by the Community institutions and bodies and on the free movement of such data (see Chapter V).[118] This Regulation was based on Art. 386 EC Treaty, which provided that (then) Community acts on data protection should bind the institutions and bodies set up by the Treaties. In addition, it prescribed the establishment of an independent supervisory authority, which would be responsible for monitoring the application of such acts to the institutions.

116 G.N. Toggenburg, 'The EU Fundamental Rights Agency: Satellite or Guiding Star?' (2007) 5 SWP Comments 1, 5. See also Kosta, (n 113), for a detailed discussion of arguments and counterarguments relating to the question of granting the FRA an ex officio legislative scrutiny role.

117 See website of the EDPS <https://secure.edps.europa.eu/EDPSWEB/edps/EDPS> accessed 11 May 2017.

118 Regulation (EC) No 45/2001 of the European Parliament and of the Council of 18 December 2000 on the protection of individuals with regard to the processing of personal data by the Community institutions and bodies and on the free movement of such data [2001] OJ L8/1.

According to Art. 41(2) of Regulation 45/2001, the EDPS is responsible 'for monitoring and ensuring the application of the provisions ... [of that] Regulation and any other Community act relating to the protection of the fundamental rights and freedoms of natural persons with regard to the processing of personal data by a Community institution or body, and for advising Community institutions and bodies and data subjects on all matters concerning the processing of personal data.'

It has been observed[119] that this wording of the Regulation setting out the mandate of the EDPS emphasises its supervisory rather than its advisory function. Further, read at face value, it is not clear that the advisory function of the EDPS should extend beyond providing advice in relation to data actually processed by the EU institutions (as contemplated by Regulation 45/2001).

However, the EDPS has itself read a broader advisory mandate into the wording of Regulation 45/2001, a view, which was crucially confirmed by the Court of Justice of the EU in the context of the famous *PNR*[120] litigation. In this case the EDPS (for the first time) applied for leave to intervene in Court proceedings based on Art 47(1)(i) of Regulation 45/2001, which gives the EDPS the power to intervene before the Court. Notably (but unsurprisingly given the specific case), the European Parliament agreed that the EDPS had the right to intervene in this case. The Court held that the advisory task of the EDPS under Art. 41(2) of the Regulation 'does not cover only the processing of personal data by those institutions or organs'.[121] This opened the way for a very broad advisory mandate of the EDPS covering all legislation (and soft law) with implications for data protection. As the EDPS explained in one of its opinions, it brings within its scope of advice '"proposals which build on, supplement or amend the existing legal framework for data protection, and [...] proposals which have a significant impact on the protection of individuals' rights and freedoms with regard to the processing of personal data." What counts is the impact on the effectiveness of the protection itself, rather than the formal impact on the existing Community framework on data protection.'[122]

119 P. de Hert and V. Papakonstantinou, 'The EDPS as a Unique Stakeholder in the European Data Protection Landscape, Fulfilling the Explicit and Non-Explicit Expectations' in H. Hijmans and H. Kranenborg, *Data Protection Anno 2014: How to Restore Trust? – Contributions in honour of Peter Hustinx, European Data Protection Supervisor (2004–2014)* (Intersentia 2014).

120 Joined Cases (C-317/04) *European Parliament v Council of the European Union* and (C-318/04) *Commission of the European Communities*, ECLI:EU:C:2006:346.

121 Order of the Court in Case C-317/04, *European Parliament v Council of the European Union*, ECLI:EU:C:2005:189, para 18.

122 European Data Protection Supervisor, 'The EDPS as an advisor to the Community institutions on proposals for legislation and related documents' (EDPS Policy Paper, 18 March 2015), at 5 <https://secure.edps.europa.eu/EDPSWEB/webdav/site/mySite/shared/Documents/EDPS/Publications/Papers/PolicyP/05-03-18_PP_EDPSadvisor_EN.pdf> accessed 11 May 2017.

This broad interpretation was thus also a basis for intervention in this case. It should be noted however that such right of intervention does not extend to proceedings within the context of the preliminary reference procedure.[123]

Once the scope of the mandate was established, every available power and task of the EDPS could be read in that light. This is true for Art. 28 (2) of Regulation 45/2001, which imposes an obligation on the Commission to consult the EDPS 'when it adopts a legislative proposal relating to the protection of individuals' rights and freedoms with regard to the processing of personal data.' When read against Art. 41 of the Regulation as interpreted by the Court, this then covers 'all matters concerning the processing of personal data'. And it is also true for Art. 46(d) of Regulation 45/2001 according to which the EDPS can advise the institutions also on its own initiative.

3.2.2. HOW TO BUILD A STRONG ADVISORY FUNCTION (ON FUNDAMENTAL RIGHTS) FOR ACHIEVING IMPACT – LESSONS FROM THE EDPS

This section will review the mechanisms that the EDPS has put in place in order to maximise its impact with a view to ensuring data protection compliant law and policy-making by the institutions.

The EDPS was given a *prima facie* narrow mandate and limited resources when it was first established. Already ten years after its inception, it was safe to say that the body was and is perceived as a major institutional player in the EU law and policy-making scene when it comes to questions of data protection.[124] Therefore, it is important to investigate how this body achieved such standing and whether there are any lessons that the other (advisory) bodies can learn from it.

It is clear that the Court's judgment confirming a broad advisory role at a good time, i.e. the very initial phase of existence of the EDPS, certainly created a favourable framework within which to operate and 'build' this office. However, it is also a question of how to make best use of that framework.

The EDPS made excellent strategic use of the Order of the Court, which confirmed the EDPS's own vision, publishing immediately (one day after the Order was issued[125]) a policy paper on how it interprets and organises this advisory task,[126] giving it the widest reading possible. Notably, after explaining the breadth of its mandate, the EDPS chose to focus its attention in this paper on its advisory role on legislative proposals (leaving the advice on internal rules and administrative measures of institutions aside). The laying out of the EDPS's mandate was carefully and strategically planned. Moreover, the fact that it was publicly

123 Order of the Court in Case C-73/07, *Tietosuoajavaltuutettu v Satakunnan Markkinapörssi Oy and Satamedia Oy*, ECLI:EU:C:2007:507.

124 See the various contributions in Hijmans and Kranenborg (n 119).

125 As noted by de Hert and Papakonstantinou (n 119), at 249.

126 EDPS Policy Paper, 'The EDPS as an advisor to the Community Institutions on proposals for legislation and related documents' (Brussels, 18 March 2005) <https://edps.europa.eu/sites/edp/files/publication/05-03-18_pp_edpsadvisor_en.pdf>, accessed 7 May 2018.

communicated proves in itself a strategic choice. As stated in the paper: '[b]y presenting this policy paper the EDPS aims to position himself as a *reliable* and *predictable* player in the process of legislation. The policy paper is an important step in a process to acquire such a position and *enhances by itself* the *effectiveness* of the EDPS as an advisor on proposals for legislation.'[127]

The EDPS also published a follow-up policy paper on the same theme building on ten years of experience.[128] The following features, which can be distilled from both papers,[129] emerge as being crucial towards achieving impact in the field; but the basic principles are applicable to other bodies with an advisory function especially in the legislative context.

Expert advice of highest quality This is self-evident. One can only achieve the standing of a reliable and useful advisor if one brings clear expertise to the table. What is needed is an impeccable analysis that goes beyond what the recipient of advice already knows (or can more easily find out via different routes) and which that recipient can trust.

Selectiveness As already noted above, the EDPS provides advice in all areas that can have an impact on data protection; by definition such broad mandate then requires taking a selective approach in view of limited resources. The EDPS organises its work according to an 'inventory', which is based on the Work Programme of the Commission and, importantly, bilateral contacts between the EDPS and the services of the Commission. The inventory flags with a colour-code the Commission proposals that the EDPS (1) will issue a formal opinion on, (2) may comment or issue an opinion on and, (3) will follow the developments. This is an essential tool for organising the work. Importantly, the inventory for each year, together with a description of priorities, is publicly available on the EDPS's website.[130]

The principle of selectiveness is applicable to CoR and EESC and is also applicable to other bodies that are facing a high workload due to the number of policy areas that follow under their mandate with limited resources, such as the FRA.

Explaining the methodology & creating accountability Building a toolkit/methodology/checklist and explaining to the various actors and institutions how to act

127 Ibid 2, emphases added.

128 European Data Protection Supervisor, 'The EDPS as an advisor to EU institutions on policy and legislation: building on ten years of experience' (EDPS Policy Paper, 4 June 2014) <https://secure.edps.europa.eu/EDPSWEB/webdav/site/mySite/shared/Documents/EDPS/Publications/Papers/PolicyP/14-06-04_PP_EDPSadvisor_EN.pdf> accessed 11 May 2017.

129 Ibid, especially 7.

130 The annual priorities and inventories are available here: European Data Protection Supervisor, 'Priorities' <https://secure.edps.europa.eu/EDPSWEB/edps/Consultation/Priorities> accessed 11 May 2017.

in a data protection (or more generally fundamental rights) compliant manner appears crucial toward achieving a shift in the working culture. The aim is here that the institutions 'internalise' the methodology, and feel themselves accountable. In order to do so, it is imperative however to have close ties and very good working relationships with the recipients of advice. As we have seen both the Commission and the Council of the European Union work with such methodology and checklists respectively and the FRA has also built fundamental rights toolkits over time.

Proactiveness The EDPS advises also on its own initiative when a matter is of significant importance. That presupposes that own-initiative interventions are mandated; but it also includes another element, namely, developing thematic or sectoral guidelines in areas where there might be a significant impact on data protection (or fundamental rights generally) and intensive legislative activity.

Involvement all along the legislative process Art. 28(2) of Regulation 45/2001 does not impart anything as to the timing of consultation. The EDPS's interpretation of this was to provide advice throughout the legislative process. In order to make interventions effective, informal early interventions, before a Commission proposal is adopted (and hence before the political bargaining between the co-legislators starts), are considered crucial. It is part of standard practice that the Commission consults the EDPS during the inter-service consultation stage and before a proposal (or measure/policy document) is adopted by the College of Commissioners. Evidently, the EDPS also provides formal and public advice to the Commission, although when a formal opinion is issued without prior informal consultation that opinion may have less of an impact on the Commission. However it can be picked up by one of the co-legislators.[131] The EDPS also undertakes both informal consultation with the European Parliament and the Council and provides formal advice to both. In this respect, keeping an 'equal distance' to all institutions is considered important in order to be a reliable and trustworthy advisor. It is one of the EDPS' proclaimed underlying values of work, namely to act with integrity.

131 As was the case for example with the European Parliament and the 'PNR Canada' file, Executive summary of the Opinion of the European Data Protection Supervisor on the proposals for Council decisions on the conclusion and the signature of the agreement between Canada and the European Union on the transfer and processing of passenger name record data [2014] OJ C51/12. See also the reference to the EDPS opinion in European Parliament, 'Draft Motion for a Resolution pursuant to Rule 108 (6) of the Rules of Procedure on seeking an opinion from the Court of Justice on the compatibility with the Treaties of the Agreement between Canada and the European Union on the transfer and processing of Passenger Name Record data (2014/2966 (RSP)), Sophie in 't Veld, Nathalie Griesbeck, Cecilia Wikström on behalf of the ALDE Group, B8–0265/2014 [19.11.2014].

With respect to the EU Data Protection Reform, and more specifically the proposed General Data Protection Regulation,[132] the EDPS has demonstrated how it takes its role as advisor at all stages in a very proactive manner seriously. The EDPS issued a formal opinion when the Proposal was first adopted.[133] Three years into the negotiation process, and when the co-legislators entered the 'trilogue' phase, the EDPS issued a new opinion because of the "need (...) to update [the] advice to engage more directly with the positions of the co-legislators, and to offer specific recommendations."[134] More interestingly, alongside the opinion the EDPS also published an Annex setting out in a comparative table the original text of the Proposal, the position of the European Parliament at first reading, the position of the Council and next to that its own proposal for the legislative text. This was also made available in form of a free mobile app.[135] It is unprecedented for an advisory body to present its own version of a legislative proposal, and moreover, to do so in the form it did. This move seems to be strategically important for several cumulative reasons: first, the co-legislators have received concrete proposals on what the actual text should look like. This is constructive and much more helpful for the actual drafters, rather than them being faced with a substantive point of criticism or suggestion, which they would have to translate into a workable legal text. At the same time, when the proposals made are sensible, it puts pressure on the respective co-legislators who would be pressed to explain why their own (deviated) position is better, especially in these circumstances where the public is made aware of the various positions through a handy tool. Finally, the EDPS managed to create attention towards its proposals, by the mere fact of having taken such an unprecedented step in terms of the form chosen for providing advice. At the same time, according to press reports,[136] the EDPS is said to have communicated this initiative to all institutions before launching it, receiving encouragement to proceed. This is in line with its by now well-established strategy, of being transparent and predictable. It also agrees with another principle underlying its work, namely, pragmatism.

132 Commission, 'Proposal for a Regulation of the European Parliament and Council on the protection of individuals with regard to the processing of personal data and on the free movement of such data (General Data Protection Regulation)' COM (2012) 11 final.

133 EDPS opinion of 7 March 2012 on the Data Protection Reform <https://edps.europa.eu/sites/edp/files/publication/12-03-07_edps_reform_package_en.pdf> accessed 11 May 2017.

134 EDPS opinion 3/2015 of 27 July 2015 and updated with an addendum on 9 October 2015, 'Europe's big opportunity – EDPS recommendations on the EU's options for data protection reform' 2.

135 European Data Protection Supervisor, 'The History of the General Data Protection Regulation' <https://secure.edps.europa.eu/EDPSWEB/edps/Consultation/Reform_package> accessed 11 May 2017.

136 David Meyer, 'Watchdog releases own version of data regulation' *Politico* (27 July 2015) <www.politico.eu/article/watchdog-releases-data-protection-regulation-buttarelli-edps/> accessed 11 May 2017.

3.3. Advice on data protection vs. advice on other fundamental rights

The EDPS is a unique body in the EU institutional landscape, in that its mandate relates to specific fundamental rights (Art. 7 and 8 of the Charter). What is also noteworthy however is that data protection in itself assumes a special position among the EU fundamental rights. In addition to it being set out in the Charter, it has its own legal basis in the Treaty (Art. 16 TFEU), and it has been regulated in secondary EU legislation. It has thus received a degree of regulation much higher than other fundamental rights in the EU.[137] This may prove an important factor in terms of achieving compliance and mainstreaming in legislative and policy action driven by the EU institutions. Having detailed 'EU home-made' laws in place defining the scope and limitations to a fundamental right will make legislative scrutiny and mainstreaming much easier than when there are other fundamental rights involved that lack such, and especially if there is not much (EU) case law in place yet, and the fundamental right is not one that corresponds to a right enshrined in the ECHR.[138]

Additionally, its implementation profits from a body like the EDPS, which, as we have seen above, acts (among others) in order to ensure that this right is complied with in legislative action. This begs then the question whether this status quo creates a 'data protection bias', given that other fundamental rights do not enjoy either of these features.

Based on the above one could conclude that there exists a structural bias. However, whether this translates into a substantive bias (in terms of the level of protection for data protection vs other fundamental rights) in legislation is a different question.

One might have grounds to argue as much if one were to find that: (a) there is considerably more legislation in place that complies with and promotes data protection than other fundamental rights; and/or (b) that the balance between data protection and other fundamental rights when the two meet within legislation is consistently struck in favour of data protection. As a final step one would have to be able to attribute these results to the two distinctive features named above (the EDPS and the high degree of existing regulation) and not say to the preferences of the legislature.

There is a principled (rather than an empirical) point to be made with respect to point (b). This concerns the role of the EDPS as an advisor on data protection issues. One could take the view that the EDPS should only be concerned with ensuring that data protection principles are complied with and that the legislation would pass judicial review. Once that is the case, it would be for the legislature to elaborate on how to strike a balance with conflicting fundamental

137 Next to equal treatment.

138 For those Charter rights that correspond to the ECHR, obviously the ECtHR jurisprudence will have to be taken into account, given that the 'meaning and scope of those rights shall be the same as those laid down by the said Convention' (art 52(3) of the Charter). However, it should be noted that the ECHR is only a ***minimum*** standard, and therefore, does not have to be identical to that of the EU.

rights. Yet, it is clear that if the EDPS wants to be influential, it would also have to engage with the fact that a measure may pursue, or may need to accommodate, other (fundamental rights) objectives. Therefore it needs to engage to a certain extent with the question on how such balance could be struck. As noted above, the EDPS follows the principle of pragmatism in its work, so it may not be surprising that it has identified this very point in its advisory function, stipulating that it 'work(s) with the institutions and other stakeholders to ensure that [it] understand[s] the priorities and objectives behind measures which have an impact on data protection, and to assist in finding solutions which minimise conflict between these priorities.'[139]

There is an argument that such (substantive bias) should not occur if the methodology for an effective implementation of the Charter is successful and has managed to achieve a fundamental rights culture across the board. There is some doubt whether that has materialised today within the legislature (consider the discussion on IAs above), even if first signs of a shift may be identified,[140] and we have seen that there is scope of improvement in the work of the advisory bodies (at section 2) and in the working structure of the FRA.

Moreover, it is clear that according to the current methodology a systematic legality check of all legislative proposals still rests with the Commission Legal Service. That is however a small unit which is moreover bound by the confidentiality of legal advice and cannot therefore act in a transparent manner. And yet, the lessons learned from the EDPS above demonstrate that transparency, and close cooperation of an expert advisor with the units drafting the legislation is key to building a fundamental rights culture.

Admittedly, there are mechanisms in place at the Commission level that seek to complement the Legal Service advice, such as fundamental rights training provided by the Fundamental Rights Officer of DG Justice to the other services, as well as the advice the DG Justice Fundamental Rights Unit can provide when receiving a query from another Service or when joining the Impact Assessment Steering Group. However, there is a clear point where the EDPS will be more effective in achieving impact, that is the fact that it is involved all along the legislative process. A Unit of a Commission Service cannot engage in that.

Secondly, the EDPS seems to be overseeing the entire legislative process based on which it chooses its interventions proactively. It is not clear to what extent the Fundamental Rights Unit at DG Justice is engaging in such a systematic and proactive advice on draft proposals for all fundamental rights contained in the Charter. To be sure, the above is not to argue for weakening the structure that is put in place for ensuring data protection compliance and promotion, but rather for strengthening the one for all other fundamental rights contained in the Charter.

139 See EDPS Policy Paper 2014, (n 128) section 4.5. 'A fair balance with other public interests and fundamental rights', at 11.

140 Kosta, (n 39).

IV Conclusions

The adoption and eventually the entry into force of the Charter has acted as a catalyst for EU fundamental rights mainstreaming – understood as a public sector duty to promote compliance with fundamental rights obligations as derived from the Charter in two ways: first, it has codified this duty in the Charter itself (section II). Secondly, that has led to the gradual establishment of mechanisms to build a fundamental rights culture in the EU institutional landscape overall but also importantly, in the legislative process (section III): from having no 'methodology' in place for building such fundamental rights culture, the Commission has gradually introduced such (CCAs and IAs). It has also put itself center-stage in this methodology due to its self-perception as the 'guardian of fundamental rights'. Thus, in its 2010 Communication, the Commission offered assistance to the other institutions to 'find an effective way to take into account the effects of their amendments on the implementation of the Charter'.[141] At the same time, it threatened that 'it will not hesitate to use all the means at its disposal, which may include requesting that the act be adopted unanimously or, where applicable, withdrawing its proposal or bringing an action for annulment of the provisions in question'.[142] In order to prevent this, it emphasised a 'transparent inter-institutional dialogue', whereby the Parliament and the Council take fundamental rights into account when assessing the impacts of their amendments, 'decisions on amendments are taken at the appropriate level' and 'the Legal Service of the three institutions are fully involved'.[143]

We have noted that at the European Parliament a new Directorate has been established, which could and arguably should be used for enhancing fundamental rights mainstreaming, and the Council of the European Union has also shown increased awareness for fundamental rights.

The advisory bodies with a legislative role (CoR and EESC) do deal with fundamental rights questions, although there are no systematic mechanisms in place to take the Charter into account. Their overall problem is one of impact in general, and thus also one of impact on fundamental rights questions. Academic authors have made proposals on how such impact in general could be improved. In that context it is submitted that, when implementing such changes, the question of maximising impact on fundamental rights questions has to be prioritised as a matter of Art. 51(1) of the Charter. Furthermore, the EDPS provides a good example on how impact on fundamental rights questions could be thus maximised. Both, the advisory bodies and the FRA could learn from this body. Although, as regards the FRA, the most pertinent issue seems one of finally giving it an *ex officio* legislative scrutiny role.

In sum, the EU has come a long way in fulfilling its duty of putting mechanisms in place that will allow fundamental rights mainstreaming; but for each of them there remains scope for improvement in their operation. Tackling these problems is equally a duty that derives from Art. 51(1) of the Charter.

141 2010 Commission Communication (n 47).
142 Ibid.
143 This point is not made in the inter-institutional agreement Council of the European Union, 'Common Approach to Impact Assessment' 14901/05 [2005].

3 The principle of gender mainstreaming

Possibilities and challenges

Eugenia Caracciolo di Torella

Introduction

Gender equality is arguably one of the most developed and elaborated general principles of European Union (EU) law. Its importance and complexity is reflected in the text of the Treaty on the European Union which aims to ensure that its application is "one of the central mission and activities of the Union".[1] It is not only one of the main principles of European Law; together with nationality, it has been one of the historical grounds protected under EU anti-discrimination law.[2] Originally encapsulated in Article 119 EEC, it was introduced in the Treaty as a device to prevent the distortion of competition.[3] Since then, the EU approach to equality law has fundamentally changed and the principle has been "deepened and widened".[4] It has deepened in the sense that it has gradually been developed into a very sophisticated principle. For example, over the years, the Court of Justice of the European Union (CJEU, previously ECJ) has distinguished between the concepts of direct and indirect discrimination.[5] Furthermore, the Treaty of Amsterdam has codified the EU's longstanding commitment to go beyond merely prohibiting discrimination in order to achieve equality. The deepening of the principle of sex equality has been matched by the widening of EU equality

1 Mark Bell, 'The Principle of Equal Treatment: Widening and Deepening' in Paul Craig, Grainne de Burca (eds), *The Evolution of EU Law* (Oxford University Press, 2012) 611–639, 629.
2 On this principle see Francesca Ippolito, 'Mainstreaming equality in the EU legal order: more than a Cinderella provision?' in this Volume.
3 Bertil Ohlin, 'Social Aspects of European Economic Co-Operation: Reports by a Group of Experts' (1956) 102 *International Labour Review* 99–123 and Catherine Barnard, 'The Economic Objectives of Article 199' in Tamara Hervey, David O'Keeffe (eds), *Sex Equality in the European Union* (Wiley, 1996) 321–335.
4 Mark Bell (n 1).
5 See Case 43/75 *Defrenne v Sabena* ('*Defrenne I*') ECLI:EU:C:1976:56, in particular para 10. For a more recent analysis see the Opinion of the AG Sharpston in Case C-73/08 *N. Bressols and Others, C. Chaverot v Gouvernement de la Communauté Française* ECLI:EU:C:2009:396 paras 43–57. See also Julia Sohrab, 'Avoiding the Exquisite Trap: a Critical Look at the Equal Treatment/Special Treatment Debate' (1993) 1 *Feminist Legal Studies* 141–162, Gillian Moore, 'Equal Treatment of the Sexes in European Law: What does "Equal" mean?' (1993) 2 *Feminist Legal Studies* 46–74.

legislation. The legislator has steadily developed a complex array of secondary legislation which has expanded the scope of application of the principle.[6] Such an expansion has ensured that the principle of sex equality is applied to a vast range of areas of life.[7] Apart from the "deepening and widening" process, the EU Charter of Fundamental Rights (the Charter)[8] has clearly established the constitutional dimension of equality[9] and this has recently been further reiterated by the European Pillar of Social Rights.[10] As a result, gender equality today is a value,[11] an objective, an aim,[12] a fundamental right,[13] a positive duty[14] and a legal competence of EU law. The importance of equality is recognised at domestic level and is supported by an increasingly powerful human rights argument.[15] This sophisticated set of provisions, however, does not *per se* guarantee the application of the principle of gender equality. Yet, equality is important to all areas of life – even those that appear to be the most gender neutral,[16] such as trade, agriculture and

6 See Sandra Fredman, 'Equality: a New Generation?' (2001) *Industrial Law Journal* 145–168, Lisa Waddington, 'The Development of a New Generation of Sex Equality Directives' (2004) *Maastricht Journal of European and Comparative Law* 11.

7 Directive 75/117 [1975] OJ L45/19 (Equal Pay Directive); Directive 76/207 [1976] OJ L39/40 (Equal Treatment Directive), as amended by Directive 2002/73 of the European Parliament and the Council [2002] OJ L269 (the amended Equal Treatment Directive); Directive 79/7 EEC [1979] OJ L6/2 (Social Security Directive); Directive 92/85 EEC [1992] OJ L348/1 (Health and Safety Directive); Directive 97/80 [1998] OJ L14/6 (Burden of Proof Directive); Council Directive 2000/43 EC [2000] OJ L180/22 (Race Directive); Directive 2000/78 EC [2000] OJ L303/16 (Employment Equality Directive); Council Directive 2004/113 EC [2004] OJ L 373/37 (Goods and Services Directive).

8 OJ [2000/C] 364/1.

9 The process of constitusionalisation of the principle of equal treatment was already described in Gillian More, 'The Principle of Equal Treatment: From Market Unifier to Fundamental Right' in Paul Craig, Grainne de Búrca (eds), *The Evolution of EU Law* (Oxford University Press, 1999) 517–553, see also Mark Bell, 'Equality and the European Union Constitution' (2004) 33 *Industrial Law Jornal* 242–260.

10 Available at https://ec.europa.eu/commission/priorities/deeper-and-fairer-economic-and-monetary-union/european-pillar-social-rights_en, accessed 11 May 2018. On the European Pillar of Social Rights see, in this Volume, Maria Eugenia Bartoloni, 'The Horizontal Social Clause in a Legal Dimension'.

11 Article 2 TEU.

12 Article 3 TEU.

13 Case C-243/95 *Hill and Stapleton v The Revenue Commissioners and Department of Finance* ECLI:EU:C:1998:298; Sophia Koukoulis-Spiliotopoulos, 'The Lisbon Treaty and the Charter of Fundamental Rights: Maintaining and developing the Acquis in Gender Equality' (2008) *European Gender Equality Law Review* 15–24. For a discussion on fundamental rights mainstreaming in the EU legal order see Vasiliki Kosta, 'Fundamental rights mainstreaming in the EU' in this Volume.

14 Sandra Fredman, 'Changing the Norm: Positive Duties in Equal Treatment Legislation' (2005) *Maastricht Journal of European and Comparative Law* 369–397.

15 See, inter alia, the European Convention on Human Rights, The International Covenant on Civil and Political Rights and the Convention on the Elimination of All Forms of Discrimination Against Women.

16 Gill Allwood, 'Gender Mainstreaming and Policy Coherence for Development: Unintended Gender Consequences and EU Policy' (2013) 39 *Women's Studies*

energy. It is crucial to ensure that the principle is applied in a meaningful and substantive fashion.

The mechanism of gender mainstreaming introduced by the Treaty of Amsterdam goes some way to ensure the effectiveness of the principle.[17] It is enshrined in Article 8 TFEU and in Article 10 TFEU that place the EU legislator under an obligation to take into account the principle of gender equality when planning and enacting legislation.[18] This is potentially a radically transformative legal principle that has generated a considerable sociological debate; it is, however, relatively underexplored by legal commentators.

This chapter aims to contribute to the legal discussion in this area. It joins those voices that maintain that the principle has not achieved the success that was hoped.[19] This is due to several interlinked reasons. To start with, gender mainstreaming is a concept that can be difficult to define and apply in practice. Furthermore, this chapter supports the view that the current interpretation has failed to (adequately) incorporate a feminist reading which is crucial to its effectiveness.[20] As a result, the concept has not been effectively implemented and, in many cases, gender mainstreaming has merely been a tick-boxing exercise. There is, however, a discrete area where gender mainstreaming has achieved some success, namely that of work-life balance. The reason for choosing this area is twofold: first, it is an area where the impact of the relevant policies and legislation on women is clear and therefore it is easier to understand why we should be mindful of its gender implications. Secondly, and perhaps more importantly, this is an area that underpins and affects any other policy. Simply put: if women do not have access to comprehensive and non-discriminatory work-life balance, their participation to any other area of life will be compromised. Work-life balance is thus particularly apt to show both the importance of the concept of gender mainstreaming as well as its potential and limitations.

To discuss these assumptions, this chapter is organised in two parts. Part one looks at the historical development of the concept, its potential and challenges before explaining why a feminist reading is important. Part two looks at how the concept has been applied to the area of work-life balance and evaluates the (admittedly limited) achievements in this area. In light of this discussion, this chapter concludes that, if certain preconditions exist, the concept *can* work. The European Pillar of Social Rights has the potential to inject new emphasis into it.

International Forum 42–52; Nitya Rao, 'Women's Rights to Land and Assets: Experience of Mainstreaming Gender in Development Projects' (2005) 40 *Economic and Political Weekly* 4701–4708.

17 There are also other mechanisms such as positive action (Article 157 (4) TFEU). These, however, will not be the focus of this chapter.

18 See 'Incorporating equal opportunities for women and men into all Community policies and activities. Communication from the Commission' COM (1996) 67 final.

19 See also Ute Behning and Maria Amparo Serrano Pascual, *Gender Mainstreaming in the European Employment Strategy* (ETUI 2001); Sylvia Walby, 'Gender Mainstreaming: Productive Tensions in Theory and Practice' (2005) 12 *Social Policy* 321–343.

20 Emanuela Lombardo and Petra Mayer, 'Gender Mainstreaming in the EU: Incorporating a Feminist Reading?' (2006) *European Journal of Women Studies* 151–166.

However, only when it incorporates a feminist reading that moves away from women to promote a broader approach can the concept truly be effective.

Gender mainstreaming: the concept

Towards a definition

There are many analyses of gender mainstreaming thus it is not difficult to find a definition[21] of the *concept*. It is more complicating to identify the *process* of gender mainstreaming.

This chapter uses Rees's definition as a starting point. Rees sees the concept of gender mainstreaming as a strategy that promotes gender equality "through its systematic integration into all systems and structures, into all policies, process and procedures, into the organisation and its culture, into ways of seeing and doing".[22] It differs from other traditionally employed strategies such as the enactment of equality legislation and positive actions. These are mainly focused on individual rights (equality legislation) and on the disadvantages of specific groups (positive actions). By contrast, gender mainstreaming seeks to challenge the very structure that gives rise to group disadvantages.[23] It does so by adding a third dimension that shifts the focus from the rights of individuals or the needs of groups to developing a structure where there are no gender hierarchies and differences are acknowledged and valued. As such, it is potentially a "paradigmatic shift" that can bring the principle of gender equality from fields traditionally considered to be "gendered" to new ones and can be more effective.[24] In other words it incorporates the gender question into traditional policy frameworks.

Gender mainstreaming is not a new concept: its history dates back to the 1990s.[25] It was first introduced as an "innovative feature" of the 1991 Third Action Programme on Equal Opportunities.[26] At this stage, however, there was no attempt to devise a structure to put it in practice. A few years later, it was established as a global strategy for promoting gender equality through the Platform for Action at the United Nations Fourth World Conference on Women in Beijing in September 1995. The European Commission that had actively

21 See inter alia, Mark Pollack and Emilie Hafner-Burton, 'Mainstreaming Gender in the European Union' (2000) *Journal of European Public Policy* 432–456; Johanna Kantola, *Gender and the European Union* (Palgrave McMillian 2010).
22 Teresa Rees, 'Reflections on the Uneven Development of Gender Mainstreaming in Europe' (2005) *International Feminist Journal of Politics* 555–574, 560.
23 Fiona Beveridge, Sue Nott and Kylie Stephen, 'Mainstreaming and Engendering of Policy Making: a Means to an End?' (2000) *Journal of European Public Policy* 385–405. Teresa Rees (n 22) 560.
24 See further Teresa Rees (n 22).
25 For an historical overview see furthermore Francesca Ippolito (n 2).
26 Commission of the European Communities, 'Equal Opportunities for Women and Men: the Third Medium-Term Community Action Programme 1991–1995' COM (90) 449.

participated at the preparation of the Conference, accepted and endorsed the concept.[27] In the same year, Austria, Finland and Sweden became members of the EU. These countries have historically demonstrated a strong commitment to equality and their membership has further boosted equality. Indeed, the following year the Commission expressly provided for the mobilisation of all Community policies for the purpose of promoting gender equality[28] and in 1997 gender mainstreaming was finally embedded in the Treaty of Amsterdam. Article 8 TFEU provides that "[i]n all its activities, the Union shall aim to eliminate inequalities, and to promote equality, between men and women" and Article 10 TFEU states that "[i]n defining and implementing its policies and activities, the Union shall aim to combat discrimination based on sex, racial or ethnic origin, religion or belief, disability, age or sexual orientation."

By codifying the principle, the EU has made a clear commitment to mainstreaming gender equality to all areas of EU law; there is, however, little guidance concerning the process on how to make this commitment effective. *Prima facie*, this is straightforward: gender mainstreaming requires the policymaker and legislator to consider gender equality aspects in any policy and legislation and to integrate it automatically and systematically into all policies and actions. In 1998, the Council of Europe offered some guidance. It held that gender mainstreaming implies "the (re)organisation, improvement, development and evaluation of policy processes, so that a gender equality prospective is incorporated in all policies, at all levels and at all stages, by the actors normally involved in policy making".[29] But, in practice, what does it mean to "(re)organise" and "develop" the policy process? And who are the actors "normally involved" in the process?

As for the process, it can safely be assumed that this entails the evaluation of gender equality at all stages of the policy or legislation making process. At the preparatory stage, it will be important to collect the practices available, statistics on the users of the proposed policy or legislation in the area, assessment of the needs of the prospective users as well as the resources available in order to gain an informed understanding to help with the planning. In the decision making stage, it will need to be evident how all the information collected is taken into consideration. At this stage, it will also be essential to have a numerical balance of the individuals involved in the decision. This will help in bringing to the table the perceptions, experience, interests of women as well as men on a particular policy. Finally, following the implementation of a given measure, it will be important to regularly review how it works and eventually adapt and/or change it. As for the

27 European Commission, 'Beijing + 5: An Overview of the European Union Follow-up and Preparations', Brussels: Directorate General for Employment and Social Affairs.

28 Communication from the Commission of 21 February 1996 'Incorporating equal opportunities for women and men into all Community policies and activities' COM (96) 67 final available at http://eur-lex.europa.eu/legal-content/EN/TXT/HTML/?uri=LEGISSUM:c10921&from=EN; accessed 5 May 2018.

29 Council of Europe (1998) 'Gender Mainstreaming: Conceptual Framework, Methodology and Presentation of Good Practice' Final Report of Activities of the Group of Specialists on Mainstreaming (EG-S-MS) 19.

relevant actors these range from the institutions responsible for a specific procedure, e.g. the Commission, to all those who are involved in its implementation.

A difficult process?

Against this background, in practice, the implementation of gender mainstreaming remains problematic and sometimes even ineffective.[30] The EU has been criticised on several occasions for failing to apply the principle of gender equality that is proclaimed in its very policy and legislation.[31] The reasons for this are multiple and interlinked. To start with, there is a considerable confusion as to what gender mainstreaming means.[32] There is a discrepancy between the level of acceptance at policy level and the confusion amongst those charged with the implementation of the process.[33] Gender mainstreaming has indeed traditionally been the responsibility of bureaucrats who have little expertise in the subject: its vague and non-specific character means that although everybody understands the general idea, no one is sure what the practical application requires.[34] This confusion can affect a number of factors such as the clarity of objectives, the use of unambiguous channels of authority, communication between the various groups as well as adequate levels of resources for its implementation.[35] This necessarily affects the way in which gender mainstreaming is framed in policy and legislation. A further difficulty is linked to the fact that the final implementation of the principle is essentially left to soft-law instruments such as recommendations and policy programmes. As these are not binding, they lack effective enforcement.[36] This in itself raises questions on the political commitment to the concept. Following from this, Kantola argues that the "soft gender mainstreaming" techniques used, such as gender budgeting and gender impact assessment, have the potential to increase the use of indicators and statistics, thus to reduce complex gender equality issues to technical concepts.[37] In addition, a meaningful approach to gender mainstreaming cannot be decoupled from a feminist reading. Only this can put in place a transformative agenda

30 Emanuela Lombardo, 'Mainstreaming Gender in the EU in Times of Crisis: Scholarly Developments and Policy Challenges' in Council for European Studies at Columbia University, *Perspective on Europe* (Spring 2013).
31 See, for example, Emanuela Lombardo, 'Integrating or Setting the Agenda? Gender Mainstreaming in the European Constitution-making Process' (2005) 12(3) *Social Politics* 412–432; Margarita León, Mercedes Mateo Diaz and Susan Millns, 'Engendering the Convention: Women and the Future of the European Union' (2003) *EUI Papers, Robert Schuman Centre for Advanced Studies.*
32 See for example Maria Stratigaki, 'Gender Mainstreaming vs Positive Action: An Ongoing Conflict in EU Gender Equality Policy' (2005) 12(2) *European Journal of Women's Studies* 165–186; S. Walby, 'The European Union and Gender Equality: Emergent Varieties of Gender Regime' (2004) 11(1) *Social Politics* 4–29.
33 Teresa Rees (n 22).
34 Alison Woodward, 'European Gender Mainstreaming: Promises and Pitfalls of Transformative Policy' (2003) *Review of Policy Research* 65–88.
35 Anne-Marie McGauran, 'Gender Mainstreaming and the Public Policy Implementation Process: Round Pegs in Square Holes?' (2009) 37(2) *Policy and Politics* 215–233.
36 Johanna Kantola (n 21) 126.
37 Johanna Kantola (n 21) 126.

setting a radical feminist potential.[38] It will ensure, that implementation of gender mainstreaming will propose fundamental changes to policy approaches to gender inequalities. In turn it will facilitate an understanding of the problems concerning the implementation of the process and thus it will enrich the debate. There is however, "resistance" to this approach by organisations, structures and policy actors which are all deeply gendered and participate in reproducing inequalities.[39]

Resistance in this case indicates not so much the refusal to accept a concept but rather the desire to preserve the *status quo* without questioning a dominant social order.[40] Resistance is more likely to occur in these organisations where cultural norms, beliefs, attitudes and values are challenged as a result of the gender mainstreaming process.[41] Simply put, gender mainstreaming is bound to fail if the very same actors who resist change and reproduce inequalities are tasked with its implementation.[42] In practice this is happening when the actors follow an integrationist policy practice[43] rather than a feminist reading which often simply results in a mere box-ticking exercise lacking substantive content.

Gender mainstreaming and work-life balance

A traditional interpretation of gender mainstreaming would see the expansion of equality from areas normally considered gendered, such as family policies to areas that are traditionally seen as gender-neutral, such as employment,[44] agriculture, energy or trade,[45] development,[46] structural fund and even the consequences of

38 Gill Allwood (n 16).

39 Lut Mergaert and Emanuela Lombardo, 'Resistance to implementing gender mainstreaming in EU Research Policy' (2014) *European Integration Papers* available at http://www.eiop.or.at/eiop/pdf/2014-005.pdf, accessed 20 April 2018.

40 Special Issue on 'Feminist Resistance-Resistance to Feminism', (2013) *Nordic Journal of Feminist and Gender Research.*

41 Yvonne Benschop and Mieke Verloo, 'Gender Change, Organizational Change and Gender Equality Strategies' in Emma Jeanes, David Knights and Patricia Yancey Martin (eds), *Handbook of Gender, Work and Organisation* (Wiley-Blackwell, 2011) 277–290.

42 Aruna Rao and David Kelleher, 'Is There Life After Gender Mainstreaming?' (2005) 13(2) *Gender and Development* 57–69.

43 Petra Meier and Karen Celis, 'Sowing the Seeds of Its Own Failure: Implementing the Concept of Gender Mainstreaming' (2011) 18(4) *Social Politics* 469–89; see also Alison Woodward, 'Too Late for Gender Mainstreaming? Taking Stock in Brussels' (2008) 18(3) *Journal of European Social Policy* 289–302.

44 Jill Rubery, 'Gender Mainstreaming and the Open Method of Coordination: is the Open Method too Open for Gender Equality Policy?' paper presented at ESRC seminar on gender mainstreaming, Leeds, October 2003.

45 Catherine Hoskyns, 'Linking Gender and International Trade Policy: Is Interaction Possible?' *CSGR Working Papers* 217/07; Jacqui True, 'Trading in Gender Equality: Gendered Meanings in EU Trade Policy' in Emanuela Lombardo, Petra Meier and Mieike Verloo (eds), *The Discursive Politics of Gender Equality: Stretching, Bending and Policymaking* (Routledge, 2009).

46 Petra Debusscher and Jacqui True, 'Lobbying the EU for Gender-Equal Development' in Jan Orbie and Lisa Tortell (eds), *The European Union and the Social Dimension of Globalisation: How the EU Influences the World* (Routledge, 2008).

snow fall! In this case, the municipality of Karlskoga was able to show how the traditional plan to clean the streets after heavy snowfall was impacting women. As the main roads were first clean, this allowed people (both men and women) to go to work on main roads. Women, however, were more likely to take children to nursery and school often situated in back roads, before going to work. As a result, women were more likely to fall and have problems requiring medical assistance. The municipality of Karlskoga was able to show the savings, in terms of hospital care and lost productivity as a result of it, by simply changing how the roads were cleaned.[47]

However, also areas where it is normally assumed that gender mainstreaming will not make an impact because they are already "gender issues", can benefit from it. This is the case of work-life balance placed on the European agenda by the 1974 Social Action Plan that called for measures to "ensure that the family responsibilities of all concerned may be reconciled with their job aspiration".[48] In practice, the principle was devised to allow *mothers* to be able to look after their young family whilst carrying on working, thus contributing to the economy. This was confirmed by the relevant legislation in this area. For example, the Equal Treatment Directive was based on the assumption that women needed to be protected: '[t]his Directive shall be applied without prejudice to provisions concerning the *protection of women*, particularly as regards pregnancy and maternity.'[49] The Pregnant Workers Directive allowed mothers paid time off in conjunction with the birth of the child, but there was no equivalent for fathers. These provisions had the effect of emphasising the role of mothers as carers. Since then, however, this assumption has gradually been challenged and this has been reflected in the relevant legislation and case law. It is now accepted that the concept is broad, flexible and covers a variety of situations. Today, it has moved away from a "mother only" approach and, to a degree, it has been extended to fathers and other carers who are not necessarily only women. The CJEU case law has been instrumental to this; for example, it has acknowledged and promoted the rights of fathers as caregivers. In the case of *Roca Alvarez*, it went as far as to hold that "the position of a male and female worker, father and mother of a young child, are comparable with regard to their possible need (…) to look after the child."[50] This is an acknowledgment that work-life balance policies and legislation are important to all employees, rather than just to mothers. There are two potential developments that commit to insert more gender equality in work-life balance. These are the proposed Work-Life Balance Directive (currently being discussed in

47 Sustainable Gender Equality – a film about gender mainstreaming in practice: https://www.youtube.com/watch?v=udSjBbGwJEg&t=17s; accessed on 27 April 2018.

48 Council Resolution of 21 January 1974 Concerning a Social Action Programme [1974] OJ C1/13. See in general a Special Issue on 'Reconciliation of Work and Family Life' (2015) 37:3 *Journal of Social Welfare and Family Law*.

49 Article 2(3) Equal Treatment Directive 76/207; emphasis added.

50 Case C-104/09 *Pedro Manuel Roca Álvarez v Sesa Start España ETT SA* ECLI:EU:C:2010:561 para 24.

the Council)[51] and the European Pillar of Social Rights.[52] Both of these initiatives place value on informal care and seek to move away from the stereotypical notion that children are women's sole responsibility. In particular the proposed Directive gives express rights to both leave and pay to fathers and the European Pillar of Social Rights specifically addresses work-life balance. It states that "*[p]arents and people* with caring responsibilities have the right to suitable leave, flexible working arrangements and access to care services. *Women and men* shall have equal access to special leaves of absence in order to fulfil their caring responsibilities and be encouraged to use them in a balanced way."[53]

Conclusions

This chapter has discussed the principle of gender mainstreaming and has highlighted its role in ensuring the full development of an equal opportunities agenda, an agenda that is vital for any democratic society.

It has argued that it has a transformative potential and can enrich any policy. Gender mainstreaming can indeed be an important principle for addressing shortcomings in many areas, such as the eradication of poverty, sustainable development, trade, governance and human rights, children's rights and disability. This chapter has used as an example a specific area, namely work-life balance, that shows that a gender mainstreaming outlook *can* be successful and is necessary and not only in those areas that are *prima facie* gender-neutral but in all areas. However, in general terms, the failure of gender mainstreaming remains well documented.[54] Despite the fact that the concept has, in the main, largely been adopted by institutions, this is not necessarily a sign of success. This chapter has sought to outline the causes that render the implementation of the principle difficult. These range from a lack of understanding of the concept to resistance to implement it. Furthermore, this chapter has emphasised that in order to be successful the principle needs to be supported by a "feminist vision".[55] When decoupled from it, as too often happens, the implementation of gender mainstreaming remains a box-ticking exercise. Thus, a transformative version of gender mainstreaming needs a feminist reading to be firmly embedded in the policy process.[56]

51 Proposal for a Directive on the EU Parliament and the Council on Work-Life Balance for Parents and Carers COM (2017) 253 final, 2017/0085(COD). See Eugenia Caracciolo di Torella, 'An Emerging Right to Care in the EU: a "New Start" to Support Work-Life Balance for Parents and Carers' (2017) *ERA Forum* 187–198.

52 Available at https://ec.europa.eu/commission/priorities/deeper-and-fairer-economic-and-monetary-union/european-pillar-social-rights_en (as of 23 June 2017) (as of 23 June 2017); accessed 27 April 2018.

53 Principle 9. Emphasis added.

54 Gill Allwood (n 16).

55 Emanuela Lombardo and Petra Meier, 'Gender Mainstreaming in the EU. Incorporating a Feminist Reading?' (2006) *European Journal of Women's Studies* 151–165.

56 Elisabeth Prügl and Audrey Lustgarten, 'Mainstreaming Gender in International Organisations' in Jane S. Jaquette and Gale Summerfield (eds), *Women and Gender Equity in Development Theory and Practice* (Duke University Press 2006) 53–70.

The shortcomings of the principle, discussed above, could be addressed with adequate information campaigns aimed at raising awareness of the importance of the principle of gender equality.

Finally, as the EU is increasingly committed to a number of cross-cutting issues, such as environmental policy and sustainable development,[57] all of which are to be mainstreamed, the principle of gender mainstreaming is arguably suffering from competition with these. This can create "mainstreaming overload".[58] Furthermore, "there is a limit to the number of issues which can be mainstreamed through all other policy areas".[59] This means that organisations have to decide which issues must take priority. In this context, gender mainstreaming might be compromised. It can be (erroneously) assumed that because gender equality has been one of the founding principles of the Treaties, gender mainstreaming is no longer a priority and other issues will take precedence. This will be a mistake as, if gender equality has made progress, it is certainly still a work in progress. In order to inject new energy in the gender mainstreaming concept, it would be necessary to focus on its very aim, namely the achievement of a fair society where equality and diversity are acknowledged and promoted.

57 See, on this issue, Beate Sjåfjell, 'The Environmental Integration Principle: A Necessary Step Towards Policy Coherence for Sustainability' in this Volume.

58 Robert Geyer and Simon Lightfoot, 'The Strengths and Limits of New Forms of EU Governance: The Cases of Mainstreaming and Impact Assessment in EU Public Health and Sustainable Development Policy' (2010) 32(4) *European Integration* 339–356.

59 Gill Allwood (n 16).

4 Mainstreaming equality in the EU legal order

More than a Cinderella provision?

Francesca Ippolito

1 Introduction. The evolutionary road of equality within the EU legal order: from non-discrimination and positive actions to positive duties

Equality has been qualified as 'the stuff of legend',[1] even the 'sovereign virtue'[2] and 'the starting point of all other liberties'.[3] Within the sphere of EU law, this principle of equality precludes comparable situations from being treated differently, and different situations from being treated in the same way, unless the treatment is objectively justified. Non-discrimination turns instead to the association between a limited number of particular characteristics (such as race, gender, etc.) and the discrimination suffered by those who have, or who are perceived to have, those characteristics and promote a version of equality defined as the absence of 'discrimination'. Thus, equality is one of the founding values of the EU together with 'respect for human dignity, freedom, democracy, the rule of law and respect for human rights, including the rights of persons belonging to minorities'. A value in a society in which *diversity* should be promoted together with equality Article 2 TEU put these values in the context of a society where 'pluralism, non-discrimination, tolerance, justice, solidarity and equality between women and men prevail'. The value of equality has been central to the development of the European Union agenda to such an extent that it is a constitutionally-embedded norm.

In particular, since the adoption of the Amsterdam Treaty the European Union has a legal mandate to 'take appropriate action to combat discrimination based on sex, racial or ethnic origin, religion or belief, disability, age or sexual orientation.' Using this article as a legal basis, in 2000 the Council adopted two directives that deal respectively with discrimination on the grounds of racial and ethnic origin[4] and with equal treatment in employment on the grounds of religion or belief,

1 N. Whitty, T. Murphy, S. Livingstone, *Civil Liberties Law: The Human Rights Act Era* (Bath: Butterworths, 2001), 377.
2 R. Dworkin, *Sovereign Virtue* (Cambridge: Harvard University Press, 2000).
3 Sir Hersch Lauterpacht
4 Council Directive 2000/43/EC of 29 June 2000 implementing the principle of equal treatment between persons irrespective of racial or ethnic origin [2000] OJ L 180/22.

disability, age and sexual orientation.[5] Before the adoption of these instruments and excluding 'nationality of another Member State' it was sex that was at the top of the list of characteristics in EU anti-discrimination legislation based on Article 21(1), combined with Article 6(1) EU and Article 157 TFEU (ex 141 EC, ex 119 EEC). EU legislation was in fact composed of the Recast Equal Treatment Directive 2006/54 (sex and employment)[6]; the Directive 2004/113,[7] which aims at combating discrimination based on sex in the access to and supply of goods and services, with a view to putting the principle of equal treatment between men and women into effect in the Member States; the Directive 79/7[8] (sex and social security) and the Directive 86/613 (sex and self-employment).[9] After the adoption of the two equality directives in 2000, the hierarchy of grounds in EU anti-discrimination legislation,[10] in relation to material scope, put sex in the middle. It would even have been dropped to the bottom had the proposed Multi-Ground Directive been adopted. The proposal[11] extends the application of the prohibition of discrimination to all persons, as regards both the public and private sectors, including public bodies, in relation to: (a) social protection, including social security and healthcare; (b) social advantages; (c) education[12]; (d) access to and supply of goods and other services which are available to the public, including

5 Council Directive 2000/78/EC of 27 November 2000 establishing a general framework for equal treatment in employment and occupation [2000] OJ L 303/16.

6 Directive 2006/54/EC of the European Parliament and of the Council of 5 July 2006 on the implementation of the principle of equal opportunities and equal treatment of men and women in matters of employment and occupation (recast) [2006] OJ L 204/23.

7 Council Directive 2004/113/EC of 13 December 2004 implementing the principle of equal treatment between men and women in the access to and supply of goods and services, [2004] OJ L 373/37.

8 Council Directive 79/7/EEC of 19 December 1978 on the progressive implementation of the principle of equal treatment for men and women in matters of social security, [1979] OJ L 6/24.

9 Council Directive 86/613/EEC of 11 December 1986 on the application of the principle of equal treatment between men and women engaged in an activity, including agriculture, in a self-employed capacity, and on the protection of self-employed women during pregnancy and motherhood, [1986] OJ L 359/56.

10 For the argument that there is a hierarchy in the grounds of EU anti-discrimination law and policy, see M. Bell and L. Waddington, 'Reflecting on inequalities in European Equality Law' (2003) 28 *European Law Review* 349 and Id., 'More Equal Than Others? Distinguishing EU Equality Directives' (2001) 38 *Common Market Law Review* 587.

11 Proposal for a Council Directive on implementing the principle of equal treatment between persons irrespective of religion or belief, disability, age or sexual orientation (COM 2008 (426) final).

12 Nevertheless Article 3(3) of the proposal admits that Member States may provide for differences in treatment in access to educational institutions based on religion or belief and Article 3(4) pinpoints how the Directive is without prejudice to national legislation ensuring the secular nature of the State, State institutions or bodies, or education ... It is equally without prejudice to national legislation promoting equality between men and women [exception for French legislation on Muslim headscarves and other 'signs or dress by which pupils overtly manifest a religious affiliation'].

housing[13] – with the note that it shall apply to individuals only insofar as they are performing a professional or commercial activity with the exclusion of private and family life.[14] Despite the significance of such a Multi Ground Directive would have had, the proposal has been blocked at the Council stage since 2009, being incoherently declared that 'some delegations would have preferred more ambitious provisions in regard to disability instead of the horizontal approach'; while 'certain delegations have put forward the view that more experience with the implementation of existing Community law is needed before further legislation is adopted at the Community level. These delegations have questioned the timeliness and the need for the Commission's new proposal, which they see as infringing on national competence for certain issues'.[15] Other issues have been underlined anyhow to require further discussion such as: the potential financial and administrative burden imposed by the provisions; the concept of discrimination by association; the question of multiple discrimination and the implementation date for the non-disability provisions.[16]

Beside such a 'negative dimension' of formal equality, through the established commitment of the EU to 'combat' any discrimination, a proactive duty of positive actions for a more substantive equality has also been recognised. They result at primary EU law from the insertion in the Treaty of Amsterdam of Article 141 (4) which reads: 'with a view to ensuring full equality in practice between men and women in working life, the principle of equal treatment shall not prevent any Member State from maintaining or adopting measures providing for specific advantages in order to make it easier for the under-represented sex to pursue a vocational activity or to prevent or compensate for disadvantages in professional careers'. The positive action model has equally been performing the EU secondary law if we consider how Article 5 of the Racial Equality Directive provides: 'with a view to ensuring full equality in practice, the principle of equal treatment shall not prevent any Member State from maintaining or adopting specific measures to prevent or compensate for disadvantages linked to racial or ethnic origin'; and similarly, Article 7(1) of the Employment Equality Directive refers to the 'positive action as compensation for past wrongs' dimension from Article 141(4) EC. This is made more specific in Article 3 of the Directive 2006/54, which permits similar measures, this time referring to measures aimed at 'ensuring full equality in

13 Ibidem, Article 3(1).

14 Article 3(2) of the Directive's proposal provides that the Directive is without prejudice to national laws on marital or family status and reproductive rights. See and compare to the Equality Employment Directive at Recital 22, and Maruko, ECJ, 1 April 2008, a specification crucial for accessing services, especially those of adoption agencies and fertility clinics, in Member States in which only married different-sex couples have access.

15 See the Progress Report: 10073/1/09 REV1 (2 June 2009), http://register.consilium.europa.eu/pdf/en/09/st10/st10073-re01.en09.pdf

16 See R. Wintemute, 'The proposal for a new anti-discrimination directive, Recent Developments in EC [now EU] anti-discrimination law: Seminar for legal practitioners Academy of European Law, Trier, Germany, 1 December 2009' available at http://www.era-comm.eu/oldoku/adiskri/01_overview/2009_wintermute_en.pdf.

practice between men and women in working life.' Similarly, Article 29 of the same Directive requires Member States to 'actively take into account the objective of equality between men and women when formulating and implementing laws, regulations, administrative provisions, policies and activities in the areas referred to in this Directive.' The preamble (para 22) expands on this by emphasising that 'given the current situation ... Member States should, in the first instance, aim at improving the situation of women in working life.' The preamble also exhorts Member States to raise public awareness of wage discrimination and changing public awareness in relation to equal treatment of men and women.

Though the Lisbon Treaty did not alter the nature of the legal basis for the adoption of harmonisation measures in the field of anti-discrimination, in some respects Article 10 TFEU partially waters down this failure. It provides that:

> In defining and implementing the policies and activities referred to in this Part, the Union shall aim to combat discrimination based on sex, racial or ethnic origin, religion or belief, disability, age or sexual orientation.

The reference is to an exhaustive list of unlawful criteria to be combated by the Union in the definition and implementation of its policies and actions: sex, race or ethnic origin, religion or belief, disability, age or sexual orientation. These criteria are valorised in such a manner to give rise to a form of hierarchisation, compared to the other criteria present in secondary law of the Union. But in this instance, the grounds for discrimination to be combated are not confined in the specific instrument that is EU anti-discrimination legislation. The duty provided in Article 10 TFEU is of mainstreaming, which seeks to change the mindset of policymakers in order that equality becomes a central concern. It not only ensures anti-discrimination in the formal sense; but it also works towards substantive equality; and managing diversity.[17]

17 See generally M. Bell, 'The right to equality and non-discrimination', in T. Hervey and J. Kenner (eds), *Economic and Social Rights under the EU Charter of Fundamental Rights. A Legal Perspective* (Oxford, Hart Publishing, 2003), 96. See also the case ECJ C-148/02 Garcia Avello [2003] (and in the same sense A.G. Jacobs in ECJ C-96/04 *Grunkin Paul* [2006]) which received much criticism for the use of the principle of non-discrimination (ex Article 13 TEC) in order to accommodate cultural diversity. According to the Court of Justice, the principle of non-discrimination requires a differentiated treatment and thus the recognition of diversity, if there are good reasons for the protection of individual identity. From a different perspective the same case had been acknowledged as playing a role in the name of cultural diversity see J.Y. Carlier, 'Regional integration and cultural diversity: the case of European citizenship', in M.C.Foblets, J.F. Gaudreault-DesBiens, A. Dundes Rentlen (eds), *Cultural Diversity and the Law. State Responses from Around the World*, (Bruylant, 2010), 763–778, at 772, according to whom the Court 'chose another way of considering diversity, laying down a rule of conflict of diversity not based "in abstracto" on the recognition of another law, but "in concreto" on the acceptance of a choice of the concerned parties wishing to connect to one particular culture.' In the same positive way EU legislation which explicitly deals with the issue of identity preservation of EU nationals respects accommodation of cultural diversity. The Council Directive 77/

The idea of Article 10 TFEU is complementary to anti-discrimination law and to the positive action model. The model of positive duties, in its variety of interpretations,[18] in particular, qualifies equality as a cross-cutting objective to be woven into all areas of law and policy,[19] and thus constitutionalising a broad political non-discrimination mainstreaming. This means a shift for equality from *static prohibition to dynamic activation* in policy areas where the EU has exclusive competence (Article 4 TFEU) but also in areas where the EU shares competences with its Member States (Article 5) in internal and external relations, or has the role of coordinating, supporting or supplementing them (Article 6), for instance in education. Equality needs to be taken into account during policy formulation, implementation and evaluation.[20]

The objectives of non-discrimination mainstreaming – following the positive duties model – are to *ex ante* evaluate and ensure that discriminatory elements of existing or proposed policies suffered by particular social groups (as well as those at risk of multiple discrimination) are identified and dismantled, or otherwise mitigated, shifting the focus from the results of discrimination towards its causes.[21] Moving in order to prevent discrimination before it happens allows for the realisation of positive duties of substantive equality upon Member States, so pushing the EU equality agenda. Thus, where EU anti-discrimination legislation is criticised for tackling the causes of inequality separately and for failing to recognize their cumulative and interrelated operation in society, equality mainstreaming presents the merit of overcoming these shortcomings. As already underlined by Beveridge and Nott, a 'mainstreaming strategy that seeks to tackle different factors of inequality together might be able to combat the law's essentialism more effectively than one focused only on gender, though the risks and practicalities of this

486/EEC OJ 1977 L 199/32 on the education of the children of migrant workers in its turn obliges host States and Member States of origin to adopt 'appropriate measures to promote the teaching of the mother tongue and of the culture of the country of origin of the above-mentioned children'.

18 See T. Rees, *Mainstreaming Equality in the European Union* (London: Routledge, 1998).

19 C. McCrudden, 'Equality', in C.J. Harvey, *Human Rights, Equality and Democratic Renewal in Northern Ireland* (Oxford: Hart Publishing, 2001), 75 indicates how this requires 'the principle that equality be seen as an integral part of all public policy-making and implementation, rather than something separated off in a policy or institutional ghetto'; and the Council of Europe 'Gender Mainstreaming: Conceptual Framework, Methodology and Presentation of Good Practices, Final Report of Activities of the Group of Specialists on Mainstreaming' EG-S-MS (98), (Strasbourg: Council of Europe 1998 May) indicates it in terms of 'the incorporation of a concern with achieving equality in all public sector policies at all levels and at all stages in policy making'

20 This was the perspective of C. McCrudden, 'Mainstreaming Human Rights', in C.J. Harvey (ed.), *Human Rights in the Community: Rights as Agents for Change* (Hart Publishing, 2005), 9 related to the human rights mainstreaming.

21 T. Donaghy, 'Mainstreaming: Northern Ireland's participative-democratic approach', (2004) 32 *Policy and Politics* 49 at 50.

require careful consideration'.[22] In so doing, equality mainstreaming will ensure compliance with equal treatment legislation (so that there is no prohibited direct or indirect discrimination against people contained within the design or implementation of the policy). But it goes beyond. It would also eliminate barriers for groups experiencing inequality (sensitively to the diversity *within* groups, as well as *across* groups), taking account of diversity in the identity, experience and situation of people within the target group adjusting the design and implementation of policy, as well as promoting positive actions that contribute to enhancing the access to resources, power and influence, status, and relationships of care and solidarity of people from disadvantaged groups currently experiencing inequality.[23]

The aim of this chapter is to shed light on these questions: how might a mainstreaming strategy interact and how is it complementary to other equality and non-discrimination laws, strategies and policies? Could it effectively overcome the limitations of established equal opportunity and positive discrimination strategies? What is good mainstreaming? Is it effectively working? The analysis will first trace the roots of non-discrimination mainstreaming before the Lisbon Treaty for then underlying the ratio behind the formal insertion of the model of positive duties within the EU primary law. Subsequently, after presenting the tools for mainstreaming – giving particular emphasis to the more representative one that is Impact Assessment(s) – the analysis will pinpoint the added value of the insertion of an equality mainstreaming clause within the treaties, first as to the tool for performing it, and then upon the institutional commitments, having an attentive look also to the indirectly progressive, directly static and potentially challenging judicial mainstreaming by the European Court of Justice.

2 The roots of non-discrimination mainstreaming before the Lisbon Treaty

Despite the anticipated programmatic relevance and significance of Article 10 TFUE, the concept that the provision introduces is not a new one at all. Namely, extending mainstreaming principles across the equality spectrum that originally were confined to gender equality mainstreaming[24] in the institutional approach of the European Commission. Since 1996 it referred to and defined gender mainstreaming as: 'mobilising all general policies and measures specifically for the purpose of achieving equality by actively and openly taking into account at the planning stage their possible effects on the respective situations of men and women (gender perspective). This means systematically examining measures and policies and taking into account such possible effects when defining and implementing

22 F. Beveridge and S. Nott, 'Mainstreaming: A Case for Optimism and Cynicism', in *Feminist Legal Studies* (2002) 10: 299–311.

23 See also N. Crowley, Final Seminar Report: Good Practice Exchange Seminar on Non-Discrimination Mainstreaming, October 2009, http://ec.europa.eu/social/BlobServlet?docId=4656&l angId=en

24 On the principle of gender mainstreaming see E. Caracciolo di Torella, 'The principle of gender mainstreaming: possibilities and challenges', in this volume.

them'.[25] In the same year the Commission also called for a disability non-discrimination mainstreaming,[26] subsequently reinforced in 2003 with the *European Year of People with Disabilities* which has triggered analogous commitments through the Action programme that has for a number of years been promoting a policy of mainstreaming in the other fields of discrimination too[27]; and then with the Action Plan 2004–2010 that called for the 'reinforcement of the mainstreaming of the disability perspective into all relevant policies at the stages of policy formulation, implementation, monitoring and evaluation',[28] and encouragingly, with a reference in the Structural Funds Regulations 2007–13[29] of the importance of taking into consideration the accessibility needs of disabled people. Nearly in the same period of time, in 1997, with the *European Year against Racism* [30] and the relative Action Plan[31] the Union was called to 'set a convincing example in combating racism, by carefully scrutinising its own policies to see whether they contain racist, xenophobic or ethnic tendencies', listing many areas where the fight against racism should be incorporated into policy considerations, including employment strategy and external relations, which adds up to a substantial commitment to a policy of mainstreaming anti-racism.

Also at the time of the 'solemn proclamation of the Charter of Fundamental Rights' in parallel with the Treaty of Nice, in 2001 the European Commission was pushed to introduce an obligation to scrutinise all new legislative proposals to ensure respect for fundamental rights.[32] Among them figures non-discrimination that therefore had the chance to be mainstreamed and considered during the early stages of policy development.

The *Draft Treaty Establishing a Constitution for Europe* expresses the need for a constitutionalisation of non-discrimination mainstreaming for the first time. First, attention was drawn to the omission of a broader and comprehensive mainstreaming principle which was originally suggested for inclusion in Part I:

25 Commission Communication 1996, *supra* n. 6, at p. 2.
26 European Commission, 'Equality of Opportunity for People with Disabilities, A New European Community Disability Strategy', (COM (1996) 406) final.
27 'Non-Discrimination mainstreaming: Instruments, Case studies and the way forward' (2007) http://ec.europa.eu/employment_social/fundamental_rights/pdf/pubst/stud/mainstr07_en. pdf
28 Commission Communication 'Equal Opportunities for people with disabilities (A European Action Plan) 2004–10' (COM(2003) 650 final)
29 For the 2007–2013 period, the instruments to pursue these objectives have their legal basis in a package of five regulations adopted by the Council and the European Parliament in July 2006 of which currently in force is Regulation (EC) No 1082/2006 of the European Parliament and of the Council of 5 July 2006 on a European grouping of territorial cooperation (EGTC) [2006] OJ L 210/19.
30 Resolution of the Council and the representatives of the governments of the Member States, meeting within the Council, of 23 July 1996, [1996] OJ C 237/1.
31 Communication from the Commission, An Action Plan Against Racism, (COM (1998) 183) final, 3.
32 On this topic see V. Kosta, 'Fundamental rights mainstreaming in the EU', in this Volume.

> In all activities falling within its competence, the Union shall aim to eliminate inequalities as well as discrimination on the basis of racial or ethnic origin, religion or beliefs, disability, age or sexual orientation, to promote equality between men and women, to promote full employment and a high level of social protection, protection of human health, advancement of education and training, and to guarantee universal accessibility of services of general interest which are financially viable, of high quality and organised on the basis of solidarity by the individual Member States.[33]

The Italian Presidency drafted a clause for possible inclusion along similar lines, and made an exception only for the non-discrimination mainstreaming principle[34]:

> In defining and implementing the policies and actions referred to in this Part, the Union shall take into account requirements linked to the promotion of a high level of employment, the guarantee of adequate social protection, the fight against social exclusion, and a high level of education, training and protection of human health.

The final formulation of a general non-discrimination mainstreaming clause found its place within Article III – 118 when it was established that

> In defining and implementing the policies and activities referred to in this Part, the Union shall aim to combat discrimination based on sex, racial or ethnic origin, religion or belief, disability, age or sexual orientation,

opting for 'combating' rather than 'eliminating' discriminatory criteria in the formulation and implementation of any EU policy. This constitutional inheritance collected by the Lisbon Treaty is what provides for the current constitutionalisation of a general comprehensive equality mainstreaming duty for EU institutions. The onus, therefore, is now on 'the effectiveness of the mainstreaming duties', which will heavily depend on their practical implementation.[35]

In parallel to the internal process of equality mainstreaming constitutionalisation, we should note that interestingly, and in a complementary manner, equality mainstreaming is treated as a duty at the EU external level.[36] There, race and gender discrimination have been addressed with a combined model of positive duty and positive actions. It originated with the call of the European Parliament in

33 See the submission from a number of members of the Social Europe working group, led by Anne van Lancker: CONV 780/03, 3 June 2003, *Text forwarded by Ms Anne van Lancker and other members of Convention working group on 'Social Europe'* (letter dated 20 May 2003).

34 See Presidency Proposals (IGC 60/03 ADD 1, 9 December 2003).

35 M. Bell, 'Equality and the European Constitution', (2004) 33:3 *Industrial Law Journal* 242, at 255.

36 See J. Beqiraj, 'Animal Welfare', in this volume for a discussion on the mainstreaming provision in Article 13 TFEU at EU external level.

1993 'for the inclusion in all association agreements of specific clauses to protect against the infringement of fundamental rights and racial discrimination.' Indeed, in 1996, the Parliament stated that it deplored 'the inability of the Union to reject and combat ethnic hatred in a consistent and effective manner through its foreign policy.' The same Barcelona declaration (1995) as to the specific case of Euromed relations highlighted that in regards to the political aspects of cooperation, the partnership aimed to establish a common area of peace and stability. In this context, the respect for human rights 'without any discrimination on grounds of race, nationality, language, religion or sex' (p. 3) is one of the basic principles. Moreover, the single EuroMed Association Agreements (hereinafter EMAAs) contain a provision which specifically addresses non-discrimination mainstreaming on the ground of race and ethnic origin within the section on cooperation in the social field. In particular, Article 62–64 Egypt AA; Article 72 Algeria, Article 69 Marocco e Tunisia provide that the dialogue and cooperation on social matters should cover 'schemes and programmes to encourage equal treatment between Algerian and Community nationals, mutual knowledge of cultures and civilisations, the furthering of tolerance and the removal of discrimination'. These provisions are also combined with the model of positive actions 'implementing and financing of exchange and leisure programmes for mixed groups of Moroccan and European young people residing in the Member States, with a view to promoting mutual knowledge of their respective cultures and fostering tolerance'.[37] Analogously, gender issues have been included in the chapters outlining the objectives and the approach towards cooperation between the EU and the ACP countries when Article 1 of the Cotonou Agreement outlining the objectives of the partnership stated that '[s]ystematic account shall be taken of the situation of women and gender issues in all areas – political, economic and social', while Article 13 on migration reaffirms the parties' obligation to eliminate sexual discrimination and Article 72 establishes that there may be no discrimination between the victims of an armed conflict on the grounds of their gender. Thus, the commitment to address discrimination as established in Article 8 into the issue areas of migration and humanitarian assistance was incorporated. That aim reflects the concept of gender mainstreaming.[38] On the other side, Article 11 (2) of the Cotonou Agreement on peace building and conflict prevention lays the basis for the active involvement of women in peace building, while paragraph 3 commits the parties to address the problem of violence against women; finally, cooperation shall ensure that the profits of economic growth will be equitably shared by men and women. This emphasis on equality of outcome constitutes a positive action approach as well as the call for specific measures to balance the disadvantaged situation of women, such as the special focus on women and girls in the area of health politics to prevent

37 See Article 71 Marocco and Tunisia AA; Article 65 Egypt AA and Article 74 Algeria AA.

38 It has to be noticed how instead as denounced by the European Parliament lastly during a review of the Cotonou Agreement in 2013 it is absent any framework for the rights of homosexuals.

female genital mutilation and to include women's rights in the fight against HIV/AIDS (Article 26 and Article 31a raising the point of 'gender inequality, gender-based violence and abuse, as drivers of the HIV/AIDS pandemic'). The same positive action tool for gender mainstreaming is available in single EMAAs agreements – i.e. the one of Egypt and Algeria, which address women's rights in the same contexts (i.e. social cooperation and education) using for their promotion the same approaches, ergo equal treatment in the field of education and positive action in matters of social cooperation; though not addressing political cooperation and women's participation.

Therefore, it is not out of the blue that Article 10 TFEU realizes in 2009 the 'constitutionalisation' of these soft internal and external institutional practices to transform a general non-discrimination mainstreaming into a legal norm as had already happened with the E.C. Treaty amendment to incorporate a legally-binding commitment to gender mainstreaming. According to ex Article 3 (2) EC Treaty, the European Union promoted: 'the systematic integration of the respective situations, priorities and needs of women and men in all policies',[39] as the Structural Funds Regulations governing the distribution of EU regeneration funds[40] and Employment Guidelines seeks to co-ordinate Member State approaches to employment and training issues.[41] The fact that gender mainstreaming was translated into a legal norm made it for a long time the most advanced form of equality mainstreaming, which saw mainstreaming initiatives 'in favour of the underrepresented sex' pledged by each Commission service in the annual work programme and then used as performance indicators of services as well as the basis for an annual report on gender equality which includes inter alia budgetary information on allocation and expenditure.[42]

A partial indication of which conceptualisation of non-discrimination is the object of the new mainstreaming duty comes from the European Charter of Fundamental Rights, and the literal interpretation of Article 151 (4) (later Article 167) of the EU Treaty. According to the latter in fact,

> The Union shall take cultural aspects into account in its action under other provisions of the Treaties, in particular in order to respect and to promote the diversity of its cultures.

39 'Incorporating equal opportunities for women and men into all Community policies and activities' (COM (1996) 67) final. For an historical overview on gender mainstreaming see E. Caracciolo di Torella, in this volume.

40 See Council Resolution of 2 December 1996 on Mainstreaming Equal Opportunities for Men and Women into the European Structural Funds, [1996] O.J. C 386/1; and subsequent 1999 Structural Funds Regulation, Council Regulation (EC) no 1260/1999 of 21 June 1999 laying down general provisions on the Structural Funds, [1999] OJ L161/1.

41 See http://europa.eu.int/comm/dg05/empl&esf/empl99/joint-en.htm

42 Cfr. S. Mazey, 'Gender Mainstreaming Strategies in the E.U.: Delivering on an Agenda?' in 2002 *Feminist Legal Studies* 10.

Since there is no effective concept of multiculturalism at the EU level and this may hamper the development of a 'equality and diversity' approach.[43] Therefore, non-discrimination mainstreaming duties should be articulated as a formal negative duty to not discriminate, as well as performing a substantive role in promoting equality, including by accommodating diversity as a 'meta-value'[44] which, in recognition of the existing diversity of values, encompasses a profile of the plurality of ethnic, linguistic and cultural groups within single Member States.[45] Not always does equality mean that people have to be treated identically, rather, religious, linguistic, ethnic differences should be taken into account by legislators and policy-makers in some circumstances, so also protecting minority cultures.[46] The next paragraphs will underline the challenges in translating this norm into consistent practice by starting to examine the main tool for mainstreaming that is Impact Assessment and then concentrating on the other EU institutional (mis)practices.

3 The main tool for mainstreaming: the impact assessment and the relative impact of the constitutionalisation of equality mainstreaming

Impact Assessments (hereinafter IA) have been compulsorily introduced in the 'better regulation' operation of the European Commission in 2003,[47] requiring all Community legislation and policies to be subject to a systematic assessment of their potential *economic, environmental and social impacts.*[48] IAs structure procedural issues in the initial legislative process for the competent DG of the European Commission that follows this scheme: problem definition, objectives, policy options, impact analysis of options, comparing options, and evaluation provisions.[49] This methodological approach has been further extended to the other co-legislators: in 2011 the Council of the EU adopted its own 'Guidelines on

43 See C. Wallace and J. Shaw, 'Education, multiculturalism and the Charter of Fundamental Rights of the European Union', in Hervey and Kenner, above n. 29; S. Benhabib, *The Claims of Culture. Equality and Diversity in the Global Era* (Princeton, NJ, Princeton University Press, 2002).

44 See B. De Witte, B. 'The Value of Cultural Diversity' in Aziz, M. and Millns, S. (eds) *Values in the Constitution of Europe* (Dartmouth) 2005.

45 See for an analysis E. Psychogiopoulou, *The Integration of Cultural Considerations in EU Law and Policies*, Leiden (Martinus Nijoff, 2008).

46 See G. N. Toggenburg, 'The debate on European values and the case of cultural diversity', in European Diversity and Autonomy Papers, 1/2004, p. 16; B. De Witte, 'The Constitutional Resources for an EU Minority Protection Policy', in G. N. Toggenburg (ed.), *Minority Protection and the Enlarged European Union, The Way Forward* (Budapest, Open Society Institute, 2004); G.N. Toggenburg, 'Minority protection in a supranational context: Limits and opportunities', in G.N. Toggenburg (ed.), *Minority Protection*, op. cit., pp. 18–20.

47 See comprehensively the Better Regulation toolbox at https://ec.europa.eu/info/better-regulation-toolbox_en

48 See on this topic J. Beqiraj, 'Animal Welfare' and V. Kosta, 'Fundamental rights mainstreaming in the EU', in this volume.

49 This Impact Assessment tool has been further extended by the European Commission also to selected implementing and delegated acts.

methodological steps to be taken to check fundamental rights compatibility in the Council's preparatory bodies'; while in 2012, the European Parliament created a new Directorate for Impact Assessment and European Added Value, responsible for guaranteeing independent impact assessment. Finally, in 2016, the three institutions agreed for a convergence and to 'carry out impact assessments in relation to their substantial amendments to the Commission's proposal'.[50] For its *rationale*, IA therefore represents the main tool for equality mainstreaming conceived as proactive duty: it takes into account the mainstreaming objectives both at the level of defining objectives of a new policy initiative and of assessing its impacts.

However, despite *de facto* IAs therefore inherently serving the scope of mainstreaming, on the one hand the system is clearly (also) geared toward other policy objectives, such as the Lisbon Strategy. On the other hand, the accompanying documents that are the Commission Guidelines on IAs, drafted and elaborated by the Secretariat General of the Commission in 2005 and 2009, do not refer to mainstreaming as an objective of the IA system, neither do they refer to the horizontal clauses in clarifying the *raison d'être* of the IA system. Eventually these Guidelines 'made reference to the core legal basis of policy competences (e.g. the TFEU's articles on social policy when considering social objectives, or, in some cases, the Charter),[51] occasionally the operational guidelines on social impacts referring to mainstreaming and the treaty articles in relation to gender and health mainstreaming, though without identifying a particular role for IAs in contributing to such mainstreaming.'[52] Only the annexes to the guidelines mention the mainstreaming objectives in relation to the IA's role of defining the problem that justifies new policy intervention. But defining the problem and defining the objectives are two separate but related aspects that each IA must include.

This brings us to another correlative consideration to be highlighted: while only social and environmental impacts are supposed to be addressed in all IAs, the other mainstreaming objectives such as the one we are analysing of non-discrimination (but also gender and consumer protection) appear as a mere subsection of these wider categories, making their systematic assessment less likely. However, given the constitutional nature of the six mainstreaming objectives, enshrined in the Treaty as integration principles, it could be argued that all of them ought to be included as primary categories of the IIA system, with the consequent necessary minimum requirement for each IA to justify explicitly if a mainstreaming objective is considered not relevant to the case in hand.

If the constitutionalisation of equality mainstreaming did not impact on the conceptual profile and rationale of the 2009 guidelines, it nonetheless produced its

50 Interinstitutional Agreement between the European Parliament, the Council of the European Union and the European Commission on Better Law-Making [2016] *OJ L 123/1*.

51 For a discussion on this issue see M.E. Bartoloni, 'The horizontal social clause in a legal dimension', in this volume.

52 S. Smismans, R. Minto, 'Are Integrated Impact Assessments the Way Forward for Mainstreaming in The European Union?' *Regulation & Governance* (2017) 11, 231–251.

impact later on, in 2015, when the guidelines were recast and renewed,[53] as well as accompanied by a strengthened governance of better regulation with a stronger oversight body (the Regulatory Scrutiny Board) and a new REFIT platform for consultation of both stakeholders and government representatives. In particular, the non-discrimination and equal opportunities dimensions in the impact assessment procedure have been increased by adding an additional chapter to the Guidelines dealing specifically with how to assess the impact of proposals in relation to equality and non-discrimination. This overcame the critical aspect that the mainstreaming objective of non-discrimination was taken into account more at the level of defining the policy objectives than of assessing impacts. Significantly, the guidelines expressly indicate the obligation to screen these impacts as a consequence of the Treaty on the Functioning of the European Union (Articles 8–14). More specifically, the detailed individual impact on equality is listed with these key questions: Does the option safeguard the principle of equality before the law and would it directly or indirectly affect the principle of non-discrimination, equal treatment, gender equality and equal opportunities for all? Does the option have (directly or indirectly) a different impact on women and men? How does the option promote equality between women and men? How does the option entail any different treatment of groups or individuals directly on grounds of sex, racial or ethnic origin, religion or belief, disability, age, and sexual orientation? Or could it lead to indirect discrimination? Does the option ensure respect for the rights of people with disabilities in conformity with the UN Convention on the rights of persons with disabilities? If so, how?

Furthermore, the new guidelines potentiate the review of possible impacts[54] and the impact on vulnerable *groups* as a factor that can, and sometimes should, be considered in impact assessments within the EU.[55] The first point of the review of possible impact could also bring the European Commission to use the tool of IAs to re-orientate some legislative instruments or to complement them. For instance, counter-terrorism policies have had a disproportionate impact on certain populations, including ethnic or religious minorities, including Muslims, people of African and Asian descent, migrants, or people perceived to be from these groups. Discrimination undermines social cohesion and society as a whole, and can reinforce radicalisation and violence. So, the welcome *commitments* made by the European Commission could also call for being complemented by a concrete follow-up in terms of obligations for Member States to address all forms of racism, including anti-Semitism, Afrophobia and Islamophobia.

53 European Commission, Commission Staff Working Document, Better Regulation Guidelines, SWD(2015) 111 final, 19 May 2015, 25

54 Id, where it reads 'wide range of possible impacts should be reviewed'.

55 European Commission, Better Regulation 'Toolbox', Tool # 16, 97 <http://ec.europa.eu/smart- regulation/guidelines/docs/br_toolbox_en.pdf> accessed 15 April 2016 in fact provides that implications of specific initiatives are to be assessed, for instance, with regard to 'youth, elderly, genders, immigrants, people suffering from discrimination or physical disadvantages'.

As to the considerations introduced in the 2015 Guidelines for vulnerable groups, they clearly open the door for making differently resilient individuals a more central goal for the EU's policies so potentiating the conceptualisation of non-discrimination as substantive equality. However, though these novelties represent an improvement, the fact that the operational guidelines on fundamental rights in the IA are steered to set off a warning light whenever policy intervention would negatively impact on disadvantaged groups, with an exception made for gender, implies that IAs still remain a negative guarantee rather than being actively used as a positive regime promoting equality in a proactive way at policy level.[56] Moreover, though the new guidelines provide that the legislator should ask how options promote equality between women and men, so realising the unique moment of positive and proactive equality, mainstreaming the gender dimension is still empirically under-conceptualised: an explicit inclusion of LGBTI people in gender mainstreaming activities, in particular, is still lacking. So, there is much room for improvement on the side of impact assessment as the elected tool for non-discrimination mainstreaming. A partial step in this direction can be seen by the special Eurobarometer on Discrimination in the EU 2015[57]: a survey which in its comprehensive update of rigorous data on citizen's acceptance of not specific groups belonging to ethnic and religious minorities, included for the first time, the social acceptance and citizens' views on the rights of lesbian, gay, bisexual and transgender people.

4. The Lisbon Treaty and the broader mainstreaming horizontal 'institutional' permeation

If we consider that the constitutionalisation of non-discrimination mainstreaming duties commits not only the European Commission through the IA but the EU institutional actors comprehensively, we should highlight that progressively a mainstreaming awareness and technique has begun to penetrate the institutions of the European Union with a variable geometry, with institutional mechanisms introduced to facilitate coordination between services of the Commission with a view to mainstreaming non-discrimination into decision-making processes. The

56 But for an exception and so a virtuous example of the employment of the concept of vulnerable groups in mainstreaming see in precedence the Directive 2012/29/EU of the European Parliament and of the Council of 25 October 2012 establishing minimum standards on the rights, support and protection of victims of crime, and replacing Council Framework Decision 2001/220/JHA [2012] OJ L 315/14. When addressing the situation of all victims of offences in Europe, and the need to consider the situation of victims of transphobic crimes as well as other bias-motivated crimes it does so by clarifying the concept of 'vulnerable victims', which was used in EU law but without being defined. The procedure identified to assess the potential vulnerability of all victims of crime includes the assessment of the possible bias motivation of the crime, as well as the victim's personal fundamental characteristics such as gender identity.

57 Special Eurobarometer 437 'Discrimination in the EU in 2015' Available at: http://europa.eu/!Rm34yd

Inter-service Working Groups set up on equality-related issues, such as disability, gender, racism and xenophobia, is an illustrator of this. But how is each institution effectively responding on the equality mainstreaming commitment?

a. The European Commission

As anticipated in the previous paragraph, a correct use of the IA appears undoubtedly the preferential mainstreaming tool at the disposal of the European Commission. But it should be underlined that other mainstreaming tools might be, and are, used by the Commission to perform the mainstreaming task. One of these appears to be standard anti-discrimination clauses, purportedly in accordance with the principle of 'mainstreaming' equality, now being inserted in a number of the Commission's legislative proposals in sensitive areas such as the Areas of Freedom, Security and Justice. However, contrary to the Commission's assertions, the approach has not been uniform. In some proposals these provisions differ,[58] while other proposals are devoid of non-discrimination clauses.[59]

Nevertheless, the *ex post evaluation* of the Commission's mainstreaming duty appears partially corrective, which is particularly significant considering the intrinsic necessity of not anchoring mainstreaming to the adoption of a legislative act or a policy but of ensuring it continues throughout the implementation process, with a need for a continuous monitoring of the impact of adopted legislation and policies (an ex post impact analysis) that includes multiple scrutinies of all the EU institutional framework. A virtuous example of this can be mentioned, *de jure condito*: the specific attention the European Commission devoted to the monitoring of the correct implementation of EU equal treatment laws. This has been done, for instance, with a particular focus on Directives 2004/113 and 2006/54 in the Annex accompanying the *Strategy for equality between women and men 2010–2015.*[60] Here the Commission underlined its commitment to 'studying the specific issues pertaining to sex discrimination in relation to gender identity', being aware of its role to play in expressly extending the meaning of sex in EU legislation to include gender identity and gender expression.

58 For example, the European Commission, Proposal for a Council Directive on minimum standards on procedures in Member States for granting and withdrawing refugee status, (COM (2000) 578) final of 20 September 2000 at p. 48 contains the following anti-discrimination clause in Article 41: 'Member States shall apply the provisions of this Directive to applicants for asylum without discrimination as to sex, racial or ethnic origin, religion or belief, disability, age, sexual orientation or country of origin'.

59 See i.e. the Commission's Proposal for a Council Directive on the right to family reunification (COM (1999) of 638) final and the amended proposal (COM (2000) 624 final) final. See further the Chapter on mainstreaming of human rights by Kosta, para II 1 (a) in this volume.

60 Communication from the Commission to the European Parliament, the Council, the European Economic and Social Committee and the Committee of the Regions of 21 September 2010 – Strategy for equality between women and men 2010–2015 (COM (2010) 491) final. Not published in the Official Journal.

But the Commission is either performing its role through the instrument of the Commission's Reports on the application of the EU Charter of Fundamental rights, a key tool for revealing and highlighting the progress made in mainstreaming the different non-discrimination grounds. For instance, the Report of 2012 specified that 'progress was made in disability mainstreaming to ensure that disability rights are reflected in legislative acts', i.e., measures in favor of persons with disabilities and with reduced mobility are included in the new Regulations on passenger rights covering maritime and inland waterways transport (entering into force on 18 December 2012) and bus and coach transport (applying from 1 March 2013). The Commission published guidelines clarifying the rights of disabled passengers and people with reduced mobility when they travel by air to ensure the correct implementation of Regulation 1107/2006.[61] On another note the Report of 2016[62] insists on the progress on the side of non-discrimination on the grounds of age and race and ethnicity recalling how the right to education was mainstreamed in particular in the EU's response to the asylum crisis. In particular, the Commission quoted its proposal for a recast of the Reception Conditions Directive, aimed at ensuring adequate reception standards for all asylum applicants throughout the Union, which obliges Member States to treat applicants who have been granted access to the labor market in the same way as their own nationals with regard inter alia to education and vocational training. Similarly, it referred to the recast Students and Researchers Directive,[63] which establishes the conditions of non-EU nationals' entry and residence for the purposes of research, study, training, voluntary service, pupil exchange schemes or educational projects, and au pairing; as well as to its proposal for a revision of the Directive on the conditions of entry and residence of third-country nationals for the purposes of highly skilled employment (blue card)[64] that upholds highly skilled workers' rights to equal treatment, in particular as regards access to education and vocational training.

Furthermore, the Commission is monitoring its performance financially as well.[65] For instance, based on the Commission's commitment to mainstreaming,

61 Regulation (EC) No 1107/2006 of the European Parliament and of the Council of 5 July 2006 concerning the rights of disabled persons and persons with reduced mobility when travelling by air (Text with EEA relevance) [2006] OJ L 204/1.

62 See in particular the Commission Staff Working Document on the Application of the EU Charter of Fundamental Rights Accompanying the document Communication from the Commission to the European Parliament, the Council, the European Economic and Social Committee and the Committee of the Regions on 2016 Report on the Application of the EU Charter of Fundamental Rights, (COM (2017) 239) final [18 may 2017].

63 Directive (EU) 2016/801 of the European Parliament and of the Council of 11 May 2016 on the conditions of entry and residence of third-country nationals for the purposes of research, studies, training, voluntary service, pupil exchange schemes or educational projects and au pairing (recast) (2016) OJ L 132/21.

64 Proposal for a Directive of the European Parliament and of the Council on the conditions of entry and residence of third-country nationals for the purposes of highly skilled employment, (COM (2016) 378) final.

65 COM (1996) 67 final (Feb. 21, 1996), *supra* note 2, at 15–19.

the 2000–2006 funding regulations were endowed with a strong mainstreaming approach, particularly in the area of gender equality.[66] Subsequently, in the 2007–2013 financial period, gender equality was complemented – and then reinforced in the 2014–2020 funding regulations – by mainstreaming action in the areas of non-discrimination and inclusion of persons with disabilities.[67] However the ex post evaluation dimension is still a feeble one considering that the Commission: (a) has never considered infringement proceedings for failure to mainstream equality and, in the current programming period, has never considered suspending payments for failure to fulfil the equality conditionalities; and that (b) the Commission's reports on the implementation of Structural Funds submitted to the European Parliament do not explicitly report on mainstreaming.[68]

Last but not least and not less significantly, *de jure condendo*, exist the potential and the challenge for the Commission in its performance of non-discrimination mainstreaming duty applied to the implementation side of EU anti-discrimination law. Let's take the example of the existent discriminatory practices targeting Roma, including residential segregation, repeated forced evictions, and discrimination in access to social housing in: (a) Italy, despite Article 3(h) of the Directive having been literally transposed into national law, and in (b) Romania where protection against discrimination is also provided for in anti-discrimination legislation but is not being implemented in practice. Thus, although housing is not explicitly mentioned in the TFEU among the list of EU competences, Article 34 of the Charter of Fundamental Rights of the European Union enshrines the right to social and housing assistance. The principle of access to housing without

66 Council Regulation (EC) No. 1260/1999 laying down general provisions on structural funds (1999) OJ L 161/1.

67 Article 16 of the Council Regulation (EC) No. 1083/2006 laying down general provisions on the European Regional Development Fund, the European Social Fund and the Cohesion Fund and repealing Regulation (EC) No 1260/1999 (but currently no longer in force) OJ L 210/25. Accordingly, the Member States and the Commission shall ensure that equality between men and women and the integration of the gender perspective is promoted during the various stages of implementation of the Funds. The Member States and the Commission shall take appropriate steps to prevent any discrimination based on sex, racial or ethnic origin, religion or belief, disability, age or sexual orientation during the various stages of implementation of the Funds and, in particular, in the access to them. In particular, accessibility for disabled persons shall be one of the criteria to be observed in defining operations co-financed by the Funds and to be taken into account during the various stages of implementation. See also i.e. Regulation (EU) No. 1303/2013, supra note 6, annex XI, pt. II, points 1–3; EU Council, Cohesion Policy Legislative Package. Presidency compromise on ex ante conditionalities, no 12543/2/11 REV 2 Annex IV (2012) 20. http://register.consilium.europa.eu/doc/srv?l=EN&f=ST%208207%202012%20ADD%202%20REV%202; Eur. Comm'n, Proposal, annex IV, COM (2011) 615 final/2 (Mar. 14, 2012) and for an excellent analysis see V. Viţă, 'Mainstreaming Equality in European Structural and Investment Funds: Introducing the Novel Conditionality Approach of the 2014–2020 Financial Framework' in *German Law Journal* 7, 2018 (4), 993–1016.

68 See for a more detailed analysis on these profile V. Viţă, Mainstreaming Equality in European Structural and Investment Funds, cit. note 67.

discrimination on grounds of nationality has also been well established by EU secondary legislation. The prohibition of racial discrimination in the area of goods and services as enshrined in EU law covers services supplied by both private and public actors and thus applies to the criteria used to allocate social housing. Social housing has been listed among the social services of general interest and Member States must regulate such services by respecting overarching principles including the principle of non-discrimination. Therefore, in the light of Articles 10 TFEU, Article 6 (3) TEU, and Article 34 EU CFR the European Commission should ensure that the principle of non-discrimination in the enjoyment of the right to adequate housing is respected in its Member States. With this aim, the Commission should ensure that the relevant provisions of the Race Equality Directive, and especially Article 3 (1) (h), are enforced in Member States.

b. The European Ombudsman

If and when the Commission performance on the mainstreaming duties is not satisfactory, the operations of the European Ombudsman might be corrective and there are already a few but relevant examples. For instance, in 2014 it reported numerous instances of discrimination (para 25) and cases where EU co-funded programs went against the EU policy on social inclusion and equality. The most visible examples are the institutionalisation of children and persons with disabilities (para 28). The European Ombudsman drew the Commission's attention to programs that, because of their deficient implementation, substantially limit the effectiveness of planned socially inclusive action. The implementation of programs that targeted the integration of women were often found counterproductive and ill-suited to promote gender equality (para 28 (iii)). The results of these findings have been acknowledged preliminary observing that 'Regulation 1303/2013 obliges not only Member States but also the Commission to 'prevent any discrimination' when preparing and implementing programmes; so improving the purely negative dimension of the preliminary IAs, at least in funding programmes. In particular, the Ombudsman derived from such a premise the relevant needed inclusion in the Commission's assessment of the success of programmes and actions financed through ESI Funds, of the 'consideration of how they have contributed to the promotion of respect for the fundamental rights enshrined in the Charter'. More specifically and operationally it has been suggested as an opportunity for the Commission to 'promote the adoption of adequate equality and fundamental rights indicators and draft checklists to evaluate the use of the funds to promote fundamental rights and non-discrimination in the broader sense'.

On another occasion[69] the Ombudsman opened an inquiry on the European Commission and its relations with its staff members with disabilities who face a wide range of obstacles that prevent them from achieving equal opportunities, independence and full economic and social integration, and in favour of whom the

69 Decision of the European Ombudsman on own-initiative inquiry OI/3/2003/JMA concerning the European Commission, 4 July 2007.

EU had been urged to strengthen its contribution to promoting equal opportunities for people with disabilities, with a view to their integration into society. The Ombudsman considered that, among the various institutions with a special responsibility to ensure that persons with disabilities are not discriminated against in their relations with the EU institution, the Commission deserved special attention because of its central role within the European Union's institutional framework. Thus, in its communication of 10 May 2000 entitled 'Towards a barrier-free Europe for people with disabilities',[70] the Commission committed itself to developing and supporting a comprehensive and integrated strategy to deal with social, architectural and design barriers that unnecessarily restrict access for people with disabilities. It not only restated the commitments set out in the Code of Good Practice but, in addition, defined new measures aimed at fostering the development of best practice within its own organisation. The actions outlined in the Communication were grouped into five themes: (i) employment; (ii) accessibility of the Commission's premises; (iii) information and communication; (iv) the European Schools; and (v) internal coordination. This strategy was indeed reinforced by the Commission with the formal adoption of a revised Code of Good Practice on 25 November 2003. Though these actions were supported by the European Parliament,[71] which called for the implementation of supplementary actions,[72] such as the creation of an inter-institutional group to examine the conditions of access for people with disabilities to EU institutions; the Ombudsman noted that good administration 'requires prompt and effective action to implement publicly stated commitments' and 'the seriousness of the situation encountered by people with disabilities demanded that the proclaimed commitments be put into practice by means of effective actions'.[73] The action of the Ombudsman was therefore centered on the acknowledged necessity of reviewing the actions undertaken by this institution in this area, and to assess whether or not they were consistent with the institution's legal obligations and stated commitments so that such commitments could be said to be effectively accomplished. The Ombudsman even made it clear that 'in light of the inquiry's outcome, he would consider whether it was necessary to widen the scope of the inquiry and include other EU institutions'. In the case at hand the efforts produced by the Commission were retained as not requiring any further steps.

Slightly differently, the same Ombudsman reviewed the European Schools' policy for the integration of children with disabilities in the context of a previous

70 Communication from the Commission to the Council, the European Parliament, the Economic and Social Committee and the Committee of the Regions – Towards a barrier-free Europe for people with disabilities, COM/2000/284 final of 12 May 2000.

71 European Parliament Resolution of 4 April 2001 on the Communication from the Commission to the Council, the European Parliament, the Economic and Social Committee and the Committee of the Regions – Towards a barrier-free Europe for people with disabilities, COM(2000) 284 – C5–0632/2000–2000/2296 (COS).

72 Ibidem, paragraph 35.

73 Ibidem, Para 1.4.

complaint (1391/2002/JMA), in which one of the allegations was that European Schools had failed to establish an integrated and unified education system to cater for the needs of all SEN children. As a result of his inquiry, the Ombudsman submitted a special report to Parliament on 27 May 2005 where he found that there appeared to be no binding legal provision requiring the Commission to set up a unified educational system. In the absence of such a legal basis, the Ombudsman could not conclude that the Commission had failed to act properly by not ensuring that the European Schools provide education programmes for all SEN children of EU officials.[74] Notwithstanding this finding, the Ombudsman also pointed to the inconsistency between the Schools' practice and the public commitments made by the EU in general,[75] and by the Commission in particular,[76] in support of an integrated educational system.

Complementary to such a monitoring and the implementation of the mainstreaming duty by the EU institution through the operational Ombudsman, the securitisation of 'citizens' rights' by the principle of good administration in the EU context, might also be able to impact on a mainstreaming clause determining a European Ombudsman inquiry for bad administrative practice, namely in case of non-respect of the IAs guidelines.

c. The co-legislators

The institution which nominates the Ombudsman, the European Parliament, has already been touched by the constitutionalisation of the non-discrimination mainstreaming duty operated by the Lisbon Treaty that has contributed to its consciousness of such a positive duty.[77] The pilot project funded by the European Parliament in the area of healthcare ('reducing health inequalities experienced by LGBTI people') is an illustrative example. The aim of the project is to better understand the specific health inequalities experienced by LGBTI people, focusing in particular on overlapping inequalities stemming from discrimination and unfair treatment on other grounds (e.g. age, disability, socioeconomic status, race and ethnicity) and the barriers faced by health professionals when providing care to those groups.

74 See point 1.5 of the Ombudsman's decision in case 1391/2002/JMA.

75 Resolution of the Council and the Ministers for Education meeting within the Council of 31 May 1990 concerning the integration of children and young people with disabilities into ordinary systems of education; (1990) OJ C 162/2. Point 2 of the Resolution recommended to Member States that, '[f]ull integration into the system of mainstream education should be considered as a first option in all appropriate cases, and all education establishments should be in a position to respond to the needs of pupils and students with disabilities'.

76 Communication from the Commission to the Council, the European Parliament, the Economic and Social Committee and the Committee of the Regions, 'Towards a barrier-free Europe for people with disabilities' (COM (2000) 284) final.

77 See, on this topic, V. Kosta, 'Fundamental rights mainstreaming in the EU' in particular para. II 1 (b), in this volume.

Moreover, the institution has taken important steps towards developing its own capacity to assess the impact of major policy initiatives since 2012, by creating a dedicated directorate (IMPA), later brought under the broader umbrella of the European Parliamentary Research Service (EPRS).[78] However, as noted by Renda, the EPRS is currently more actively involved in providing early assessments of the European Commission's own impact assessment than in evaluating the impacts of major amendments proposed by parliamentary committees[79]; also, the work of the above mentioned Service is often ignored by the members of the European Parliament, what Renda describes as 'also due to the wide distance between the logic of cost-benefit analysis and that of political decision-making'.[80] Anyhow, the European Parliament has also been able to impact on equality mainstreaming positively, for instance in sensitive areas such as the Area of Freedom Security and Justice in the recasting process of EU asylum legislation. An example of such an attitude might be the impact on gender identity non-discrimination within the so called Qualification Directive and the Procedure Directive. In particular, gender identity has been included as a recognised reason for persecution on the one hand (Qualification Directive), and more sensitivity towards gender identity related asylum cases has been introduced thanks to a new definition of 'asylum seekers with special needs' on the other hand (Procedure Directive). In both cases, while the initial proposals of the Commission (October 2009) included no new provisions regarding gender identity, the European Parliament used its co-decision powers procedure introduced by the Lisbon Treaty and called for these amendments. In the case of the Qualification Directive, in particular, this vote was an orientation vote which defined the Parliament's position in its negotiations with the Council.

Moving then to consider the other co-legislator, in 2015 the Council of the European Union[81] set up a High Level Group on Non-Discrimination, Equality and Diversity (HLG) directly linked to thematic priorities of the Presidency of the Council and gathering representatives from all EU Member States and EEAS countries dealing with non-discrimination, equality and diversity issues. It meets twice a year (one meeting per EU Presidency). Its agenda in 2015 focused mostly on LGBTI policies. More generally, it is positively making more use of Commission impact assessments.

However, in so doing, it is still impermeable to its own capacity for impact assessment and ex post evaluation. This fundamentally undermines the possibility for Member States of having a fully evidence-based justification for the legislative acts that are adopted. Rather, even impact assessments are reduced to give evidence of the 'original' rationale that backed the Commission proposal, not the

78 See http://www.europarl.europa.eu/thinktank/en/home.html
79 See A. Renda, How can Sustainable Development Goals be 'mainstreamed' in the EU's Better Regulation Agenda? In CEPS Policy Insights n. 2017/12.
80 Ibidem.
81 See V. Kosta, 'Fundamental rights mainstreaming in the EU', para II 1 (c), in this volume.

rationale that backs the final text approved at the end of the ordinary legislative procedure.

d. The Court of Justice: indirectly progressive, directly static and potentially challenging

The attitude of the Court of Justice as to the judicial equality mainstreaming, rather distinctly from other integration principles or mainstreaming clauses, in particular Articles 9 and 11 TFEU,[82] has not been pervasive but rare. In particular, Article 10 TFEU has been invoked by the parties or mentioned *en passant* by the Advocate Generals in their Opinion only in a few cases. Let's see how and with what implications but first we shall underline that such a reluctance should not be exaggerated: indirectly the Court of Justice jurisprudence has in fact impacted on the constitutionalised non-discrimination mainstreaming duty, and thus is progressive in that regard. In particular, this is true for the grounds of discrimination that is sexual orientation. In fact, some lines of case law show an indirect impact on non-discrimination mainstreaming, favoring the Court's decision and pushing the performance of the EU legislator mainstreaming duty. Illustrative is the case where the Court of Justice pushed the legislator in the direction of a more targeted approach to sexual orientation non-discrimination mainstreaming in the field of asylum. Thus, it was in the joined cases *A, B and C* [83] that the Court of Justice pointed out that, while questions based on stereotyped notions of homosexuality may be useful, 'the assessment of applications for the grant of refugee status on the basis solely of stereotyped notions associated with homosexuals' would not satisfy the right to be heard. Furthermore, this requirement would be breached if an applicant was not considered credible on the grounds that they did not reveal their sexual orientation at the first possible opportunity.[84] This has influenced the EU legislator in the recasting of EU provisions for asylum seekers to orientate the provisions for interviewing asylum seekers towards a requirement that such interviews be carried out in a sensitive manner, by competent, trained officials.[85]

The line of the Court of Justice jurisprudence concerning the age ground of discrimination, where the Court shows its willingness to treat age discrimination as a 'suspect' ground of discrimination and to rigorously apply the objective justification test as is done with the other non-discrimination grounds has also been commented on as possibly finding its rationale in the willingness of the Court to

82 See chapters of Bartoloni and Seijfell. For a discussion on the judicial review of the 'provisions having general application' articulated in Articles 7–13 TFEU, see Nic Shuibhne, 'Deconstructing and reconstructing Article 7 TFEU', in this volume, in particular Section III A.

83 Joined Cases C-148/13 to 150/13, *A., B., C.*, ECLI:EU:C:2014:2406.

84 Ibidem, paras 70–71.

85 Article 15 (3) Directive 2013/32/EU of the European Parliament and of the Council of 26 June 2013 on common procedures for granting and withdrawing international protection OJ L 380/60.

make clear the commitment of the EU legal order to non-discrimination norms, 'the rhetorical and moral significance of the language of equality', and the Court's strong commitment in the past to gender equality'.[86] After all, it was the Court of Justice which suggested that the Court has a duty to interpret anti-discrimination directives in a way that is consistent with the gender mainstreaming provision of Article 3(2) of EC Treaty. Or, when the Court of Justice has had the opportunity – though very rare – to be confronted with Article 10 TFEU directly, what has its attitude been? What area and discrimination grounds do these case laws cover and concern? So far, there have been only Advocate Generals to use Article 10 TFEU in their reasoning, and very rarely. The rationale and aim has been, however, to grant and recognize a 'fundamental' and constitutional status to the equality principle together with Article 3 (3) TEU.[87] It remains instead so far to be clarified if the model of positive duties recalled in Article 10 TFEU is more than a political commitment and especially a veritable legal duty with the annexed consequences and legal effects.[88]

A partial orientation has nonetheless been provided by the same Court of Justice, though only with reference to the gender mainstreaming and its integration clause contained in Article 8 TFEU. In that regard, the Court held that *the obligation to mainstream* did not require the EU to take immediate action – achieving equality must be done progressively. But when the Union decides to take mainstreaming action, the mere mention of equality is not enough. In particular, according to the Court of Justice, both the EU and its Member States must ensure that 'it ... contribute[s], in a coherent manner, to the achievement of the intended objective',[89] so that the institutions must ensure that mainstreaming measures are actually effective. Deductively, if a coherence among the specific (though more advanced) commitment to the gender grounds of discrimination and the other comprehensive grounds of non-discrimination, the same clarification should be considered valid also for the general equality mainstreaming clause provided by Article 10 TFEU. Is that the case?

Explicitly the Court has not replicated the idea in cases where Article 10 TFEU was at stake. First, some Advocates General, when provided an interpretation of Article 10 TFEU, proposed to see in the provision a general clause which articulates a particular *policy aim* to which the European Union is committed[90]; further

86 See C. O'Cinneide, *Age Discrimination and the European Court of Justice: EU Equality Law Comes of Age*, in ERA COMM available at http://www.era-comm.eu/oldoku/Adiskri/08_Age/2010_09_OCinneide%20EN.pdf.

87 Case C-236/09 *Association Belge des Consommateurs Test-Achats ASBL and ot.* E.C.R I-00773. For a discussion on Article 3, para 3 TEU see Nic Shuibhne, 'Deconstructing and reconstructing Article 7 TFEU', in this volume.

88 For the question on whether there is legal obligation to mainstream fundamental rights under EU law see V. Kosta, 'Fundamental rights mainstreaming in the EU', in this volume.

89 Case C-236/09 cit. supra note 87, paras 20 e 21.

90 Opinion of Advocate General Wahl in *Z*, Case C-363/12, EU:C:2013:604, para 112; Opinion of Advocate General JÄÄskinen in Case C-354/13, FOA, ECLI:EU:C:2014:2106, point 23.

establishing the insufficiency of the clause for establishing an incidence of Member State implementation of EU law in the sense of Article 51 of the Charter of fundamental Rights.[91] On another note, Advocate General Tanchev in *Egenberger*, [92] with respect to the judicial protection of the prohibition on discrimination on the basis of religion, when a religious organisation relies on Article 4(2) of Directive 2000/78, used Article 10 TFEU to contrast an interpretation of Articles 17 (1) and (2) TFEU as some kind of *meta* principle of constitutional law[93] that binds the Union to respect the status under Member State law of churches, religious associations and communities, and philosophical and non-confessional organisations, whatever the circumstances. He highlighted that 'account should also be taken of Article 10 TFEU and the EU's aims in defining and implementing its policies and activities'[94] next to Articles 22 and 47 of the Charter, the former supporting pluralism and the latter reflecting the general principle of the right to an effective judicial remedy in the event of violation of the rights and freedoms guaranteed by EU law. This was relevant in order to suggest to interpret Article 4 (2) of Directive 2000/78/EC 'as meaning that an employer, such as the defendant in the present case, or the church on its behalf, may not itself authoritatively determine whether adherence by an applicant to a specified religion, by reason of the nature of the activities or of the context in which they are carried out, constitutes a genuine, legitimate and justified occupational requirement, having regard to the employer/church's ethos'.

Looking to the cases where Article 10 TFEU appears in the Court's reasoning, only two cases have been acknowledged so far. On one occasion the provision has just been mentioned among the EU law sources.[95] In the other case, the Court has indirectly shed light on the uncertainty of the possibility that the legitimacy of actions of the Council, European Parliament, and Commission be reviewed by the Court in the light of the non-discrimination mainstreaming clause of Article 10

91 Opinion of Advocate General JÄÄskinen in FOA, cit. supra note 90 point 23.

92 Opinion of Advocate General Tanchev in Case C-414/16, *Egenberger*, ECLI:EU:C:2017:851.

93 See L. Alexander, 'Introduction' in L. Alexander (ed), *Constitutionalism: Philosophical Foundations* (Cambridge University Press, 1998) p. 1, and his discussion at pp. 2 to 4 of the distinction between the meta constitution, the elements of which are relatively fixed (e.g. the separation of powers) and the symbolic constitution, the content of which may change without alteration to the meta constitution.

94 Opinion of Advocate General Tanchev in *Egenberger*, cit. supra note 92, para 93.

95 In the *Minority SafePack* case law, T-646/13, judgment of 3 February 2017 ECLI:EU:T:2017:59 the General Court in reality limits to refer to the provision as one of the EU law sources upon which the European citizens' initiative (ICI) was based. Thus, at para 24 it is acknowledged how 'after a first section dedicated to the importance given by the EU to respect for, and the protection of, minorities and respect for cultural and linguistic diversity through, in particular, a certain number of provisions contained in the Treaties, such as Articles 1 TEU to 3 TEU and Articles 9 TFEU and 10 TFEU, sections 2 to 7 of the annex to the proposed ECI outline 11 areas in which the proposed acts should be developed by the institutions of the European Union and give, to that end, precise suggestions on the types of act to adopt, the content of those acts and the corresponding legal bases in the FEU Treaty'.

TFEU. Thus, in the *Z.* case, mentioned earlier, the Court of Justice was probably influenced by the formulation of the preliminary ruling having been asked 'having regard to Article 10 TFEU', and/or Articles 21, 26 and 34 of the Charter of Fundamental rights if Article 3 (1) and 5 of the Directive 2000/78 should be interpreted as meaning that there is discrimination on the grounds of disability where a woman – who suffers from a disability which prevents her from giving birth, whose genetic child has been born through a surrogacy arrangement, and who is responsible for the care of her genetic child from birth – is refused paid leave from employment equivalent to maternity leave and/or adoptive leave. The Court itself in fact underlined that: 'the referring tribunal asks, in essence, whether Directive 2000/78, interpreted it necessary in the light of the UN Convention, must be understood as meaning that a refusal to provide paid leave equivalent to maternity leave or adoptive leave to a female worker who is unable to bear a child and who has availed of a surrogacy arrangement constitutes discrimination on the ground of disability, and, if the answer is in the negative, *whether that directive is valid in the light of Article 10 TFEU, Articles 21, 26 and 34 of the Charter, and the UN Convention* (emphasis added)'.[96] When the Court declared it 'not necessary to examine the validity of Directive 2000/78 in the light of Article 10 TFEU and Articles 21, 26 and 34 of the Charter',[97] it admitted the legitimacy of a request to indicate the non-discrimination mainstreaming clause as a yardstick for the judicial review Article 10 TFEU – and so indirectly a judicial review of EU secondary law under – among others primary law provisions. More in detail, the Court based such a line of reasoning on a precedent case law (related that time to Article 8 TFEU and so to the gender mainstreaming clause and the validity of Directive 2006/54) where it motivated the dismissed decision on the point not on its inadmissibility on the merit but because 'the Court may decide not to give a preliminary ruling where the provision whose validity is the subject-matter of the reference manifestly has no bearing on the outcome of the main proceedings'.[98] So, *a contrario*, if instead the provision requested to be annulled because of a contrast with the non-discrimination mainstreaming clause bears an outcome on the main proceeding, it might be the case that the Court of Justice examines the question, even possibly considering the illegitimacy of the European regulatory act, for instance, because of a failure to respect procedural requirements in relation to the Impact Assessment proceeding as to equality mainstreaming. In these cases, the possibility of an annulment might neither require a balance between the relative importance of non-discrimination objectives and other Union objectives. A possible advantage (convenience) of using 'Article 10 TFEU bedrock' for a judicial review of EU secondary law could be that with the model of positive duty instead of positive actions, the judicial review becomes no more limited to the question of whether the Union legislator committed 'a manifest error of appraisal,'

96 Case C-363/12, *Z.*, ECLI:EU:C:2014:159, para 68.
97 Ibidem, para 83.
98 See Case C-222/04 *Cassa di Risparmio di Firenze and Others* [2006] ECR I-289, paragraph 75.

because these are not positive duties rendered subject to compliance with the proportionality requirement.

A last further space for the use of Article 10 TFEU by the Court of Justice seems to be its incorporation into future cases that might allege *indirect* discrimination or that address *multiple* inequalities[99] both in the context of migration and enlargement,[100] and in response to concerns around how public policy addresses intersecting inequalities.[101] It would be interesting to see if that would be the judiciary attitude in the near future.

Conclusions

'Integration principles' are those principles in the TFEU that are 'overarching', i.e. that must be taken into account in all areas in which the EU undertakes activities. The main purpose of such principles is to 'harmonize' or 'streamline' the EU's own actions in such a way that certain central values or objectives of the Union can be reached more effectively. Title II of the TFEU brought together a series of principles of 'integration character'. This chapter has focused on Article 10 TFEU and its integration principle and carried out an assessment of the impact of the new provision in the Lisbon Treaty concerning the non-discrimination mainstreaming in the main EU policies, from the legislative making, judicial interpretation and enforcement perspectives.

Analysis has shown, with an evolutionary picture from the equality mainstreaming before and after Lisbon, in contrast with the underlined 'inherent danger' as to the environment that under the disguise of integration, certain

99 Multiple discrimination addresses the problem and profile of 'intersectionality' which is about the interaction of categories of 'difference'. On the philosophical concept of intersectionality see N. Yuval-Davis, 'Intersectionality and Feminist Politics', 13 *European Journal of Women's Studies* (2006) pp. 193–209; on the concept applied to the EU see M. Verloo, 'Multiple Identities, Intersectionality and the European Union', 13 *European Journal of Women's Studies* (2006) pp. 211–228; S. Fredman, 'Positive Rights and Duties: Addressing Intersectionality,' in D. Schiek, V. Chege (eds), *European Union Non-Discrimination Law: Comparative Perspectives on Multidimensional Equality Law*, (Routledge Cavendish, 2008); U. Vieten, 'Intersectionality scope and multidimensional equality within the European Union: traversing the national boundaries of inequality?' in D. Schiek, V. Chege (eds) *European Union Non-Discrimination Law*, cit., pp. 93–135; D. Schiek, J. Mulder, 'Intersectionality and EU Law: A Critical Appraisal', in D. Schiek, A. Lawson (eds), *EU Law and Intersectionality: Investigating the Triangle of Racial, Gender and Disability Discrimination* (Farnham: Ashgate, 2011); D. Schiek, 'Intersectionality and the Notion of Disability in EU Discrimination Law' in *Common Market Law Review* 53 (2016), 1: 35–64.

100 S. Fredman, 'European Community Discrimination Law: A Critique' 1992 *Industrial Law Journal* 21(2): 199–134; R. Evans Case, T.E. Givens, 'Re-engineering Legal Opportunity Structures in the European Union? The Starting Line Group and the Politics of the Racial Equality Directives' 2010 *Journal of Common Market Studies* 48 (2): 221–241.

101 E. Lombardo, P. Meier, M. Verloo, (eds), *The Discursive Politics of Gender Equality: Stretching, Bending and Policymaking* (London: Routledge, 2009).

standards will be diluted or offset against other interests and policy considerations[102]; a rather positive 'tentative' outcome, with good intentions but still some gaps and areas of further improvements for the potential of the new provision.

In particular, the chapter has shown how, if the constitutionalisation of equality mainstreaming had not impacted on the equality conceptual profile and rationale, it has nonetheless significantly – though not entirely adequately – impacted on the institutional and procedural performance of such a positive duty. It has been pinpointed how the principal tool for mainstreaming as to the European Commission, the IA, has been improved through the recast of the 2015 guidelines – accompanied by a strengthened governance of better regulation by a stronger oversight body (the Regulatory Scrutiny Board) and a new REFIT platform for consultation of both stakeholders and government representatives. The addition of a chapter within these renewed guidelines dealing specifically with how to assess the impact of proposals in relation to equality and non-discrimination overcomes the critical aspect that the mainstreaming objective of non-discrimination was taken into account more at the level of defining the policy objectives than of assessing impacts. Moreover, the analysis has demonstrated how the attitude of the European Commission towards an adequate non-discrimination mainstreaming appears to be reinforced with the entry into force of the Lisbon Treaty. Also reinforcing this attitude is the new comprehensive integration principle regarding equality as different tools appear to be used for implementing the duty ranging from the *ex ante* to an *ex post evaluation* throughout the implementation process, and a continuous monitoring of the impact of adopted legislation and policies, eventually mixing the two profiles and perspectives in the financial practice of the Commission. The analysis has described how the positiveness of these attitudes has been proven by the application of the same mainstreaming duty by the European Ombudsman. But there are areas for further improvements, and also for the performance of the mainstreaming duty by EU institutions other than the Commission. Thus, looking from the side of the European Parliament, though some good practices, also in the sensitive Area of Freedom Security and Justice, the internal organisation of the institutions has been underlined as still too much more actively involved in providing early assessments of the European Commission's own impact assessment than in evaluating the impacts of major amendments proposed by parliamentary committees. Analogous terms of criticism stem for the European Council that though remarkably is making more use of Commission impact assessments, in so doing, is still impermeable to its own capacity for impact assessment and ex post evaluation. The attitude of the Court of Justice neither can be qualified as 'audacious' as to a formal incorporation of the integration principle in its reasoning. As the chapter has indicated, so far, if the Court has sometimes

102 J. Jans, 'Stop the integration principle?' (2011) 33 *Fordham International Law Journal* 1533, speaks in terms of 'reversed integration', a process by which certain environmental standards, such as environmental quality standards or emission standards, are lowered as a consequence of the requirement that other than environmental interests are to be taken into account.

indirectly judicially mainstreamed equality, it has been rather cautionary in mentioning Article 10 TFEU in its mainstreaming duty performance. Only indirectly a judicial mainstreaming has been achieved, and essentially as to the ground of age and sexual orientation discrimination, but not, for instance, as to other sensitive grounds such as religious discrimination.[103] However, from the single case where the Court has made use of Article 10 TFEU concerning disability, the analysis has deductively underlined some possible room for improvement. Thus, *a contrario*, the words of the Court have here been interpreted as admitting a possibility for a challenging judicial review of a EU regulatory act for violation of the non-discrimination mainstreaming duty. And this would present the further positive aspect that no severe proportionality compliance should be required and a role for positive duty might be judicially explored in intersectional discrimination. We must wait to see if that will really be the case so that the potential of equality positive duty model could achieve an effective and proper comprehensive exploitation by all the main EU institutional levels, so avoiding what Shakespeare had already pinpointed in *King Lear* that 'virtue itself turns vice being misapplied'.

103 See Case 157/15, *Samira Achbita and Centrum voor Gelijkheid van Kansen en voor Racismebestrijding v G4S Secure Solutions NV*, ECLI:EU:C:2017:203 and Case C-188/15 *Asma Bougnaoui, Association de Défense des Droits de l'Homme (ADDH) v Micropole Univers SA* EU:C:2017:20

5 The horizontal social clause in a legal dimension

Maria Eugenia Bartoloni[1]

I. Introduction

As a significant step forward regarding the organisation of interests in previous versions of the Treaties, the Lisbon Treaty provides a fresh new emphasis on social needs. The most significant changes though lie not so much in the sphere of the EU's regulatory powers which, as will be seen below, remain almost unchanged[2] within the social sector more generally as in the different approach in which social values are recognised and expressed in the broader context of the objectives and priorities that shape the EU.[3]

A glance at the opening provisions of the Treaty on European Union (TEU) shows that the values and goals that traditionally belong to the EU, and which lie at the heart of the integration process, are pervaded by an unprecedented social dimension which is largely absent from the previous text of the Treaty of European Community (TEC). The increasing weight given to social values and objectives becomes readily apparent when the pre-existing version is compared with the current Arts 2 and 3 of the TEU, and is even more marked in comparison with the corresponding provisions relating to the sphere of market integration

1 Many thanks to Francesca Ippolito for her suggestions.
2 See the last paragraph of the present contribution.
3 For a discussion see S. Garben, 'The Constitutional (Im)balance between "the Market" and "the Social" in the European Union' (2017) 13 *European Constitutional Law Review* 22; M. Dawson and B. de Witte, 'Welfare policy and social inclusion' in A. Arnull and D. Chalmers (eds), *The Oxford Handbook of European Union law* (OUP 2015) 964–990; B. Cantillon, H. Verschueren, P. Ploscar (eds), *Social Inclusion and Social Protection in the EU: Interactions between Law and Policy* (Intersentia 2012); M. Daly and P. Copeland, 'Poverty and Social Policy in Europe 2020: Ungovernable and Ungoverned' (2014) 42(3) *Policy and Politics* 351; C. Barnard, 'EU Employment Law and the European Social Model: The Past, the Present and the Future' (2014) 67 (1) *Current Legal Problems* 199; E. Guild, S. Carrera, K. Eisele (eds), *Social Benefits and Migration: A Contested Relationship and Policy Challenge in the EU* (CEPS 2013); U. Neergaard, R. Nielsen, L. Roseberry (eds), *Integrating Welfare Functions into EU Law: From Rome to Lisbon* (DJØF Publishing 2009); F. Pennings, *European Social Security Law* (5th edn, Intersentia 2010); D. Schiek, U. Liebert, H. Schneider (eds), *European Economic and Social Constitutionalism after the Treaty of Lisbon* (CUP 2011).

and to what could be called the hard core of the European economic constitution.[4]

Art 2 introduces a strong social connotation into the fabric of EU values where it states that it is based – first and foremost – on the values of respect for human dignity, freedom, democracy, equality and protection of human rights, and where it also acknowledges the inclusion of pluralism, non-discrimination, tolerance, justice, solidarity and gender equality that are common to all Member States.[5] Art 3, para 3, advances the EU's objectives with the idea – much debated due to its ambiguous ordoliberalism,[6] but clear at least in its principled political inspiration[7] – of 'a highly competitive social market economy, aiming at full employment and social progress', and that 'shall combat social exclusion and discrimination, and shall promote social justice and protection.'[8]

At the same time, in the opening provisions of the new TEU, the reference to the 'open market economy with free competition', which strongly characterised the principles of the European economic constitution[9] and was found in the text of the earlier treaty, has been suppressed and symbolically relegated to Protocol 27 annexed to the Treaties. The idea – formally expunged from the heart of the values, objectives and general principles of the EU – survives in Art 119 of the TFEU, which opens Title VIII on economic and monetary policy. This would also seem to confirm the weakening and downgrading of the idea of an 'open market economy with free competition' from a general principle to a more narrow principle related to a specific sector, that is, the sphere of legislative competence and action to which it specifically refers. However important this sphere might be, it could no longer claim to be central or even dominant in the interpretation of the European (economic) constitution.

This overall constitutional rebalancing stems from, and indeed is specifically reinforced by, the definitive acquisition of the Charter of Nice – and, in particular, of the rich catalogue of fundamental social rights and principles enshrined therein – along with the European Union's primary law. The moment when fundamental social rights were constitutionalised in the EU signalled the most substantial revision of the overall supranational legal order, which would finally allow a certain balance to be made, no longer systematically favourable to the free

4 A. Williams, *The Ethos of Europe: Values, Law and Justice in the EU* (CUP 2010) 283.
5 See F. Ippolito, 'Mainstreaming equality in the EU legal order: more than a Cinderella provision?' in this volume.
6 Cf. Ch. Joerges, F. Rödl, '"Social Market Economy" as Europe's Social Model?' in L. Magnusson, B. Stråth (eds), *A European Social Citizenship? Preconditions for Future Policies from Historical Perspectives* (Lang 2004) 125.
7 Which tends to rebalance 'the internal asymmetries between market integration at supranational level and social protection at national level'. See M. Monti, *A New Strategy for the Single Market at the Service of Europe's Economy and Society: Report to the President of the European Commission* (Brussels, 9 May 2010) 71.
8 For a discussion on Art 3, para 3, TEU see Nic Shuibhne, 'Deconstructing and reconstructing Article 7 TFEU' in this volume.
9 Cf. e.g., J. Baquero Cruz, *Between Competition and Free Movement: The Economic Constitutional Law of the European Communities* (Hart 2002).

market.[10] It is not unreasonable to suppose then how the general provisions of the new treaties might open up a strong potential to reverse the relationship between social Europe and economic Europe. The interpreter, and more specifically the EU Court of Justice (ECJ) in the first place, stands before a framework of values, objectives and principles which have been significantly modified by the Treaties, extending beyond the functional and economic dimension of European integration, and recognising a co-essential social *finalité* of the EU. In this new axiological platform shaped by the opening provisions of the Treaties, the market ceases to act as supreme within the EU and competition shifts from being a protected value to a tool of the 'social market economy.'[11]

In this context, on 17 November 2017 the Commission, the European Parliament and the Council launched the 'European Pillar of Social Rights', a policy initiative in the social field.[12] The Pillar consists of a set of social rights and principles and is accompanied by a package of proposals, comprising pre-existing initiatives, new legislation and soft law measures. However, while the Pillar's precise implications are still unclear, it has the potential to significantly improve the overall balance between social and economic values in the EU's output in substantive terms.[13]

In this shortly defined context, particular relevance is given to the clause contained within Art 9 of the Treaty on the Functioning of the EU (TFEU), which states that '[i]n defining and implementing its policies and activities, the Union shall take into account requirements linked to the promotion of a high level of employment, the guarantee of adequate social protection, the fight against social

10 On the uncertain effects of the Charter, see S. Robin-Olivier, 'La contribution de la Charte des droits fondamentaux à la protection des droits sociaux dans l'Union européenne: un premier bilan après Lisbonne' (2013) 1 *European Journal of Human Rights* 109.

11 D. Damjanovic, 'The EU Market Rules as Social Market Rules: Why the EU Can Be a Social Market Economy' (2013) 50 *Common Market Law Review* 1685.

12 The 'official text' can be found online at <ec.europa.eu/commission/sites/beta-political/files/social-summit-european-pillar-social-rights-booklet_en.pdf>. The consultation on this initiative of the European Commission was launched in March 2016 (COM (2016) 127 final, 8 March 2016). On 26 April 2017 the Commission issued a series of documents including a Recommendation on the European Pillar of Social Rights (C (2017) 2600 final), a Communication on 'Establishing a European Pillar of Social Rights' (COM (2017) 250 final and a Proposal for an 'Interinstitutional Proclamation on the European Pillar of Social Rights' (COM (2017) 251 final). A 'Reflection paper on the social dimension of Europe' (COM (2017) 206 final) was also published the same day. At the social summit in Gothenburg on 17 November 2017, the Pillar was proclaimed by the European Parliament, the Council and the European Commission.

13 For a discussion see S. Garben, 'The European Pillar of Social Rights: Effectively Addressing Displacement?' (2018) 14(1) *European Constitutional Law Review* 210–230. For a critique see S. Robin-Olivier, 'Fundamental Rights as a New Frame: Displacing the Acquis' (2018) 14(1) *European Constitutional Law Review* 96–113. Furthermore see E. Caracciolo di Torella, 'The Principle of Gender Mainstreaming: Possibilities and Challenges' in this Volume on the implications of the European Pillar of Social Rights on gender mainstreaming.

exclusion, and a high level of education, training and protection of human health'.[14] This is the so-called *Horizontal Social Clause* which, inserted in Title II of the TFEU among the provisions of general application, requires that the objectives of social policy be considered within the framework of other EU policies and actions. The clause thus tends to settle the tension between liberalism and solidarism that has been at the centre of the debate on the nature of European integration since its origins. The liberalist philosophy tends to see market integration as the predominant if not the only factor of integration, and has the obvious effect of isolating free competition from the influence of EU social policy. The solidarist philosophy tends rather to suggest that social policy is not only a distinct policy of the EU, but also constitutes an imperative that should permeate the aims of any other policy.

In line with the changes introduced by the Lisbon Treaty (see above), the clause thus presents a clear, strong political significance when it introduces the need to balance economic and market goals with social objectives.[15] In this sense, the clause reflects the need to repair the breach – also reflected in a series of ECJ rulings[16] – between market interests and social protection.[17]

Not so simple, however, is its legal significance since the clause raises many issues. First, it is unclear whether the institutions and actors called upon to implement EU policies and actions have a 'legal duty' (to take account of social objectives) which may be disputed judicially or what kind of control EU judges may exercise (para II). Secondly, assuming that Art 9 TFEU does not constitute an *ad hoc* legal basis for the realisation of its objectives, it is not clear whether the

14 The importance of the *Horizontal Social Clause* and its strict relationship with the objective of the 'social market economy' is highlighted in the communication of the European Commission, 'Towards a Single Market Act. For a highly competitive social market economy' COM (2010) 608 final, 27 October 2010.

15 P. Vielle, 'How the Horizontal Social Clause Can Be Made to Work: The Lessons of Gender Mainstreaming' in N. Bruun, K. Lorcher, I. Schornann (eds), *The Lisbon Treaty and Social Europe* (Hart Publishing 2012) 105.

16 Case C-341/05 *Laval un Partneri Ltd v Svenska Byggnadsarbetareförbundet* [2007] ECR I-11767; Case C-438/05 *International Transport, Workers' Federation and Finnish Seamen's Union v Viking Line APB* [2007] ECR I-10779. See D. Leczykiewicz, 'Conceptualising Conflict between the Economic and the Social in EU Law after *Viking* and *Laval*' in M. Freedland, J. Prassl (eds), *Viking, Laval and Beyond* (Hart Publishing 2014) 307–322; S. Giubboni, *Social Rights and Market Freedom in the European Constitution. A Labour Law Perspective* (CUP 2006) 7–40; C. Barnard, 'EU Social Policy: From Employment Law to Labour Market Reform' in P. Craig, G. de Búrca (eds), *The Evolution of EU Law* (2nd edn, OUP 2011) 641.

17 See European Commission 'A strategy for smart, sustainable and inclusive growth' COM (2010) 2020, of 3 March 2010, which, as is well known, contains the future strategy to transform the EU into a smart, sustainable and inclusive economy characterised by high levels of employment, productivity and social cohesion. See M. Ferrera, 'Mapping the Components of the Current Institutional Patchwork' in E. Marlier, D. Natali (eds), *Europe 2020. Towards a More Social EU?* (Peter Lang, 2010) 45. See, also, European Economic and Social Committee, 'Strengthening EU cohesion and EU social policy coordination through the new horizontal social clause in Art 9 TFEU' (Opinion) (2012/C 24/06), 26 October 2011.

clause, in indicating the need to integrate social objectives within other EU policies, determines an extension of purpose congruent with each material legal basis, or whether it is intended to disregard the principle of conferral (para III). There is also the matter of examining how EU legislature actually integrates social needs with other competences (para IV) and how the ECJ has reconciled social objectives with economic integration and what kind of status has been given to the purposes indicated by Art 9 (paras V and VI). This analysis will therefore concentrate on the clause from a strictly legal perspective by examining the key issues that it raises. In the light of our findings, an attempt will be made to provide a brief reflection on the function that Art 9 carries out in relation to the context of the competences outlined by the Treaties (para VII).

II. Constraints falling upon EU institutions and Member States

In defining and implementing its policies and activities, the EU 'shall take into account' the social needs set out in the clause. As mentioned, however, the rule does not clarify the extent of 'commitment' required.[18] In its recent *Pillbox* judgment[19] the ECJ, in stating that Art 9 'require[s] it to ensure' the objectives set down,[20] appears to suggest that the EU is subject to an 'obligation' and that this amounts to an 'obligation of result'. It is thus reasonable to conclude that the expression used by the ECJ is not limited to guiding the conduct of the EU, but has the added function of binding it to the achievement of social objectives.[21] From this perspective, the scope of integrating the needs of Art 9 into the context of other policies translates into a general obligation to evaluate the possible negative impact that such a measure can produce as compared to the achievement of standards of social rights protection.

This constraint should lead, in turn, to a duty on the part of the institutions to balance the need for protection of social values with competing interests, both in policy-making and policy implementation.[22] As for the definition phase, the ruling should imply a substantial *ex ante* examination involving a systematic assessment of the impact of the measures to be taken on the achievement of

18 The position of the *Horizontal Social Clause* in provisions of general application seems to argue for its strictly legal and not simply political nature. See, on this point, J.C. Piris, *The Lisbon Treaty: A Legal and Political Analysis* (CUP 2010) 310 who stresses the binding nature of HSC also for the European Union Court of Justice. About the binding nature of HSC see also F. Lecomte, 'Embedding employment rights in Europe' (2011) 11 *Columbia Journal of European Law* 20.

19 See infra, Case C-477/14 *Pillbox v Secretary of State for Health* ECLI:EU:C:2016:324.

20 Ibid. para 116. Specifically, it should guarantee 'a high level of protection of human health in the definition and implementation of all Union policies and activities'.

21 See European Parliament Resolution (2012/C 380 E/08), 8 June 2011.

22 See European Parliament Resolutions (2012/C 188 e/09), 17 February 2011; (2012/C 70 E/04), 20 October 2012. See on this issue B. Sjåfjell, 'The environmental integration principle: A necessary step towards policy coherence for sustainability' in this volume para 3.1.

social goals.[23] The outcome of such an examination would likely occur, within the reasoned grounds of the decision, in the exposition of how social considerations have been integrated and balanced with interests of a different nature.[24] Similar conclusions should be drawn at the time of preparation of the implementing measures of the EU's policies.

Even more problematic might be the subsequent monitoring of compliance with the obligation laid down by Art 9. The main difficulty lies not so much at policy level or with an impact assessment of the Commission's proposals,[25] but rather the possibility to seek judicial review concerning an act that might fail to take due account of, or even undermine the interests of, Art 9.[26] In this case, the ECJ would be called upon to assess the adequacy, in terms of social protection, of measures which, requiring 'political, economic and social choices' and towards which the legislator is called upon to undertake 'complex assessments', would

23 For a discussion see F. Ippolito (n 5).

24 The characteristic horizontal, or better cross, effect of this clause derives from the concept of mainstreaming as it has been developed by the EU Commission with regard to the principle of equality between men and women and the fight against discrimination. As is well known, 'to mainstream' means to integrate something or someone in a context which is considered the general and dominant paradigm. In the EU documents mainstreaming means to act in order that the principle of non-discrimination and the promotion of equal opportunities become a general and paradigmatic way in the process of policy-making. Similarly, the social mainstreaming clause under Art 9 TFEU has a cross nature because through an integrated approach it aims to make the protection of social objectives a general paradigm in the public action, ensuring that these goals are guaranteed not only through specific measures, but also through their systematic incorporation in all public policies.

25 See European Parliament Resolutions (2012/C 188 e/09), 17 February 2011, http://www.europarl.europa.eu/sides/getDoc.do?pubRef=-//EP//TEXT+TA+P7-TA-2011-0068+0+DOC+XML+V0//IT. See, also, European Economic and Social Committee, 'Strengthening EU cohesion and EU social policy coordination through the new horizontal social clause in Art 9 TFEU' (n 17) 29; European Economic and Social Committee, 'The open method of coordination and the social clause in the context of Europe 2020' (Opinion) (2011/C 44/04) of 15 July 2010. The Belgian Presidency of the European Union in 2010 underlined the importance of this clause as a tool for increasing the focus on the European social dimension through a structured dialogue on the social impact of policies and actions within and outside the EU, identifying the Impact Assessment as a valid tool for implementing the HSC. Belgian Presidency of the European Union, *The Horizontal Social Clause and Social Mainstreaming in the EU. The Horizontal Social Clause as a Call for Intensified Cooperation and Exchange of Knowledge Through the Commission's Impact Assessment* (26–27 October 2010, Background Paper) www.socialsecurity.fgov.be/eu/docs/agenda/26-27_10_10_sia_en.pdf. For a discussion see E. Muir, 'Drawing Positive Lessons From the Presence of "The Social" Outside of EU Social Policy Stricto Sensu' (2018) 14(1) *European Constitutional Law Review* 75–95; M. Dawson, 'Better regulation and the future of EU regulatory law and politics' (2016) 53 *Common Market Law Review* 1209.

26 M.D. Ferrara, 'Social Justice Through Social and Economic Mainstreaming: The Role of the Horizontal Social Clause of TFEU'. Social Justice Conference: The institutions that make social justice, London School of Economics, 1–2 August 2014. See Nic Shuibhne (n 8) Section III A.

leave room for 'broad discretion'.[27] It is reasonable to wonder, then, just what kind of test the ECJ might adopt when the legislator, in view of the wide discretion available, has to balance social needs with other interests.[28]

Since Art 9 imposes an obligation to integrate social objectives in the EU as a whole, a significant role should also be assigned to Member States when implementing existing EU measures.[29] In this case, failure to abide by the obligation arising from Art 9 should, in principle, justify any claim against infringement. Again, however, such an action could prove problematic. The biggest challenge could lie in the difficulty of reviewing a failure, in breach of the obligation in Art 9, to integrate and reconcile the social objectives identified at EU level.[30]

III. Legal basis

Art 9 is difficult to place within a theoretical framework also as regards its legal scope. In establishing a series of social objectives, which should guide the EU's activities and policies as a whole, it is open to diametrically opposed interpretations.

One line of argument is that since '[i]n defining and implementing its policies and activities, the Union shall take into account' the various objectives set down in Art 9, it might be reasonable to suppose that one of the functions of Art 9 TFEU is to assign different objectives to each policy and activity, which go beyond those specifically established by each legal basis. From this perspective, in extending the range of objectives pursued by each policy beyond what is indicated by the specific legal basis, Art 9 would have the effect of eliminating or at least mitigating the functional link which, by virtue of the principle of conferral, exists between powers and purposes. In this light, the generally univocal correspondence that each legal basis establishes between powers of action and objectives, either explicitly or implicitly, would give way to an overall conception of the various competences conferred so as to 'rebuild the Union as an entity of general competence … in the context of spheres of competences conferred'.[31] From this perspective, the actual competence of the Union in the context of various concrete policies would have to be derived from a joint reading of the objectives of Art 9 (and other general clauses) and the powers assigned by each specific legal basis considered overall and balanced one against the other. The limitations of such an approach are obvious: an integrated approach to the system of the Union's objectives – assuming that

27 Case C-157/14 *Société Neptune Distribution v Ministre de l'Économie et des Finances* ECLI:EU:C:2015:823 para 76.

28 On this profile see, infra, para V.

29 See P. Vielle (n 15). The interpretation that extends the binding scope of Art 9 TFEU and its objectives also towards the Member States is founded on the principle of sincere cooperation.

30 This would mean upholding the failed or correct transposition of a directive that already addressed the balancing of interests. See B. Sjåfjel (n 22).

31 This very effective expression can be attributed to E. Cannizzaro, 'Gerarchia e competenza nel sistema delle fonti dell'Unione europea' (2005) 8 *Il Diritto dell'Unione europea* 651.

they are not clearly assigned to each competence, but rather help to determine the overall picture of the objectives that the Union must pursue through all of its competences taken together – would make it extremely difficult, if not impossible, to identify the relevant legal basis for each individual measure taken, and would inevitably run counter to the principle of conferral, which continues to be a key feature of the legal system of the EU.[32]

A second line of argument suggests a more cautious approach. Rather than widening the scope of other policies, the function of Art 9 TFEU is to suggest a series of objectives to guide the overall action of the Union, merely providing a framework in which individual policies should be conducted. From this point of view, Art 9 would then be a non-competence-specific and non-power-conferring statement; rather it would be an attempt to substantially increase overall policy coherence of the Union. On this basis, Art 9, since it does not confer competence, would not be a suitable means to broaden the objectives pursued by each material policy beyond what is indicated by the specific legal basis. It follows that the social policy objectives would have the limited function of guiding the development and implementation of policies of a material nature, but could not be considered an integral part of them.[33]

This reading does seem to be in line with Art 7 TFEU, which opens Title II on provisions of general application. In establishing that '[t]he Union shall ensure consistency between its policies and activities, taking all of its objectives into account and in accordance with the principle of conferral of powers', the rule would appear to indicate that the integration of social objectives within the exercise of other policies is simply to make the various policies consistent, without entailing any change in the scope of each material competence.[34]

IV. Regulatory practice

Even a cursory examination of regulatory practice shows that EU legislature, after the introduction of Art 9 into the Treaties, has used the *Horizontal Social Clause* cautiously. Up until now, four acts alone have made explicit reference to the clause.[35] In these cases, the intention of the EU legislator to include and integrate social considerations in the exercise of the powers it enjoys becomes apparent. The omitted mention of the clause should however not imply, in principle, the legislator's intention to exclude social considerations through a mutual balance from the purposes pursued

32 For a discussion on the principle of conferral of powers see Nic Shuibhne (n 8).
33 See, for an analogous approach, J. Beqiraj, 'Animal welfare' in this volume.
34 For the approach adopted by the Court of Justice see infra paras V and VII. On this topic see Nic Shuibhne (n 8).
35 The references to HSC were more frequent when the introduction of this clause was only in gestation. For example, see Commission, 'Reforming Europe for the 21st century' (Communication) COM (2007) 412 final, and 'Opportunities, Access and Solidarity: towards a new social vision for 21st century Europe' (Communication) COM (2007) 726 final. Surprisingly, the Commission does not mention the HSC in the recent Communication 'Strengthening the social dimension of the Economic and Monetary Union' COM (2013) 690 final.

by the measure. In this case, however, it is not always clear whether the inclusion of social values in the context of the act derives from Art 9 or from other sources.

This difficulty emerges, for example, with regard to Directive 2014/40/EU on the approximation of the laws, regulations and administrative provisions of the Member States concerning the manufacture, presentation and sale of tobacco and related products.[36] The Directive, based on Arts 53, para 1, 62 and 114 TFEU concerning, respectively, the right of establishment and approximation of laws, significantly modifies regulations on the manufacture, presentation and sale of tobacco and related products within the European market. The legislation is designed to ensure that such products are placed on the market under uniform conditions, ensuring, at the same time a high level of health protection. Nor is it clear whether this additional concern for health protection,[37] which must be duly taken into account and reconciled with the needs of the market,[38] derives from the *Horizontal Social Clause* or from Art 114 TFEU. The latter provision – to which the Directive expressly refers – requires a high level of protection such that the harmonisation measure affects 'health, safety, environmental and consumer protection.'[39]

The Art 9 clause, however, is currently cited in very few legal acts. Among these is Regulation (EU) No. 1304/2013 of the European Parliament and the Council of 17 December 2013 on the European Social Fund,[40] which, in defining the

36 Directive 2014/40/EU of the European Parliament and of the Council of 3 April 2014 on the approximation of the laws, regulations and administrative provisions of the Member States concerning the manufacture, presentation and sale of tobacco and related products and repealing Directive 2001/37/EC [2014] OJ L127/1 (Tobacco Directive). In the same vein see, e.g., the acts on the approximation of laws on regulations regarding food products.

37 See Art 1 of the directive which points out that the objective is 'to approximate the laws, regulations and administrative provisions of the Member States ... in order to facilitate the smooth functioning of the internal market for tobacco and related products, taking as a base a high level of protection of human health'.

38 See also further references to the interest of 'health' in the directive. Recital 13 refers to the 'obligation placed on the Union to ensure a high level of protection for human health'; recital 36, with reference to tobacco products states that 'A high level of public health protection should be taken into account when regulating these products'; recital 43 states that 'it is necessary to approximate the national provisions on advertising and sponsorship of those products having cross-border effects, taking as a base a high level of protection of human health'.

Similar considerations count, e.g., for Regulation (EU) 2016/589 of the European Parliament and of the Council of 13 April 2016 on a European network of employment services (EURES), workers' access to mobility services and the further integration of labour markets, and amending Regulations (EU) No 492/2011 and (EU) No 1296/2013 [2016] OJ L107/1. Based on Art 46 TFEU (freedom of movement for workers), the regulation establishes a framework for cooperation in order to ease the freedom of movement of workers within the Union also aimed at 'achieving a high level of quality employment' (Art 1, letter c).

39 Art 114, para 3, TFEU.

40 Regulation (EU) 1304/2013 of the European Parliament and of the Council of 17 December 2013 on the European Social Fund and repealing Council Regulation (EC) No 1081/2006 [2013] OJ L347/20 (European Social Fund Directive).

tasks of the European Social Fund (ESF), the scope of its support as well as the specific provisions and types of eligible expenditure, must take into account '[i]n accordance with Art 9 TFEU, ... requirements linked to the promotion of a high level of employment, the guarantee of adequate social protection, the fight against social exclusion, and a high level of education, training and protection of human health'.[41] The reference to Art 9 does not, however, appear to be particularly significant. The various interests that the regulation aims to promote, and which partly coincide with those mentioned in the clause, do not actually derive from the obligation arising from this clause,[42] but from the legal basis employed which 'shall aim to render the employment of workers easier within the Union'.[43] Significant in this regard is recital 2, which, in indicating that the ESF 'should improve employment opportunities, strengthen social inclusion, fight poverty, promote education, skills and life-long learning and develop active, comprehensive and sustainable inclusion policies', clearly indicates that these are objectives that correspond to 'the tasks entrusted to the ESF by Art 162 of the Treaty on the Functioning of the European Union'.

Another act that invokes the clause is the Council Decision (EU) 2015/1848 of 5 October 2015 on guidelines for the employment policies of the Member States for 2015.[44] Based on Art 148 TFEU, the decision lays down guidelines which should be taken into account by Member States in their policies on employment on the understanding that it is national policies on employment that help to define the policy of the Union on the area in question through mutual cooperation. As is clear from Decision 2015/1848, these guidelines not only regard '[b]oosting demand for labour', '[e]nhancing labour supply, skills and competences', and '[e]nhancing the functioning of labour markets',[45] but should also accord with the 'requirements linked to the promotion of a high level of employment, the guarantee of adequate social protection, the fight against social exclusion, and a high level of education and training'[46] aimed at '[f]ostering social inclusion, combatting poverty and promoting equal opportunities'.[47] Unlike the previous case, here the reference to the clause appears to take on more significance: the objective of promoting employment must be achieved not only

41 Ibid. Recital no 2.
42 Based on Art 164 TFEU, the regulation "shall promote high levels of employment and job quality, improve access to the labour market, support the geographical and occupational mobility of workers and facilitate their adaptation to industrial change and to changes in production systems needed for sustainable developments, encourage a high level of education and training for all and support the transition between education and employment for young people, combat poverty, enhance social inclusion, and promote gender equality, non-discrimination and equal opportunities, thereby contributing to the priorities of the Union as regards strengthening economic, social and territorial cohesion" (Art 2).
43 Art 162 TFEU.
44 [2015] OJ L268/28.
45 Ibid. Guidelines Nos 5, 6, 7.
46 Ibid. Recital No 2.
47 Ibid. Guideline No 8.

through market and economic means, but also through instruments of social protection, on the basis therefore, of an approach that integrates and reconciles different needs. In other words, the guidelines clearly indicate, consistent with Art 9, that the promotion of employment is a goal whose achievement requires the reconciliation of both economic demands and social needs.

Even more significant for our purposes, are Regulations 472 and 473 of 2013[48] which, along with other measures, in order to reassure the markets, curb speculation and restore stability to the Euro, combined to redefine the governance of the EMU in the aftermath of the 2008 economic crisis.[49] Founded on Arts 136 and 121, para 6 TFEU, the two regulations (so-called Two Pack) are intended, respectively, to step up economic and budgetary surveillance of Member States within the Eurozone facing difficulties and risks to their stability or requesting or receiving financial assistance, and to establish common provisions between Member States of the Eurozone for the monitoring and assessment of draft budgets and for the correction of excessive deficits. Both regulations expressly refer to Art 9 TFEU.[50]

As for Regulation 472/2013, among other provisions, this establishes that any State intending to access financial assistance measures from Member States or third-party States or on the basis of other financial instruments should draw up 'in agreement with the Commission, acting in liaison with the ECB and, where appropriate, with the IMF, a draft macroeconomic adjustment program'.[51] This draft – aimed 'at rapidly re-establishing a sound and sustainable economic and financial situation and restoring the Member State's capacity to finance itself fully on the financial markets' – not only relies on a constantly reviewed assessment of the sustainability of the government debt,[52] but also takes into account 'the practices and institutions for wage formation and the national reform programme of the Member State concerned in the context of the Union's strategy for growth and jobs'.[53]

48 Regulation (EU) 472/2013 of the European Parliament and of the Council of 21 May 2013 on the strengthening of economic and budgetary surveillance of Member States in the euro area experiencing or threatened with serious difficulties with respect to their financial stability [2013] OJ L140/1 (Economic and Budgetary Surveillance Regulation); Regulation (EU) 473/2013 of the European Parliament and of the Council of 21 May 2013 on common provisions for monitoring and assessing draft budgetary plans and ensuring the correction of excessive deficit of the Member States in the euro area, [2013] OJ L140/11 (Draft Budgetary Plans Regulation).

49 See Fritz W. Scharpf, 'Monetary Union, Fiscal Crisis and the Preemption of Democracy' (MPIfG Discussion Papers, 2011, 11).

50 See Recitals Nos 2 and 8.

51 Art 7 para 1 of the Regulation.

52 Art 7 para 1 states: 'The draft macroeconomic adjustment programme shall be based on the assessment of the sustainability of the government debt referred to in Art 6, which shall be updated to incorporate the impact of the draft corrective measures negotiated with the Member State concerned, and shall take due account of any recommendation addressed to that Member State under Arts 121, 126, 136 or 148 TFEU and of its actions to comply with any such recommendation, while aiming at broadening, strengthening and deepening the required policy measures'.

53 Art 7 para 1.

And this is not all: in preparing its drafts concerning the macro-economic adjustment program, the 'Member State shall seek the views of social partners as well as relevant civil society organisations ..., with a view to contributing to building consensus over its content'.[54] Given these overall directions, it is reasonable to suppose that the Art 9 clause comes into play precisely wherever it requires the Member State (and the Commission) to found the draft program based on an extensive evaluation that takes into account and balances the various interests at stake: sustainability of the government debt, on the one hand; preserving national systems of collective bargaining, on the other.[55]

Regulation 473/2013, for its part, establishes a framework to strengthen the monitoring of budgetary policies in the Eurozone and to ensure the consistency of national budgets with economic policy guidelines.[56] The actions taken on the basis of the regulation, however, have some limitations: in accordance with Art 152 TFEU, they must recognize and promote the role of the social partners, respect current national systems and practices in the determination of wages and avoid undermining the right to negotiate, conclude or enforce collective agreements or take collective action in accordance with law and national practices.[57] Again, it seems reasonable to suppose that in balancing overall conflicting interests, the enhancement of the need to ensure respect for social values derives from Art 9.[58]

V. ECJ practice: the clause and objectives of general interest

As with regulatory acts, references to Art 9 TFEU in European case law are few and far between.[59] The ECJ has invoked and 'employed' the *Horizontal Social Clause* in only four judgments in order to balance the goal of 'a high level of protection of human health' with other interests at stake. Although references in case law are limited, they do offer significant clues as to the legal scope of the clause. It is thus worth referring to these four cases, albeit briefly, retracing the ECJ's arguments.

In all four preliminary rulings the ECJ had to determine whether approximation norms regarding nutrition and health claims made on foods, in particular

54 Art 8.

55 See D. Chalmers, G. Davies, G. Monti, *European Union Law* (3rd edn, CUP 2014) 745: 'The guarantees provided in EU law are greater than under the ESM. The programme must respect national system of collective bargaining. The Member State must also seek the views of social partner as well as civil society organisations in drafting this programme'.

56 See Art 1 para 1.

57 See Art 1 para 2.

58 For a discussion see M. Dawson, 'New governance and the displacement of Social Europe: The case of the European Semester' (2018) 14(1) *European Constitutional Law Review* 191–209, 196.

59 The trend of the ECJ in relation to the Art. 10 is not dissimilar. See F. Ippolito (n 5).

concerning the use and marketing of natural mineral waters, on the one hand,[60] and the manufacture, presentation and sale of tobacco and related products, on the other,[61] violated certain provisions of the Charter of Fundamental Rights. It should be noted that none of the acts subject to review makes any reference to Art 9.

In particular, in the first judgment, taken chronologically (*Deutsches Weintor*)[62] the Court was asked to verify the validity of Art 4, para 3, first clause of Regulation (EC) No. 1924/2006[63] – which prohibits, without exception, the producer or distributor of alcoholic beverages from making 'health claims'[64] – in the light of Art 15, para 1 and Art 16 of the Charter. Such provisions ensures that everyone has the right to work and to pursue a profession, and conduct business. The Court was therefore called upon to ascertain whether such individual rights and freedoms had been unlawfully restricted by the legislation concerned.

With concise and linear argument, the Court first stated that 'the compatibility of the prohibition … must be assessed in the light not only of the freedom to choose an occupation and the freedom to conduct a business, but also of the protection of health'.[65] Consequently, such an assessment must be carried out 'in accordance with the need to reconcile the requirements of the protection of those various fundamental rights protected by the Union legal order, and striking a fair balance between them'.[66]

On the one hand, freedom to pursue a profession or conduct a business are not absolute rights but must be considered in relation to their 'social function'. They can therefore be restricted 'provided that those restrictions in fact correspond to objectives of general interest pursued by the European Union and do not constitute, with regard to the aim pursued, a disproportionate and intolerable interference, impairing the very substance of those rights'.[67] On the other, the protection of human health 'constitutes, as follows also from Art 9 TFEU, an objective of general interest justifying, where appropriate, a restriction of a fundamental freedom'.[68]

Thus, in describing the protection of health – and with it the other interests protected by Art 9 – as 'objectives of general interest', the Court resorted to a conceptual method commonly used in its case-law whenever it might be necessary

60 Regulation (EC) 1924/2006 of the European Parliament and of the Council of 20 December 2006 on nutrition and health claims made on foods [2006] OJ L404/9 (Nutrition and Health Claims Regulation); Directive 2009/54/EC of the European Parliament and of the Council of 18 June 2009 on the exploitation and marketing of natural mineral waters [2009] OJ L164/45 (Natural Mineral Waters Directive).

61 Tobacco Directive.

62 Case C-544/10 *Deutsches Weintor eG v Land Rheinland-Pfalz* ECLI:EU:C:2012:526.

63 Nutrition and Health Claims Directive.

64 'Beverages containing more than 1.2 % by volume of alcohol shall not bear health claims'. In this case what was controversial was the wording 'easily digestible'.

65 Para 46.

66 Para 47.

67 Para 54.

68 Para 49.

to reconcile conflicting interests. Traditionally, the objectives of general interest are those values/parameters that measure the degree of protection of fundamental rights. Although it would be wrong to speak of an elaboration of an independent notion of general interest of the Union,[69] with this statement the Court referred to those interests that are inherently ingrained within the nature and functions of the Union and that, as such, are capable of justifying the restriction of individual fundamental rights and freedoms.[70]

One issue that traditionally lies behind this method concerns the discretion enjoyed by the legislator when, in adopting a certain discipline, he is called upon to balance fundamental rights with the objectives of general interest. Clearly, the greater or lesser extent of the discretion conferred on the legislator will consequently determine the scope of judicial review reserved to the ECJ.

To this regard, in its *Deutsches Weintor* ruling the Court confined itself to stating that the contested legislation 'must be regarded as complying with the requirement that is intended to reconcile the various fundamental rights in this instance and to strike a fair balance between them'.[71] Indeed, '[f]ar from prohibiting the production and marketing of alcoholic beverages, the legislation at issue merely controls, in a very clearly defined area, the associated labelling and advertising'.[72]

Some more detail on this point is provided by the subsequent judgment in the *Société Neptune Distribution* case.[73] Here, too, the Court was called upon to establish the compliance of certain provisions of Directive 2009/54 and Regulation No. 1924/2006[74] with the freedom of expression and information (Art 11 of the Charter) and the freedom to conduct business (Art 16 of the Charter), in particular those which prohibit certain claims on packaging, labelling and advertising of natural mineral waters.[75]

After pointing out that fundamental rights can be restricted when they are incompatible with objectives of general interest, the Court reaffirmed that '[i]n those circumstances, the determination of the validity of the contested provisions must be carried out in accordance with the need to reconcile' the protection of individual liberties invoked with a high level of health protection.[76] The Court, however, added that '[w]ith regard to judicial review of the conditions of the

69 On this topic, see C. Boutayeb, 'Une recherche sur la place et les fonctions de l'intérêt général en droit communautaire' (2003) 39.4 *Revue Trimestrielle de Droit Européen* 587.

70 Case 44/79 *Hauer* [1979] ECR 3727; Case 5/88 *Wachauf* [1989] ECR 2609; Joined Cases C-143/88 and C-92/89 *Zuckerfabrik* [1991] ECR I-415; Case C-44/89 *von Deetzen* [1991] ECR I-5119.

71 Para 59.

72 Para 57.

73 Case C-157/14 *Société Neptune Distribution v Ministre de l'Économie et des Finances* ECLI:EU:C:2015:823.

74 Natural Mineral Waters Directive and Nutrition and Health Claims Regulation.

75 See Art 9 paras 1 and 2 of Natural Mineral Waters Directive, in addition to annex III and annex to Nutrition and Health Claims Regulation.

76 Para 75.

implementation of the principle of proportionality, the EU legislature must be allowed a broad discretion in an area such as that involved in the present case, which entails political, economic and social choices on its part, and in which it is called upon to undertake complex assessments'.[77]

This premise sufficed for the Court to conclude that 'the actual content of the freedom of expression and information of the person carrying on the business is not affected by those provisions',[78] and that 'far from prohibiting the production and marketing of natural mineral waters, the legislation at issue in the main proceedings merely controls, in a very clearly defined area, the associated labelling and advertising. Thus, it does not affect in any way the actual content of the freedom to conduct a business'.[79]

The Court, therefore, not only confirmed that where human health is at stake the protection of individual rights must be weighed against this and if necessary yield, but also provided a further indication. It recognised that where the assessments to be made are complex, such broad discretion has the effect of producing little control over the necessity and appropriateness of the measure adopted as it relates to the objective of general interest pursued. In concluding that the essential content of the freedoms in question is not affected, the ECJ clearly showed that it was unwilling to demonstrate the effective need that binds the measures taken to the fulfilment of the general interest or the impossibility of replacing such measures with alternative but equally effective instruments that might be less detrimental to fundamental rights.

In the subsequent *Pillbox* and *Philip Morris* cases,[80] the Court was asked to rule on the alleged conflict of certain provisions of Directive 2014/40/EU with the EU Charter of Fundamental Rights and the principle of proportionality.[81] Again, the directive, adopted to completely redefine the rules of harmonisation on tobacco products, overcame hindrances to its validity posed by the two cases. The dispute concerned the ban on certain labels on tobacco products; the ban on placing tobacco products with certain flavourings on the market; the requirements for warnings concerning health hazards to appear on packaging; the ban on promoting electronic cigarettes. The arguments relating to these regulations concerned the violation of the principle of proportionality; incompatibility with the freedom of expression and information (Art 11 of the Charter),[82] the freedom to conduct a business (Art 16 of the Charter) and the right to property (Art 17 of the Charter).[83]

77 Para 76.
78 Para 70.
79 Para 71.
80 Case C-477/14 *Pillbox 38* ECLI:EU:C:2016:324; Case-547/14 *Philip Morris* ECLI:EU:C:2016:325.
81 Tobacco Directive. On the content of the Directive and incidents accompanying legislative process see T.K. Hervey and J.V. Hale, *European Union Health Law* (CUP 2015) 393.
82 *Philip Morris* para 146.
83 *Pillbox 38* para 152.

According to the Court, restrictions on fundamental rights and freedoms that the directive actually causes appeared appropriate and necessary in relation to the legitimate objectives pursued. Some of the arguments put forward to reach these conclusions were unprecedented. After pointing out that the protection of public health, in accordance with Art 9, is a general interest objective recognised by the EU,[84] the Court did not limit itself to reiterating that the legislature's task is to strike a 'fair balance'[85] between the different needs at stake, despite the likely negative impact on the profits of tobacco companies. It turned to a fresh argument, reasoning that in determining this balance, the discretionary power available to the legislature 'varies for each of the goals justifying restrictions on that freedom and depends on the nature of the activities in question'.[86]

By introducing an evaluation criterion of the discretionary margin reserved to the legislature, the Court thus employed two parameters: the scope of the general interest objective, and the nature of the activity affecting the individual right or freedom. In this case the first parameter concerned the interest of 'health protection in an area characterised by the proven harmfulness of tobacco consumption'.[87] The second related to the exercise of individual freedoms 'to spread information in the pursuit of commercial interests'.[88]

Once the Court had identified the scope and nature of the competing interests in this manner, it concluded that the protection of human health 'outweighs the interests put forward by the claimants in the main proceedings'.[89] Indeed, as is clear from certain articles, and in particular Art 9 TFEU, 'a high level of human health protection must be ensured in the definition and implementation of all the European Union's policies and activities'.[90]

Through the dual parameter deriving from the objective of general interest and the nature of the activity affecting individual rights, the ECJ accepted the balance operated by the legislature. It basically means that individual freedoms may yield, and in doing so are subject to a restriction, as a result of the higher importance, in accordance with Art 9, of the protection of health compared with the exercise of freedom to pursue commercial interests.[91] The impression, difficult to dispel, is

84 *Philip Morris* para 152; *Pillbox 38* para 116.
85 *Philip Morris* para 154.
86 Ibid. para 155.
87 Ibid. para 156.
88 Ibid. para 155.
89 Ibid. para 156.
90 Ibid. para 157.
91 Ibid. para 190, where the Court states that the legislature 'weighed up, on the one hand, the economic consequences of that prohibition and, on the other, the requirement to ensure, in accordance with the second sentence of Art 35 of the Charter and Arts 9 TFEU, 114(3) TFEU and 168(1) TFEU, a high level of human health protection with regard to a product which is characterised by properties that are carcinogenic, mutagenic and toxic to reproduction'. See also Case C-358/14 *Polland v European Parliament and Council* ECLI:EU:C:2016:323, para 102, and the Opinion of AG Kokott delivered on 23 December 2015 (ECLI:EU:C:2015:848) on the same case, para 130.

that setting health protection above other interests may further reduce judicial control, already ineffective as it is, over the necessity and appropriateness of the restrictive measure adopted in relation to the general interest objective being pursued.[92]

VI. … and what about overriding reasons?

The rulings that have been examined summarily attribute to the interest relating to health protection (and indirectly to all other interests identified in Art 9) the status of 'general interest objectives', that is, interests liable to restrict the enjoyment of fundamental individual rights and freedoms with which they come into conflict. The rulings also recognize a particular relevance to such interests where the individual rights at stake have a purely economic nature.[93]

That said, defining social objectives as 'public interest objectives' is justified in relation to the individual nature of the rights with which these objectives may enter into conflict within a certain discipline. If so, it is reasonable to suppose that the various social objectives may become 'overriding reasons' where they come up against so-called fundamental freedoms. An overriding reason applies when a national measure, though detrimental to the freedom guaranteed by the Treaty, is justified as it pursues a general interest according to that nation's legal system.[94]

In this view, *objectives of general interest* and *overriding reasons* are frequently two sides of the same coin: both tend to limit individual rights or the four fundamental freedoms in order to protect an interest worthy of protection according to the EU, in the first case, or national law, in the second. Consequently, when such an interest is recognised and protected in both legal systems it may represent either an 'objective of general interest' or an 'overriding reason', depending on the function it performs.

Based on this premise, the social objectives of the clause, which apply to Member States in the application of EU law, may be configured as 'overriding reasons' where they justify government measures restricting fundamental freedoms. Although the Court did not, at the time, refer to the objectives of the clause as 'overriding reasons', this line of argument was held by Advocate General Villalón in his opinion regarding the *Santos Palhota* case.[95]

92 In similar terms, see P. Koutrakos, 'Reviewing Harmonization: the *Tobacco Products Directive* Judgments' (2016) 3 *European Law Review* 305.

93 It is worth asking oneself whether the conclusion to consider the interest of health of 'greater importance' would be applied if the other interests referred to in Art 9 were at stake. A definite solution is not easy. The Court would appear to derive this 'greater importance' not only from the fact that it is recognised by primary law, but also by the required standard that must be high. If so, only the objectives related to employment, education and training could gain greater importance, once established that they require a high degree of protection.

94 See B. Sjåfjel (n 22).

95 Case C-515/08 *Santos Palhota and Others* ECLI:EU:C:2010:245, Opinion of AG Cruz Villalón.

In this case, doubts were raised as to the compatibility of national legislation to monitor the intra-Community movement of workers with Treaty rules on the free movement of services.[96] It is well know that case-law, on the one hand, has accepted a broad notion of 'restriction' to the freedom to provide services – ranging from the actual prohibition of an activity to the mere loss of advantage to the latter[97] – while on the other it has provided a restrictive interpretation of the conditions justifying the use of national restrictive measures, based on overriding reasons of general interest.[98]

According to the Advocate General, the restrictive approach of the Court regarding the interpretation of the conditions that justify the invocation of 'overriding reasons' should be softened because of the clause. The 'overriding reasons' based on the need to protect the interests identified in Art 9 – like, for example, the social protection of workers – appear, according to the Advocate General, to outweigh other 'overriding reasons'. In the words of the Advocate General, the existence of the clause means that:

> when working conditions constitute an overriding reason relating to the public interest justifying a derogation from the freedom to provide services, they must no longer be interpreted strictly. In so far as the protection of workers is a matter which warrants protection under the Treaties themselves, it is not a simple derogation from a freedom, still less an unwritten exception inferred from case-law. To the extent that the new primary law framework provides for a mandatory high level of social protection, it authorises the Member States, for the purpose of safeguarding a certain level of social protection, to restrict a freedom, and to do so without European Union law's regarding it as something exceptional and, therefore, as warranting a strict interpretation. That view, which is founded on the new provisions of the Treaties cited above, is expressed in practical terms by applying the principle of proportionality.[99]

The social objectives of the clause thus confer a special significance not only to the *objectives of general interest*, as expressly recognised by the ECJ in the *Philip*

96 Basically, doubts were raised as regards the legitimacy of the employer's obligation to present the Belgian authorities with a prior declaration of posting, or to keep available copies of documents such as an individual account or payslip.

97 This fundamental freedom requires not only the elimination of all discrimination on grounds of nationality against providers of cross-border services, but also the abolition of any restriction, even if it applies without distinction to national providers of services and to those of other Member States, which is liable to prohibit, impede or render less advantageous the activities of a service provider established in another Member State, where he lawfully provides similar services (see, e.g., Case C-76/90 *Säger* [1991] ECR I-4221, para 12; Case C-398/95 *SETTG* [1997] ECR I-3091, para 16; Case C-244/04 *Commission v Germany* [2006] ECR I-885, para 30; and Case C-219/08 *Commission v Belgium* [2009] ECR I-0000, para 13).

98 See, e.g., Case C-319/06 *Commission v Luxembourg* [2008] ECR I-4323.

99 Case C-515/08 *Santos Palhota and Others* (n 95) para 53.

Morris case,[100] but also to the *mandatory requirements* that States are entitled to rely on in order to restrict freedom of movement that may infringe a substantial State interest. Indeed, from this perspective, where requirements regarding the protection of social values are in opposition to the interests of the market, the clause should be appreciated to the full, in accordance with the spirit that inspired its inclusion in the Treaties.

VII. Concluding remarks

At this point it is not easy to draw definitive conclusions on the legal scope of the clause, hampered by poor legislation and equally limited case law.[101] Indeed, current EU acts referring explicitly to the clause or implicitly to the social interests that it protects are few and far between. Case law too has shown a preference for moderate 'use', for the moment, focused mainly on the interest of health protection. This interest, in the absence of the clause, in all probability would be enhanced through alternative routes in case law, provided that different provisions of the Treaties, whether of general[102] or specific scope,[103] recognize its importance.

The fact remains that the indications that may be generally drawn do contribute significantly – if not to clarify the overall legal dimension of the clause – at least to reveal its most relevant aspects. Two aspects in particular are worth focusing on.

First, since the clause was invoked when acts concerning different sectors were adopted, the question arises as to whether the function that it has to play is the same in all cases, or may vary depending on the regulatory context at work. A cursory analysis of the acts analysed shows that while its policy function is undisputed, its legal effects may be cause for concern. This is clear in relation to Regulation (EU) No. 1304/2013 regarding the European Social Fund, where the clause appears to carry out a merely *promotional* function.[104] As noted earlier, the social objectives that the regulation aims to promote, and which are partly overlapping with those of Art 9, correspond to 'the tasks entrusted to the ESF by Art

100 Case-547/14 *Philip Morris* (n 80).

101 For the same conclusion see F. Ippolito (n 5): 'It remains instead so far to be clarified if the model of positive duties recalled in Art 10 TFEU is more than a political commitment, and especially a veritable legal duty with the annexed consequences and legal effects'.

102 See Art 36 TFEU where, among the exceptions that Member States may invoke to maintain or introduce measures restricting free movement of goods, is one that refers to 'protection of health'; see, also, *supra*, Art 114 TFEU.

103 See Art 168 TFEU which, as regards public health, establishes in para 1, that a 'high level of human health protection shall be ensured in the definition and implementation of all Union policies and activities'; Art 169, para 1, which states that '[i]n order to promote the interests of consumers and to ensure a high level of consumer protection, the Union shall contribute to protecting the health ... of consumers'; Art 191, para 1, TFEU, regarding the environment establishes that 'Union policy on the environment shall contribute to pursuit of the following objectives: ... protecting human health.'

104 European Social Fund Directive.

162 of the Treaty on the Functioning of the European Union'.[105] A similar conclusion may be drawn in relation to Council Decision (EU) 2015/1848 on guidelines for Member States' employment policies for 2015.[106] Among the approved guidelines to guide the choices of Member States in matters of employment, is one related to '[f]ostering social inclusion, combating poverty and promoting equal opportunities' in accordance with Art 9.[107] However, as the objectives translate into a mere guideline, the clause seems to play a merely *guiding* role in the act in question.

Instead, an autonomous function going beyond pure policy is carried out by the clause where, as in regulations 472 and 473 of 2011,[108] it provides for a greater emphasis to be placed on the need to ensure respect for social values within the framework of an overall balance of conflicting interests. In these cases, and far from producing effects at policy level only, the clause seems to fulfil a *prescriptive* function. Similarly, a function of this kind is carried out by the clause even when it limits the enjoyment of positions related to economic interests or implies restrictions on the fundamental freedoms of the market. Its *regulatory* function is evident in relation, for example, to the acts of harmonisation in which EU legislature, in restricting the promotion or marketing of certain products for reasons of health, attempts to reconcile the two opposing economic and social dimensions. In this respect, the first significant signs of openness are visible on the part of the ECJ's case law opting for a more balanced assessment of the contentious matters while also taking into account the regulatory value of the clause. Thus, while in most cases the value of the clause lies at a policy level, in other cases it plays a merely regulatory/prescriptive function. What cannot be overlooked within this perspective is the strong potential that social values may fulfil in regulating the market in the future.

Another issue that deserves clarification concerns the possible effects that the clause produces or may produce on the distribution of competences between the Union and Member States. Protection interests under Art 9 are inherent in the fields of competence defined as *supporting* or *complementary* competences, which leave the regulatory powers of the Member States virtually untouched, reserving a mere coordination function for the Union.[109] Based on this premise, it

105 Ibid. recital 2.
106 n 44.
107 Ibid. guideline 8.
108 Economic and Budgetary Surveillance Regulation and Draft Budgetary Plans Regulation (n 48).
109 It regards those competences which, variously named, still retain a markedly national character. The actions taken by the Union are simply of a coordinating nature, complementing and reinforcing those of the Member States, though this does not mean that the acts adopted by the institutions lead to harmonisation of national laws or regulations, or that the competence of the Union replaces the competences of the Member States in the relevant sectors. Employment policies and a part of social policies fall within those policies for which the EU has a coordinating role (see, in particular, Art 5, paras 2–3 TFEU, Arts 145–150 TFEU included in Title IX concerning 'Employment', Arts 151–161 TFEU regarding 'Social Policy'). Education/training

is reasonable to suppose that the obligation for EU legislature to graft social values identified in the clause onto the fabric of other policies may, in some cases, amount to a genuine exercise of competence, determining the corresponding expropriation of the regulatory powers of the Member States.[110]

This hypothesis seems to hold true, for example, where the EU's measures entail harmonisation of national regulations governing the marketing of products that may have a negative impact on health, as in the context of Directive 2014/40 regarding harmonisation rules on tobacco products.[111] The problem that arises relates to the fact that Art 168, para 5, TFEU (regarding 'public health') states specifically 'excluding any harmonisation' in the specific matter of the 'protection of public health regarding tobacco'. The regulation allows for incentive measures only on the part of the EU, in compliance with what is expected for the exercise of supporting, coordinating or complementary competences (Art 2, para 5, TFEU), which leads back to health policy and, in general, the protection of human health (Art 6 TFEU).

The making of an act for the approximation of legislations in this field thus poses the problem of coordination between the general rules on harmonisation (first and foremost, Art 114 TFEU)[112] and the aforementioned Art 168, para 5 TFEU. The contradiction could be resolved by giving preference to the latter provision in view of its speciality (*ratione materiae*), thus excluding the eligibility of acts of harmonisation. The opposite is the case in the solution that has emerged in EU case law, also reiterated in the judgments given in the *Philip Morris* and *Pillbox* cases.[113] The Court recognised the legitimacy of the acts approximating the laws also in the specific matter of tobacco products.

The basis for the position taken by the ECJ lies in the affirmation that it is legitimate to adopt an act of regulatory harmonisation where the conditions for recourse to Art 114 TFEU are met (i.e. when the act contributes to the objective of eliminating the existing or potential obstacles to the functioning of the internal market), despite the presence of health objectives. Thus, an act such as Directive 2014/40, which simultaneously pursues 'two objectives in that it seeks to facilitate the smooth functioning of the internal market for tobacco and related products,

and the protection and improvement of human health fall within the so-called support competences in which the EU restricts itself 'to carry[ing] out actions to support, coordinate or supplement the actions of the Member States' (see Art 6, letters a), e) TFEU; see, also, Arts 165–166 TFEU included in Title XII concerning 'Education, Vocational Training, Youth and sport' and Art 168 TFEU regarding 'Public Health').

110 For the 'blocking effect of EU law' see Nic Shuibhne (n 8).

111 See, for example, the Court's points in the judgment of 5 October 2000 Case C-376/98 *Germany v European Parliament and Council* ECLI:EU:C:2000:544 para 76 concerning legislative harmonisation of Member States in relation to advertising of tobacco products: '[t]he national measures affected are to a large extent inspired by public health policy objectives'.

112 This issue could also arise with the other general provisions on harmonisation in Arts 51, para 3, and 62 TFEU, cited as a legal basis along with Art 114 TFEU in Tobacco Directive.

113 n 80.

while ensuring a high level of protection of human health', may be based on Art 114 TFEU.[114]

Far from being neutral, this conclusion determines some very significant consequences. First, if the function of health protection is not simply to outline the framework underlying the regulation of tobacco products, but, like the smooth functioning of the internal market, is an equally predominant goal of the Directive, the clause would appear to extend the scope of other substantive policies, as well as those outlined in the Treaty. Seen from this perspective, Art 9 would be a clause conferring powers, contrary to earlier readings.[115]

Second, the expansion of the sphere of application of other substantive policies would, in turn, have the effect of determining, as mentioned, a creeping erosion of the competence which the Member States retain in matters of health protection. Holding that the adoption of an act of harmonisation is justified by the mere occurrence of a need for legislative approximation, irrespective of the fact that 'public health protection is a decisive factor in the choices to be made' means[116] in some way allowing the circumvention of the prohibition laid down by Art 168, para 5, TFEU.

To wind up, it is not unreasonable to suppose that besides disclosing a strong potential to reverse the relationship between economic Europe and social Europe through, in particular, its political but also regulatory dimension, the clause has the effect, at least in certain cases, of an expropriation of the competences that Member States continue to maintain in the social sector more generally. The need to extend the Union's action beyond the purely functional or economic aspects would therefore appear to assign the clause a limiting role as well: that of justifying intervention that is poorly compliant with the principle of conferred powers. And it is in this direction that the Court seems to be cautiously heading, giving 'greater importance' to social rather than economic objectives.

114 *Philip Morris* para 220. See J. Beqiraj (n 33) for a discussion on the correct use of the internal market legal basis (Art 114) in relation to animal welfare.

115 V., *supra*, para III.

116 *Philip Morris* para 60.

6 The environmental integration principle

A necessary step towards policy coherence for sustainability

Beate Sjåfjell[1]

1. Introduction

Article 11 in the Treaty on the Function of the European Union (TFEU) sets out that:

> Environmental protection requirements *must be integrated* into the definition and implementation of the Union policies and activities, in particular with a view to promoting *sustainable development.* [2]

The environmental integration that this rule mandates for the EU is arguably a necessary contribution to achieve policy coherence for sustainable development, or sustainability – as it is currently often denoted. However, the mere existence of this provision is clearly not sufficient to achieve the environmental integration in all EU policies and activities, let alone policy coherence to facilitate global sustainability.

For the duty of environmental integration to make a significant contribution to achieving such policy coherence, the environmental integration must have a clearly defined goal. Including environmental concerns at some level or other, an attempted 'greening' of European policies, is insufficient. Article 11 TFEU sets out

1 Professor Dr. Juris at the University of Oslo Faculty of Law; Professorial Research Fellow at Deakin University Law School. As the Project Coordinator of Sustainable Market Actors for Responsible Trade (SMART), with funding from the European Union's Horizon 2020 research and innovation programme under Grant Agreement No 693642, I gratefully acknowledge its support. The views expressed in this chapter are my own and do not necessarily coincide with those of the European Union. I would like to thank Francesca Ippolito for her encouragement and guidance, without which this chapter would not have been completed.

2 Emphasis added. The Treaty on the functioning of the European Union, last amended by the Treaty of Lisbon, OJ 2008 C115 (consolidated version), abbreviated TFEU. Julian Nowaq, 'The Sky is the Limit: On the Drafting of Article 11 TFEU's integration obligations and its intended reach', in Beate Sjåfjell and Anja Wiesbrock, *The Greening of European Business under EU Law: Taking Article 11 TFEU Seriously* (Routledge, 2015), Ch. 2, gives an introduction to the enhancement of the environmental integration rule over time and also sets out the Member States' clear intention with the rule.

the goal as one of 'promoting sustainable development'. This goal, of sustainability development, or sustainability, must be defined in light of natural science. This is necessary to mitigate the problem of sustainability being an extremely overused and broad concept with multiple definitions, and to reduce the danger of regulatory and policy capture. The reference to natural science is not to say that sustainability only has an environmental dimension; it clearly does not. However, the environmental literally must set the framework within which the balancing of sustainability requirements must take place. Section 2 draws on state-of-the-art natural science to flesh out what this means, Section 3 discusses the potential of Article 11 TFEU in that light, while Section 4 concludes with some reflections on how to realise the potential.

2. Environmental integration and the Goal of Sustainable Development

Sustainable development is an overarching, global societal goal, encompassing the search for a balance between economic development, social justice and environmental protection. The ultimate objective is the achievement of the best possible world for all of humanity and the boundaries within which the balancing must take place is the preservation of our ecosystems as the very basis of our existence. We see indications of a global consensus through the adoption of the United Nations Sustainable Development Goals (SDGs).[3] The European Union's follow up of the SDGs is particularly interesting, as it appears to have inspired a broadening of the former somewhat niche work on policy coherence for development to an emphasis on the cross-cutting nature of sustainability issues, as expressed in The New European Consensus on Development: 'Our World, Our Dignity, Our Future'.[4]

However, the SDGs do not draw up an analytical framework or suggest any order of priority, or discuss whether it is conceivable to achieve 'sustained, inclusive and sustainable economic growth'[5] for all countries while mitigating the dire environmental issues, including biodiversity reduction and climate change.[6] To understand what the goal of sustainability entails requires therefore a research-based understanding of what we are trying to achieve, the constraints on the

3 United Nations General Assembly resolution 70/1, *Transforming Our World: The 2030 Agenda for Sustainable Development*, A/RES/70/1, (25 September 2015), available at: www.undocs.org/A/RES/70/1. More on the SDGs here: http://www.un.org/sustainabledevelopment/sustainable-development-goals/

4 The New European Consensus on Development: 'Our World, Our Dignity, Our Future', Joint statement by the Council and the representatives of the governments of the Member States meeting within the Council, the European Parliament and the Commission (2017/C 210/01).

5 United Nations Sustainable Development Goals, United Nations Resolution adopted by the General Assembly on 25 September 2015, A/RES/70/1 2015, § 70/1: Transforming our world: the 2030 Agenda for Sustainable Development, www.un.org/sustainabledevelopment/sustainable-development-goals/, Declaration item 9.

6 Ibid.

achievement of our aims, and the relationship between them. Accordingly, in this new geological epoch that is suggested denoted the Anthropocene, as the era where human activity changes geological processes,[7] we may define sustainable development as 'development that meets the needs of the present while safeguarding Earth's life-support system, on which the welfare of current and future generations depends'.[8]

The grand challenge of our time may be formulated as that of achieving a safe and just operating space for humanity: of securing the social foundation for humanity now and in the future while staying within planetary boundaries.[9] If we are to achieve this, we cannot continue with incremental improvements; neither can we focus on whichever environmental or social challenges are given the most attention at any one time. The concept of planetary boundaries, state-of-the-art natural science,[10] embodies this fundamental recognition of planet-level environmental dynamics presenting non-negotiable ecological limits, which should form the space within which all economic and social development is to take place.

Planetary boundaries as a term used for the limits of our planet is the result of the work of an international multidisciplinary group of environmental scientists, who in 2009 pooled their knowledge of different Earth system processes to inform the world about the space for sustainable action within planetary boundaries.[11] Their work reflects the growing scientific understanding that life and its physical environment co-evolve. This pioneering effort brought together evidence of rising and interconnected global risks in several different contexts where environmental processes are being changed by human activities. The planetary boundaries framework flags a set of sustainability-critical issues. It gives a dashboard of issues

7 Yadvinder Mahli (2017) 'The concept of the Anthropocene', *Annual Review of Environment and Resources*, 42, 77–104, https://doi.org/10.1146/annurev-environ-102016-060854

8 David Griggs et al, 'Policy: Sustainable development goals for people and planet', *Nature*, 495, 305–307 (21 March 2013), doi:10.1038/495305a. This is a step on from the famous definition of sustainable development as development that 'meets the needs of the present without compromising the ability of the future generations to meet their own needs.' World Commission on Environment and Development *Our Common Future* (Oxford University Press, 1987) 43.

9 M. Leach, K. Raworth and J. Rockström, 'Between social and planetary boundaries: Navigating pathways in the safe and just pathway for humanity', *World Social Science Report 2013: Changing Global Environments*, pp. 84–90 (OECD, 2013), available at: www.worldsocialscience.org/activities/world-social-science-report/the-2013-report/ [last accessed 26 Jan. 2017].

10 J. Rockström et al. (2009) 'Planetary boundaries: exploring the safe operating space for humanity', *Ecology and Society*, 14(2), 32, www.ecologyandsociety.org/vol14/iss2/art32/ [last accessed 24 July 2015], and updated and revised in W. Steffen et al. (2015) 'Planetary boundaries: Guiding human development on a changing planet', *Science*, 347(6223), www.sciencemag.org/content/347/6223/1259855.abstract [last accessed 24 July 2015].

11 Sarah Cornell, 'Planetary boundaries and business: putting the operating into the Safe Operating Space for Humanity' (draft paper on file with current author); see Rockström et al., and Steffen et al., n. 10 above.

where our collective humanity is changing the fundamental dynamics of the Earth system most profoundly.[12]

Through this work, it is estimated that humanity has already transgressed or is at risk of transgressing at least four of the currently identified nine planetary boundaries, including climate change, biosphere integrity, biogeochemical flows and land-system integrity.[13] The planetary boundaries work is a continuous natural-science work-in-progress, as scientists gradually understand more of the complex interactions and feedback mechanisms in the global ecological systems.[14] Planetary boundaries as a concept forms the rationale by which new boundaries may be identified and better quantifications or metrics adopted. In line with this, the conceptual framework for planetary boundaries itself proposes a strongly precautionary approach, by 'setting the discrete boundary value at the lower and more conservative bound of the uncertainty range'.[15]

Sustainable development has a strong legal position among the ultimate objectives of the European Union, underpinned by the growing recognition in the EU of the inextricable entity of humanity, our natural environment and our economic system.[16] That this requires a recognition of ecological limits may be found expressed in the EU's Seventh Environment Action Programme 'Living well, within the limits of our planet', where this vision is formulated:

> In 2050, we live well, within the planet's ecological limits. Our prosperity and healthy environment stem from an innovative, circular economy where nothing is wasted and where natural resources are managed sustainably, and biodiversity is protected, valued and restored in ways that enhance our society's resilience. Our low-carbon growth has long been decoupled from resource use, setting the pace for a safe and sustainable global society.[17]

Implementing the natural science understanding of planetary boundaries into the interpretation of Article 11 TFEU has significance on three levels: firstly and most importantly, it brings to the forefront that there indeed are ecological limits, and that loosely attempting to 'green' EU policies is inadequate. Secondly, it highlights the complex interaction between planet-level environmental processes and

12 Cornell, ibid.

13 The other five being global freshwater use, ocean acidification, atmospheric aerosol loading, stratospheric ozone depletion, and novel entities such as nano particles and micro plastic; Steffen et al., n. 10 above.

14 See also T. Häyhäa, P.L. Lucas, D.P. van Vuuren, S.E. Cornell, H. Hoff (2016) 'From planetary boundaries to national fair shares of the global safe operating space — how can the scales be bridged?' *Global Environmental Change*, 40, 60.

15 Rockström et al, n. 10 above.

16 Articles 3(3), 3(5) and 21(2)(d) and (f) of the Treaty on European Union (1992), last amended by the Treaty of Lisbon, OJ 2008 C115 (consolidated version), hereinafter referred to as the EU Treaty (abbreviated TEU).

17 Environment Action Programme to 2020, Decision No 1386/2013/EU of the European Parliament and of the Council of 20 November 2013 on a General Union Environment Action Programme to 2020 'Living well, within the limits of our planet', OJ L 354, 28.12.2013, p. 171–200.

that for example climate change, however topical (and difficult to mitigate), is only one aspect of the convergence of crises we are heading directly into. Thirdly, it continuously reminds us that state-of-the-art natural science must continue to inform our decisions on a work-in-progress basis. For policy-makers it therefore should stress the unacceptability of ignorance in the face of these severe environmental risks and the necessity of a knowledge-based precautionary approach.

3. The sustainability potential of Article 11 TFEU

The principle of sustainable development, with its core codified in the environmental integration rule in Article 11 TFEU,[18] contains within itself a potential transformational effect through the duties it arguably sets out for the EU institutions and the rights, and emerging duties, for Member States. The full realisation of its potential could have led to cross-sectorial discussions on necessary changes to achieve policy coherence for sustainability.

However, in practice this is only partially realised, as we shall see in this section. Notably, while there are significant decisions from the Court of Justice of the European Union, the Court has not taken upon itself clearly enough the role Article 11 TFEU bestows upon it: to be a guardian of the planetary boundaries. There are even some contradictory statements in the case-law. As regards policy-making, while we have seen some indications of plans for horizontal environmental integration, EU policy-making is still influenced by the compartmentalisation that perpetuates the illusion that environmental protection can be left to environmental law, while other areas of law do not have to concern themselves with environmental protection. This section will elaborate on the potential of Article 11 TFEU for the transformation of the EU institutions' contribution to sustainability – and of the potential for the Member States.[19]

3.1 Article 11 TFEU and the EU institutions

The *European Council* is an important political institution, an institutionalisation of the former summits,[20] which is to 'provide the Union with the necessary

18 For an analysis of its predecessor, Article 6 of the EC Treaty, see Sjåfjell *Towards a Sustainable European Company Law* (Kluwer Law International, 2009), Sect.s 10.5 and 10.7. See also *inter alia* L. Krämer 'The Genesis of EC Environmental Principles' in *Principles of European Environmental Law* ed. R. Macrory (Europa Law Publishing, 2004) 29–47. See Christina Voigt, 'Article 11 TFEU in Light of the Principle of Sustainable Development in International Law', in Beate Sjåfjell and Anja Wiesbrock, *The Greening of European Business under EU Law: Taking Article 11 TFEU Seriously* (Routledge, 2015), Ch. 3, on sustainable development as a principle of international law, and its relevance for Article 11 TFEU.

19 This section draws on Beate Sjåfjell, 'The Legal Significance of Article 11 TFEU for EU Institutions and Member States', in Beate Sjåfjell and Anja Wiesbrock, *The Greening of European Business under EU Law: Taking Article 11 TFEU Seriously* (Routledge, 2015), Ch. 4.

20 See Art. 13(1) and Art. 15 TEU.

impetus for its development and shall define the general political directions and priorities thereof'.[21] The overview here concentrates on the main institutions of the EU[22] and those that, as opposed to the European Council, have the core legal decision-making powers.[23] Suffice it to say therefore that the legal obligations flowing from the environmental integration rule apply to the European Council as they do to the other institutions, i.e. within the realm of its competence. Although the European Council has been a driving force for the recognition of sustainable development as an overarching objective of the European Union,[24] the Council can undoubtedly do more to ensure that the overarching objective of a sustainable development is not lost sight of in the day-to-day politics and practice of the European Union.[25] Illustrative are for example the March 2014 conclusions of the European Council, where the focus on 'Climate and energy' seems to be driven more by geopolitical reasons for ensuring energy security than the threat of global warming, and where sustainable development is not mentioned at all.[26] Similarly, the June 2017 conclusions illustrate the lack of attention paid to other planetary boundaries through an overly narrow focus on climate change and the significance of the Paris Agreement for modernising EU industry and economy, although mention is made of the broader New European Consensus on Development.[27]

The three main institutions of the Union legislator: The Council, the Commission and the Parliament must 'act within the limits of the powers conferred on it in the Treaties, and in conformity with the procedures, conditions and objectives set out

21 Art. 15(1) TEU.

22 The Council, the Commission, the European Parliament and the Court of Justice of the European Union; delimiting against, for reasons of space and time, the also important EU institutions of the European Central Bank and the Court of Auditors (Art. 13(1) TEU).

23 Although the Treaties give the European Council competence in exceptional cases, see Art. 48 TEU and e.g. Art. 48(2) and 82(3) TFEU, the European Council has no general legislative powers, Art. 15(1) TEU.

24 As early as from the Presidency Conclusions of the European Council, Rhodes, 2–3 December 1988 (DOC/88/10).

25 That the European Council had to amend its Lisbon Agenda may serve to illustrate its lack of proper focus: In 2001 the European Council stated that sustainable development is a 'fundamental objective under the Treaties', agreed on a strategy for sustainable development and expressly added an environmental dimension to the Lisbon agenda; Presidency Conclusions of the Gothenburg European Council 15–16 June 2001 (SN 200/1/01 Rev 1) paras. 1 and 19–21.

26 'A coherent European energy and climate policy must ensure affordable energy prices, industrial competitiveness, security of supply and achievement of our climate and environmental objectives', Conclusions of the European Council, Brussels, 20–21 March 2014 (EUCO 7/14). 7. Although meeting the 'ambitious' targets of reduction of greenhouse gas emissions are discussed and the international climate negotiations emphasise and renewable energy is emphasised, the context of 'renewable and other indigenous' energy sources gives the impression that the European Council is focused more on energy security in the current geopolitical situation, rather than combating global warming; see e.g. the discussion of import of natural gas from North America to Europe.

27 Conclusions of the European Council, Brussels, 22–23 June 2017 (EUCO 8/17).

in them'.[28] The overarching objectives are however so broad, that they only very rarely will hinder new initiatives from the European Union.[29] The converse is of special interest for environmental protection. With reference to the environmental protection objective and the environmental integration rule (now in Article 11 TFEU) the Court of Justice found that the EU law-maker can also adopt secondary law provisions within the area of criminal law, when necessary to ensure an effective environmental protection.[30] The Court has also established that the environmental integration rule has the following implication: Environmental protection measures can be validly adopted under any legal basis of the Treaties, as long the relevant requirements of that basis otherwise are fulfilled.[31]

The EU law-maker also has a duty to actively promote the objectives and to strike a balance between them, and under certain circumstances a duty to undertake specific action.[32] The Council has a policy-making and coordinating function in the EU law system, and holds legislative functions,[33] with the aim of advancing the objectives of the European Union.[34] The Council has a central position in the legislative process. The Commission normally has the right of proposal, though – the Council can only rarely adopt legislative measures without prior proposals from the Commission.[35] The Commission is thus, with the aim of promoting 'the general interest of the Union' and of ensuring 'the application of the Treaties', to participate in the EU law-making process.[36] The EU Parliament has through a remarkable development[37] been given an ever larger role in the EU law-making process.[38]

28 Art. 13(2) TEU; cp. Ex Art. 5 EC. See also Art. 3(6) TEU.

29 The division of labour in accordance with the principle of subsidiarity may on the other hand affect the competence of the EU institutions to put forward initiatives in certain areas, see Art. 5 TEU. That is not a topic for this chapter.

30 See C-176/03 *Commission v. Council* [2005] ECR I-7879 and C-440/05 *Commission v. Council* [2007] ECR I-9097.

31 See C-62/88 *Greece v. Council (Chernobyl I)* [1990] ECR I-1527, C-300/89 *Commission v. Council (Titanium Dioxide)* [1991] ECR I-2867, C-440/05 *Commission v. Council* [2007] ECR I-9097.

32 See Sjåfjell, 'The Legal Significance of Article 11 TFEU for EU Institutions and Member States'.

33 And also budgetary functions, both together with the Parliament.

34 Art. 16(1) and 13(1)-(2) TEU.

35 See Art. 289 TFEU and the ordinary legislative procedure as set out in Art. 294 TFEU. Note also the Council's competence to 'request the Commission to undertake any studies the Council considers desirable for the attainment of the common objectives, and to submit to it any appropriate proposals', Art. 241 TFEU.

36 Art. 17(1) TEU, cp. ex 211 EC. The Commission of course also has a number of other duties, see further below.

37 See pre-Lisbon P. J. G. Kapteyn and P. VerLoren van Themaat *The Law of the European Union and the European Communities* (4th rev. edn., Kluwer Law International, 2008), 207.

38 Through the codetermination procedure in ex Art 251 EC, now the ordinary legislative procedure in Art. 294 TFEU, see also Art. 14(1) TEU. In addition, the Parliament has a general competence to discuss any EU relevant issue, adopt resolutions thereto and ask the Member States to act thereupon.

On all the various levels, the duty to seek a balance and promote a sustainable development is relevant. The duty applies to the chosen approach and the scope of the preparatory work in connection with new secondary legislation. To achieve integration of environmental protection requirements with the aim of sustainability in the secondary legislation, it should be included in the very first planning phase. That this is a part of the duty is clear from the wording of Article 11 TFEU: Environmental protection requirements are to be integrated into the 'definition and implementation of' policies and activities. Article 11 TFEU, taken seriously, thereby requires action in general for the law-making institutions to ensure the integration of environmental protection requirements in legislative processes that are initiated for other reasons. Especially for the Commission, which has direct competence to propose new legislative initiatives,[39] the rule then also entails a duty to act specifically to promote a sustainable development – i.e. to take action where action otherwise would not have been taken (and not only to include environmental considerations in legislative initiatives planned for other reasons). The European Parliament is also subject to this rule, within its competence to request that the Commission 'submit any appropriate proposal on matters on which it considers that a Union act is required *for the purpose of implementing the Treaties*'.[40]

Although the legal bases set out a competence to act and not a duty to act expressly, the competence interpreted in light of the overarching objectives and particularly Article 11 TFEU entails that the institutions must use their competence where necessary. The Parliament must therefore request that new proposals are submitted by the Commission where necessary to promote the overarching aim of a sustainable development, and the Commission must submit such proposals, whether or not it is requested to do so by the Parliament.

It follows logically, then, that the duty to act also will be a specific duty to undertake specific action in certain circumstances.[41] It is clear that *business as usual* is a very certain path towards a very uncertain future; continuing on the same track cannot then be in compliance with Article 11 TFEU and the obligation to promote a sustainable development.[42]

Article 11 TFEU applies also for the institutions that play a role in the legislative process after a proposal has been put forward, that is the Council, the Parliament, the Commission and the Conciliation Committee, as the case may be.[43]

39 See the ordinary legislative procedure in Art. 294(1) TFEU.

40 Art. 225 TFEU (emphasis added), ex Art. 192(2).

41 For a discussion of what this entails for the EU's regulation of business, see Beate Sjåfjell, 'Corporate Governance for Sustainability: the Necessary Reform of EU Company Law', in Beate Sjåfjell and Anja Wiesbrock, *The Greening of European Business under EU Law: Taking Article 11 TFEU Seriously* (Routledge, 2015), Ch. 6.

42 See e.g. Will Steffen, Johan Rockström Robert Costanza, 2011 'How defining planetary boundaries can transform our approach to growth' *Solutions*, 2, 3, thesolutionsjournal.com/node/935.

43 Art. 294 TFEU.

This gives rise to the question of whether the environmental integration duty is procedural or substantive. When the Parliament is to decide whether to approve, reject or suggest amendments in the legislative proposal, a procedural requirement could entail that it was sufficient for the Parliament to check whether environmental concerns had been considered in the making of the proposal. The environmental integration rule's emphasis of the goal of sustainable development combined with the position of sustainable development as an overarching goal,[44] which the institutions have a duty to act to achieve, indicates a substantive duty to carry out the integration necessary to achieve a sustainable development. The non-negotiable ecological limits which must be respected if sustainable development is to be achieved, supports the argument.[45]

Article 11 TFEU is further relevant for the choice of rules and the formulation of the rules, which would require ex ante thorough impact assessments. Not implemented properly, the principle of sustainable development – instead of making environmental law less marginal – may serve to 'subsume environmental considerations' and 'perpetuate an approach' to economic activities that encourages environmental problems.[46]

Each institution, when carrying out its tasks according to the treaties, has an independent obligation to ensure that the environmental integration duty is carried out and that sufficient action is taken to promote a sustainable development. Indubitably this is demanding. In some cases this will entail that the whole idea of a secondary legislative initiative needs to be reassessed. Correctly implemented this integration could prevent more 'path-dependent' results, and maybe – for a while – lead to fewer legislative proposals and more discussions on a higher level, and thereby better preparatory work.

The Court of Justice of the European Union, including the Court of Justice, the General Court and specialised courts, is the guardian of EU law.[47] When the Court deals with Treaty infringement cases against a Member State, reviews the legality of legislative acts by the other EU institutions, handles actions against other EU institutions for infringement of the Treaty through passivity and gives preliminary rulings concerning the interpretation of the treaties and of secondary legislation,[48] the Court must as a matter of law itself comply with the environmental integration rule and ensure that the other EU institutions[49] do the same.

The Court of Justice has shown in its practice, employing a dynamic, contextual and teleological method, that it is capable of taking the objectives of the Treaties

44 Art. 3 TEU.

45 See also Christina Voigt, 'Article 11 TFEU in light of the principle of sustainable development in international law'.

46 P. Sands *Principles of International Environmental Law* (Cambridge University Press, 2003) 9.

47 Art. 19(1) TEU, including the Court of Justice, the General Court and specialised courts.

48 Especially Articles 258–260, 262, 265 and 267 TFEU, see ex Articles 226, 230, 232 and 234 EC.

49 And the Member States, as far as applicable, see below, Section 3.2.

seriously. Even before inclusion as such in the Treaties, the Court elevated environmental protection from a position of neglect to one of the 'essential objectives' of the European Union.[50] Based on its case law and the position of environmental protection as an objective, the Court in 1988 declared environmental protection to be a mandatory requirement, i.e. an objective that may justify restrictions on free movement.[51] *PreussenElektra* is a landmark case in its acceptance of discriminatory measures, with reference to the environmental integration rule and its significance for priority objectives in accordance with international climate change obligations.[52]

The overarching objectives have proven to form a framework for EU law and the Court has shown that the objectives require balance.[53] The environmental integration rule, now in Article 11 TFEU, has been emphasised and accorded significance in a number of cases before the Court, also before the rule was strengthened and moved to the elevated position in then Article 6 of the EC Treaty. The overarching objective of environmental protection and the environmental integration rule have formed an important part of the Court's reasoning in the cases where the Court expanded the framework of EU law (at least in comparison to what many perceived as the limits of EU law at the time), by finding that the EU law-maker is competent to include requirements of criminal penalties in secondary legislation where necessary to achieve an effective environmental protection.[54] In its quest for a balance between the overarching objectives, the Court has shown a number of times that environmental protection may substantiate restrictions on free movement.[55]

Taking Article 11 TFEU seriously, the Court should to a greater extent and also *ex officio* focus on what the objective of sustainable development and the reference thereto in Article 11 TFEU entails with regard to a duty to integrate environmental protection in all EU law areas – also in areas where environmental concerns traditionally have not been even considered. *Concordia Bus* is a now quite dated case which gave hope for the future direction of the case-law of the Court, as the Court of Justice here, in a traditionally economic area emphasised the objective of environmental protection with reference to the environmental

50 Case 240/83 *ADBHU* [1985] ECR 531 para. 13. E.g. Jacobs 'The Role of the European Court of Justice' and Sjåfjell *Towards a Sustainable European Company Law* Sect. 10.5.

51 Case 302/86 *Commission v. Denmark* [1988] ECR 4607 para 8–9. See also J. Scott *EC Environmental Law* (London, Longman, 1998) 67–68, Jans *European Environmental Law* 247–248 and 258–262, and Krämer *EC Environmental Law* 105–106.

52 C-379/98 *PreussenElektra* C-379/98 [2001] ECR I-2099.

53 See the overview of case-law in Sjåfjell *Towards a Sustainable European Company Law* Sect. 10.1.3.4.

54 C-176/03 *Commission v. Council* [2005] ECR I-7879 and C-440/05 *Commission v. Council* [2007] ECR I-9097; F. Jacobs (2006) 'The role of the European Court of Justice in the protection of the environment' *Journal of Environmental Law*, 185–205.

55 See briefly below.

integration rule, and indirectly initiated a revision of relevant secondary legislation.[56]

There is also a need to clarify the confusion that has arisen on the level of the General Court. In Castelnou Energía v Commission the Court concluded that there was not a duty to assess the environmental impacts of decisions made in other areas.[57] This ignores Article 11 TFEU and the overarching of the EU set out in Articles 2 and 3 TEU, and is not in line with the Court of Justice decision, for example, in *Nuova Agricast.* [58]

The potential for the use of Article 11 TFEU, taken seriously, in the Court is apparent. If a well-founded case against a legislative act, based on non-compliance with the environmental integration rule, is brought before the Court sufficiently early, the secondary legislation may – and shall, as a matter of EU Treaty law – be declared void.[59] More specifically, this entails that secondary legislation may be declared void if – which would be the simplest variety – the environmental integration duty has not even been considered,[60] or – and more difficult, except in the obvious cases of violation – where the environmental integration duty has been considered, but where the environmental integration, as a matter of substance, has not been carried out properly.[61]

Where the Court cannot or will not declare the secondary legislation to be void (for example because the action is brought too late or the Court finds the integration effort too difficult to assess or within the legislative margin of appreciation), the integration rule and the duty to seek a balance between the relevant objectives are of significance as Treaty-based principles for the interpretation of the secondary legislation, and as guidelines for the discretion exercised by the EU institution or a Member State, as the case may be.

The EU institutions that have the competence to bring a case before the Court of Justice obviously have as a part of their mandate to ensure, in this manner, compliance with the environmental integration rule. This brings us to the Commission as a supervisory body.

56 See C-513/99 *Concordia Bus Finland* [2002] ECR I-7213. See Anja Wiesbrock (2013) 'An obligation for sustainable procurement? Gauging the potential impact of Article 11 TFEU on public contracting in the EU' *Legal Issues of Economic Integration*, 40, 2, 105–132, and Beate Sjåfjell and Anja Wiesbrock, *Sustainable Public Procurement under EU Law: A New Role for the State as Shareholder* (Cambridge University Press, 2015).

57 Castelnou Energía v Commission, T-57/11, ECLI:EU:T:2014:1021.

58 Nuova Agricast Srl and Cofra Srl v Commission, C-67/09 P, ECLI:EU:C:2010:607, see further J. Nowag, *Environmental Integration in Competition and Free-Movement Laws* (Oxford University Press, 2016), Ch. 4.

59 Art. 264 TFEU.

60 As the case is with the Takeover Directive, see Sjåfjell *Towards a Sustainable European Company Law* Sect. 18.3.2.

61 Discussed also by Krämer *EC Environmental Law* 22–23, Dhondt *Integration of Environmental Protection* 484–485, and J. H. Jans *European Environmental Law* (2nd rev. edn., Europa Law Publishing, 2000) 21.

The Commission has a number of tasks and a wide competence to 'promote the general interest of the Union'.[62] Article 11 TFEU is relevant for the Commission as a legislative body, as discussed above, and of course very much so in the Commission's control function, i.e. its task of overseeing the application of EU law, which it is to carry out to 'ensure the application of the Treaties, and of measures adopted by the institutions pursuant to them'.[63] The Commission is a key player, together with the Court,[64] in safeguarding the Treaties, ensuring their correct application and moving EU law forward, through its Treaty-given competence and because of its independence in relation to the Member States.[65]

In practice, the Commission has often been the applicant bringing cases against Member States before the Court in the cases where the Court of Justice subsequently has ruled in favour of the Member States in determining that the objective of environmental protection, with reference to the environmental protection rule, has justified Member State restrictions of free movement. On the other hand, the Commission has also brought actions against Member States in a number of cases where Member States were in violation of their duty to protect the environment (concerning lack of proper implementation of secondary legislation aiming to protect the environment).[66]

In a proper search for a balance between the overarching objectives, the Commission's approach should integrate an understanding of the necessity of working to stay within planetary boundaries to achieve the EU's overarching goals. As is the case with the Court,[67] the Commission also fails in the *ex officio* application of the environmental integration rule in non-environment cases, i.e. in policy areas where environmental interests traditionally are not considered, and where environmental protection and sustainable development as Treaty-based objectives and the environmental integration rule in Article 11 TFEU actually require integration. In this respect, the Commission fails in its duty to ensure the application of the Treaties.

3.2 *Article 11 TFEU and the Member States of the EU*

The Court of Justice has declared that the overarching objectives of the Treaties,[68] in themselves and seen in isolation, neither impose legal obligations on Member

62 In addition to the important legislative and control functions, the Commission is to 'execute the budget and manage programmes', have 'coordinating, executive and management functions', represent the Union externally (with the exception especially of the common foreign and security policy), and 'initiate the Union's annual and multiannual programming with a view to achieving interinstitutional agreements', see now Art. 17(1) and (2) TEU. Pre-Lisbon, see P. J. G. Kapteyn and P. VerLoren van Themaat *The Law of the European Union and the European Communities* (4th rev. edn., Kluwer Law International, 2008), 193 seq.

63 Art. 17(1) TEU.

64 That is, 'under the control of the Court of Justice of the European Union', Art. 17(2) TEU.

65 Art. 17(3) TEU.

66 See B. Sjåfjell *Towards a Sustainable European Company Law* Sect. 10.9.3.3.

67 Sect. 4.2. above.

68 In then Art. 2 EC, now Art. 3 TEU.

States nor confer rights on individuals.[69] Correspondingly, it is clear that Article 11 TFEU does not directly address the Member States. It should be just as clear however, that the obligations for the EU institutions indirectly may entail both duties and rights for the Member States. The scope of these duties and rights is the topic of this section.

The duty of loyalty and cooperation in Article 4(3) TEU[70] is an important part of the basis for the argument that the Member States have duties that flow from the overarching objectives and the principle-based rules of the Treaties, beyond those duties that follow directly and narrowly from the provisions of the Treaties and the secondary legislation. Already in the 1970s, the Court of Justice found that the Member States had duties based on the predecessor of Article 4(3) TEU.[71] Article 4(3) TEU (and its predecessors) refers to the 'attainment of the Union's objectives' and similar phrases,[72] entailing that the obligations of the Member States have developed and will continue to develop in pace with the scope and the legal significance of the overarching objectives of the European Union, as set out in the Treaties.[73]

The obligations (and the rights) for the Member States apply on all levels and to all their institutions: the legislative bodies, administrative and supervisory authorities and courts, although it will vary from institution to institution which duty (or right) is the most relevant to discuss.

This topic may be discussed as an issue concerning implementation of secondary legislation, but it is also significant for the interpretation of the Member States' obligations flowing directly from the Treaties.

Secondary legislation must be interpreted in light of the Treaties, which are to be understood as a coherent system.[74] This may be seen as one of the most profoundly important constitutional principles of EU law, supported inter alia by (now) Article 4(3) TEU.[75] Research into the significance of the overarching objectives of EU law strengthens this argument.[76]

Member States accordingly have the right and the duty to follow the principle of sustainable development, as codified in the environmental integration rule, in their interpretation, implementation and application of EU law.[77] Member States

69 Case 126/86 *Zaera* [1987] ECR 3697 para 10 and 11. See also C-339/89 *Alsthom Atlantique* [1991] ECR I-107 para 8–9, Joined cases C-72/91 and C-73/91 *Firma Sloman Neptun Schiffahrts* [1993] ECR I-887 para. 28 and C-293/03 *Gregorio My v. Office national des pensions* [2004] ECR I-12013 para. 29.

70 Ex Art. 10(2) EF, before that: Art. 5 EC.

71 Then Art. 5 EC, later: Art. 10(2) EC.

72 Art. 4(3) third paragraph.

73 See P. J. G. Kapteyn and P. VerLoren van Themaat *The Law of the European Union and the European Communities* (4th rev. edn., Kluwer Law International, 2008), *The Law of the European Union* 153.

74 See e.g. the Court's reasoning in Albany, and see also Art. 13(1) TEU.

75 See J. Temple Lang 'The development by the Court of Justice of the duties of cooperation of national authorities and community institutions under Article 10 EC' *Fordham International Law Journal* (2007–2008) 1483–1532 at 1483.

76 Sjåfjell *Towards A Sustainable European Company Law*.

77 See ibid. Sect. 18.3.2.

should be obligated to comply with the environmental integration rule also when the EU institutions have not expressly fulfilled their duty according to the rule. Each institution of the EU and each Member State are obligated to do what they can to 'assist each other in carrying out tasks which flow from the Treaties' and refrain from doing anything that may 'jeopardise the attainment of the Union's objectives'.[78] The principle of loyalty requires cooperation, but it also entails that one party's failure cannot be used to justify another party's failure. This has primarily been expressed concerning the relationship between the Member States, but arguably the same must apply between the Member States and the EU institutions. The Court of Justice has used the predecessors of Article 4(3) TEU as a basis to develop a number of constitutional principles and a finely knit web of obligations to act, to cooperate and to be loyal for both the Member States and the EU institutions.[79] Even though the duty of cooperation originally was interpreted in such a way to entail that a Member State has violated EU law if the Member State was under a sufficiently clear and precise obligation to do something and did nothing, this has developed into a more general obligation in pace with the Court of Justice's development of its understanding of (now) Article 4(3) TEU.[80] As is apparent from the wording of the provision itself, the loyalty is not owed to the EU institutions, but to the Treaties and the overarching objectives.

Accordingly, the Member States' institutions must as far as possible, and in all relevant areas, interpret national law in light of the objectives and the wording of secondary legislation, and in general, in a way that is in accordance with EU law requirements.[81] Further, the Treaties themselves require that the Member States institutions must interpret and apply secondary legislation in light of the objectives and obligations flowing from the Treaties. This has often been expressed in cases concerning free movement and arguably the same principles apply to other Treaty obligations meant to promote the same overarching objectives. The Member States therefore have both a duty to implement, interpret and apply EU law rules in light of the Treaty. More specifically, there is a legal foundation for the establishment of a right and a duty to act in accordance with the environmental integration rule as far as possible, within the framework of the treaties and of the secondary legislation.

For national legislators this means that the (other) general Treaty rules and the secondary legislation must be implemented in as environmentally-friendly a way as possible, aiming to promote sustainable development. All Member State institutions (on state and local level) must interpret national law (as far as relevant) in light of the rules flowing from the Treaties themselves. The Treaty rules themselves must be interpreted and understood in light of EU law's own general and constitutional principles, including the principle of sustainable development as

78 Art. 4(3) TEU.

79 See Temple Lang 'The Development by the Court of Justice'.

80 K. Lenaerts and P. Van Nuffel *Constitutional Law of the European Union* (ed. R. Bray, 2nd edn., Sweet & Maxwell, 2005) 117 and Temple Lang 'The Development by the Court of Justice'.

81 Lenaerts and Van Nuffel *Constitutional aw* 119.

codified in Article 11 TFEU – also where the EU institutions have failed to do so in a proper manner. This applies correspondingly to administrative authorities' implementation and application of the law (whether in the form of administrative regulations or administrative decisions) and national supervisory authorities' control in light of EU law rules.

The national courts are, as we know, all – within their areas of competence – EU law courts, with a right and a duty to apply all relevant EU law rules in each case, regardless of whether these rules have been the subject of arguments presented by the parties in the case.[82]

The environmental integration rule, and its links to the overarching objective of the EU as well as to international climate change obligations, may be seen as broadening the Member States' scope of action, compared to the perceived scope if the rule and its possibilities are not properly considered. The basis for justification also indicates the direction in which the broader scope of action may be applied – it is the objective of the environmental dimension of sustainable development that provides a (perhaps) broader basis for justifying restrictions, and the Member State initiative must therefore contribute to that overarching objective. Member States may on another basis, in national law, EU law or international law (or politically or even morally), be obligated to use this possibility.

This is of significance for the legislator, for the public administration and for the courts of the Member States, and emphasises the importance of understanding EU law rules in their full context.

When the EU institutions have violated Article 11 TFEU by adopting secondary legislation without considering or properly implementing necessary environmental protection requirements, a Member State may and should then bring action for 'infringement of the Treaties' within the two-month deadline,[83] whereupon the Court may declare the secondary legislation to be void. Probably stipulating a duty in the strongest sense and on a general basis for Member States to do this would be too strict, as that would make the Member States responsible for their own infringement if they did not realise that the environmental integration rule had been violated before the two months had passed. However, based on for example a Member State's Constitutional duties to protect the environment, it may be a duty where that Member State that *is* aware of the Article 11 TFEU violation, to either bring the case before the Court or at least refuse to implement or apply the relevant secondary legislation or other rule of EU law. Certainly, each Member State has a right to do so. That will lead to conflict – to infringement cases being brought before the Court of Justice – but in conflict lies the possibility for a change in a positive direction.

We may also ask whether the Member States are obligated to bring action against an EU institution that does not do enough to promote a sustainable

82 Reflecting the principle of Roman law: *Juva novit curia*. See also Temple Lang 'The Development by the Court of Justice', 1532 and 1507.
83 Art. 261 TFEU.

development.[84] Again, certainly the Member States have a right to do so – and may be obligated to do so, based on other legal arguments.

The discussion above gives rise to the general question of whether the Member States have a duty to act – on national level – to promote sustainable development through the integration of environmental protection requirements in all areas, if the EU institutions do not take sufficient action.[85]

There is EU case-law going back to the 1980s, with the predecessors of Article 4(3) TEU as a point of departure, that indicates that a Member State is obligated to take initiative to achieve an EU law objective. This is also in areas where the entire policy area is within the competence of the EU law, and when an EU institution fails to do what it should. In such cases, the Member State must act in cooperation with the EU institutions.[86] In the further line of cases, the Court emphasised that the Member States have a duty of action in the form of conservation measures where this is in the common interest.[87] The foundation was that the conservation of the fish stock in question was a clearly accepted EU law objective, and that there was 'clear scientific advice' indicating that the measures (stop fishing of a certain type of fish) should be adopted.[88]

This is directly relevant for the situation today where transgressing the core planetary boundaries of climate change and biodiversity may jeopardise the EU law objective of a sustainable development. If there is 'clear scientific advice' that a certain measure must be adopted or stopped to achieve the objective, the argument could be made that the Member States individually have a duty to act, based on Articles 3 and 4(3) TEU and Article 11 TFEU. However, to stipulate a duty in accordance with Article 4(3) TEU, the context must be a strengthening of an already existing Treaty obligation. Article 4(3) TEU has not been perceived as providing a basis for establishing completely new duties where there is no Treaty-based (or secondary law-based) obligation to start with.[89] When the Court of Justice has declared that the general objectives of the EU do not in themselves give duties for the Member States, it is difficult to argue that Article 4(3) gives sufficient basis to declare that the Member States individually must adopt measures to achieve the overarching objectives in accordance with Article 3 TEU.

On the other hand, it follows directly from Article 4(3) EU that the Member States must refrain from doing anything that will jeopardise the achievement of

84 Art. 263 TFEU.

85 Whether in violation of the Treaties or due to the limits imposed by the principle of subsidiarity.

86 See Case 13/83 *Parliament v. Council* [1985] ECR 1513 and Temple Lang 'The Development by the Court of Justice'.

87 Lenaerts and Van Nuffel *Constitutional Law* 120, with reference to Case 32/79 concerning marine conversation measures, quote from para 15: 'In such a situation, it was for the Member States, as regards the maritime zones within their jurisdiction, to take the necessary conservation measures *in the common interest* and in accordance with both the substantive and the procedural rules arising from Community law' (emphasis added).

88 Ibid.

89 Temple Lang 'The Development by the Court of Justice'.

the objectives of the EU. This gives rise to the question whether it nevertheless will be an infringement of the Treaties to adopt or allow new national measures that will, for example, dramatically increase greenhouse gas emissions. Arguably, this is the case when we include in the equation the environmental integration rule in Article 11 TFEU as a link in the chain between the general objectives of Article 3 TEU and the obligation to act, to cooperate and to be loyal in Article 4(3) TEU. At the end of the day, and especially in terms of an enforceable obligation, the answer will depend on whether the necessary action to promote the objective (or refrain from jeopardising the achievement of the objective) can be spelled out concretely enough for a court to feel comfortable in calling it an obligation.

4. Realising the potential of Article 11 TFEU

Undoubtedly, the situation today is nowhere near a true integration in all sectors.[90] Article 11 TFEU, setting out a clear duty to integrate environmental protection requirements in all policies and activities of the EU, with the aim of achieving sustainability development, is often ignored. However, lack of true integration does not constitute an argument against the existence of these legal duties set out here, rather it shows the necessity of spelling them out clearly and repeating the message until it gets through.

Not everything that has been put forward as obligations flowing from Article 11 TFEU in this chapter, can be substantiated, directly or fully, with reference to case-law from the Court of Justice (although some of the obligations can). Legal science will not contribute to developing the law, or can only with much difficulty do so, if our perspective is only to be retrospective. If we are to contribute to solving the challenges of today and of the future, we as legal scholars cannot primarily base ourselves on retrospective, static understanding of the law. It is our responsibility to look forward.

The EU legal method is teleological and dynamic. Although much is left to be desired still also on EU law level, EU law may provide a greater opportunity for a way forward than many a national legal system through the EU law focus on the overarching objectives and the dynamic interpretation of the legal requirements flowing from them. Through the implementation of EU secondary legislation and the recognition of the significance of EU Treaty law, the supranational level of EU law may influence national legal method and thereby lead to greater awareness of the significance of overarching international and supranational goals. This may in turn influence the national methodologies of law, leading to a greater significance being attached also on national level to overarching objectives. Many Member States today have the protection of the environment and even the goal of a sustainable development included in their constitutions. Through the influence of

90 A situation which has been pointed out also by earlier contributions, see L. Krämer *EC Environmental Law* (6th edn., Sweet & Maxwell, 2007) 396–400 and 402–410 and N. Dhondt *Integration of Environmental Protection into other EC policies: Legal Theory and Practice* (Europa Law Publishing, 2003) 479–480. For a more recent analysis, see Julian Nowag, *Environmental Integration in Competition and Free-Movement Laws* (Oxford University Press, 2016).

EU law methodology, these objectives may be given greater weight. The constitutional objectives of environmental protection and sustainability may be interpreted in the light of the overarching objective of a sustainable development and a high level of environmental protection in the EU Treaties, while the Treaty objectives themselves may be seen as strengthened through the recognition of these objectives being common to the constitutions of many Member States.

The supranational level of EU law may on several levels function to make national law disciplines comply with and work towards the sustainable development objective and the principle of a sustainable development that flows from international treaties, provided that EU law follows up on the requirements within its own system. Taking its own environmental integration rule seriously, EU law has the potential of taking the lead globally and turning the trend of short-term growth mania into a reflective, long-term sustainable development.

There are some positive indications of a broader understanding of these issues in the EU.[91] The 2015 adoption of the SDGs and the EU's follow up in the form of The New European Consensus for Development in 2017, may be a platform for change.[92] With its shift from policy coherence for development towards the cross-cutting integration of the SDGs, the EU has the chance of implementing the systematic and comprehensive integration that is necessary to achieve the global sustainability goals.

Article 11 TFEU may prove to be key in achieving the fundamental transformation away from a fossil fuel-based with its linear business models towards a renewables-based, circular and just economy within planetary boundaries. To realise the potential of Article 11 TFEU requires recognition that 'business as usual' is not an alternative, that path-dependency is an explanation, not an excuse, that incremental improvement may be a dangerous deflection device, and that the achievement of policy coherence for sustainability must be sought. This intrinsically demands that Article 11 TFEU, as the EU's codification of the core of the principle of sustainable development becomes a part of a broader recognition of a general principle of sustainable development as a guideline for all policies. The realisation of this potential requires concerted efforts on several levels, where sustainability-oriented civil society, business and finance, policy makers, media, as well as academia, must engage in new and unprecedented ways.

We face a convergence of crises. We are on the brink of several types of disasters, and yet, if we grasp this occasion and use this opportunity to all work together in a different way to complete the jigsaw puzzle of sustainability, we can be the generation that leads humanity away from its destructive trajectory and onto a sustainable path towards a better world for us all. Taking seriously the EU's environmental integration rule with its aim of achieving sustainability, may be one small but crucial step towards this goal.

91 See e.g. Eléonore Maitre Ekern, 'Towards an Integrated Product Regulatory Framework Based on Life-Cycle Thinking', in Beate Sjåfjell and Anja Wiesbrock, *The Greening of European Business under EU Law: Taking Article 11 TFEU Seriously* (Routledge, 2015), Ch. 8.

92 See notes 3 and 4 above.

7 On the current meaning and potential effects of the horizontal consumer clause of Article 12 of the TFEU

Francesco Seatzu

I Preliminary remarks

To the best of our knowledge, no discussion of the consumer features of the Treaty of Lisbon has failed to recognize the insertion of the so-called horizontal consumer clause ('HCC') into the Title II of the Treaty on the Functioning of the EU (TFEU), named 'Provisions Having General Application'. The reason behind this is clear: the 'Provisions Having General Application' (Articles 7 to 17) are important since they require the EU to guarantee consistency of its different policies, taking all of its aims into consideration and in accordance with the general principle of conferral of powers. This assertion, incidentally, is certainly accurate, albeit some uncertainties persist concerning the application of the 'Provisions Having General Application' to the policies encapsulated in the TFEU in addition to to those encompassed in the TEU.[1]

Legal academics and policy observers have often claimed that the new horizontal consumer clause, also frequently called the 'consumer integration clause', has to be seen as a truly original innovation able to give visibility and strength to the EU's engagement to consumer protection.[2] They claim this notwithstanding

1 For a discussion of this issue, see e.g. Marise Cremona, 'The Two (or Three) Treaty Solution: The New Treaty Structure of the EU', in Andrea Biondi, Piet Eeckhout, Stefanie Ripley (eds), *EU After Lisbon* (Oxford: OUP, 2012), p. 48 ff.

2 See *ex multis* M. Ioannidou, *Consumer Involvement in Private EU Competition Law Enforcement* (Oxford: OUP, 2015), p. 25; I. Benoehr, *EU Consumer Law and Human Rights* (Oxford: OUP, 2014), p. 41 ff; Sybe A. De Vries, 'The Court of Justice's "Paradigm Consumer" in EU Free Movement Law', in D. Leczykiewicz, S. Weatherill (eds), *The Images of the Consumer in EU Law: Legislation, Free Movement and Competition Law* (Oxford: Hart Publishing, 2016), p. 416, stressing in particular that the placement of the consumer integration clause on an equal footing with the environmental integration clause makes consumer protection requirements stronger and more fundamental than before the entry into force of the Lisbon Treaty. See also E. Psychogiopoulou, *Integration of Cultural Considerations in European Union Law and Policies* (Leiden and Boston: Martinus Nijhoff Publishers, 2008), p. 64, note 170, stressing that: 'the specific objective under the common agricultural policy of agricultural products reaching the consumer at reasonable prices, inserted in the original Treaty of Rome … could be seen as a first, concrete example of mainstreaming consumer protection'.

the fact that the exact normative consequences of this clause (other than the delimitation of the EU's discretionary powers in the sense that the full effect of the single market should be mitigated when horizontal policy interests such as consumer protection are at stake[3]) are far from being evident for a number of sound reasons.[4]

Grounded in the examination of the general principles and rules of EU treaty law, other EU official documents including EU Commission guidelines, as well as the pertinent jurisprudence of the CJEU, reflections of legal academics and autonomous experts and comparisons with other horizontal integration clauses that share common ingredients such as Articles 9, 11 and 13 of the TFEU, this chapter aims to carry out a more extensive survey of the usefulness and potential of this new 'competence to protect' consumers' welfare[5] alias of the consumer integration clause encapsulated in Article 12 of the TFEU for the establishment of a sustainable European consumer market. In its first introductory part, it concentrates on the normative status and meaning of the engagement indicated for the European Union institutions, bodies and organs in the normative texture of Article 12. The second part provides a critical account of the results achieved, if any, from the use of the consumer integration clause in the EU's practice. The third and final part of the chapters suggests changes that would help to better realise HCC's potential. The general objective of each part is to find a satisfactory answer to the following query: is the HCC a clause that can only raise false expectations in the supporters of a 'pro-consumer' European Union, or is it a clause that might become a valid legal tool for re-orienting the EU towards a substantial equilibrium between pro-consumer measures and actions and its internal single market? Or, said alternatively and more specifically: is Article 12 of the TFEU only meant to be interpreted as a procedural provision requiring the EU legislator to consider the consumer dimension of other EU policies and activities, or might it be interpreted and applied as requiring a substantive integration of consumer concerns?

II The genesis, legal meaning and normative content of the consumer protection clause in Article 12 of the TFEU

The starting point here is that the horizontal consumer clause, embodied in Article 12 of the TFEU, almost literally follows the language of Article III-120 of the Treaty Establishing a Constitution for Europe. Article III-120 reads as follows:

3 See Sybe A. De Vries, above n. 2, p. 416.

4 See Bernardo Hernández Bataller, 'Report of the Single Market Observatory on The horizontal clause in consumer protection policy', available at: https://www.eesc.europa.eu/resources/docs/ces3209-2013_00_01_tra_tcd_en.doc. For analogous remarks on Article 11 of the TFEU, see Nicolas de Sadeleer, *EU Environmental Law and the Internal Market* (Oxford: OUP, 2015), p. 25 ff.

5 This expression has been borrowed by Bruno de Witte, 'A competence to protect. The pursuit of non-market aims through internal market legislation'. In Phil Syrpis (ed.), *The Judiciary, the Legislature and the EU Internal Market* (Cambridge: Cambridge University Press, 2010), p. 25.

'Consumer protection requirements shall be taken into account in defining and implementing other Union policies and activities'.[6]

The consumer protection goals of the EU as emerging from a combined reading of Article 12 and Article 169 of the TFUE (such as consumers' health, safety, economic interests, and the possibility for consumers to organize themselves to protect their interests, etc.) that should always be taken into consideration in the definition and implementation of any EU policies and activities, are not the only provisions possessing general application. The same Title II of the TFEU also indicates, amongst several others, the fight against any discrimination (Article 10), the promotion of environmental protection and sustainable development (Article 11), animal welfare and respect of traditions (Article 13) and the principles of good governance and transparency (Article 15).

It seems almost superfluous to state that the size of the obligation of the general application of the above-mentioned articles cannot be derived exclusively from their wording. For instance, while Article 15 of the TFEU, which provides that: 'the EU institutions, bodies, offices and agencies shall conduct their work as openly as possible', obliges EU institutions and organs stringently, Article 12 of the TFEU, in contrast, uses a rather generic language of good intentions (e.g., consumer protection requirements shall be 'taken into account') to describe the duty of EU institutions and organs. Therefore, the question here is to establish how the insertion of such a horizontal consumer integration provision in the TFEU may directly impact on the functioning and activities of the European Union and indirectly on the work of its member countries in selecting the most appropriate instruments for enforcing EU measures and actions. Or, to say it more precisely, the question is if the horizontal consumer integration clause in Article 12 of the TFEU can lead (or not) to a better equilibrium in the EU between consumer protection and economic efficiency.[7]

Some EU lawyers and, though only implicitly, also the EU Commission in its Agenda of 2012 for a European Consumer Policy,[8] seem to suggest that the consumer integration clause of Article 12 of the TFEU operates as an instrument primarily aimed at helping the enforcement of the goals of Article 3 (3) of the TEU in all EU acts and activities, in particular the goals of a competitive social market economy[9] aiming at full employment and social progress as well as a high

6 Amplius on this provision, see Steve Weatherill, *EU Consumer Law and Policy* (Cheltenham: Edward Elgar Publishing, 2005), p. 18 ff.

7 On the necessity to find an equilibrium between consumer protection and economic efficiency, see Hans-Wolfgang Michlitz, Norbert Reich, Peter Rott, *Understanding EU Consumer Law* (Mortsel: Intersentia, 2009), ch. I; Thierry Bourgoignie, 'Vers un droit européen de la consommation: unifié, harmonisé, codifié ou fragmenté?' (2005) 46 *Cahiers de droit*, pp.153–174.

8 The text of the Agenda of 2012 is available at: https://ec.europa.eu/info/live-work-travel-eu/consumers_en

9 See *ex multis* Dragana Damjanovic, 'The EU market rules as social market rules: why the EU can be a social market economy' (2013) 50 *Common Market Law Review*, p. 1685 ff; Fausto Pocar, 'Gli obiettivi dell'Europa nel nuovo Trattato: un compromesso tra luci e ombre' (2007) 4 *Guida al diritto*, p. 8 ff.

level of protection and improvement of the environment.[10] But this is a view that can hardly be updated, at least if one not only looks at the very inclusion of the HCC in the TFEU, but also at the language used in Article 12, which is significantly weaker than that of Article 3 of the TEU.[11] One may not be sure, nevertheless, if such a comparison has any positive sense. For example, Article 169 of the TFEU (formerly Article 153 of the EC) on consumer protection refers (though indirectly) to the objectives of Article 3 (3) of the TEU,[12] while Article 114 of the TFUE on approximation of laws speaks of 'consumer protection', not of a 'high level of consumer protection' like Article 169 of the TFUE. Yet, analogous wording to that of Article 169 of the TFEU can be found in Article 38 of the EU Charter of Fundamental Rights (EUCFR) regarding the fundamental rights and freedoms of consumers.[13] It seems highly controversial that the use of adjectives such as high, proper, vulnerable[14] etc. may have any practical effect since the both the TFEU and TEU employs these words rather freely or generically.

If we commence from the usually recognized explanation of the role of the consumer integration clause in the TFEU as an enforcement instrument of the goals embodied in Article 3 (3) of the TEU,[15] it then follows that the consumer

10 See e.g. J. Stuyck, E.Terryn, 'Le droit européen de la consommation (développements récents)' (2007) 143 *Journal de droit européen*, p. 257; F. Chaltiel, 'Le droit européen de la protection du consommateur' (2007) 197 *LPA* 2, p. 5. POCAR.

11 Article 3 (3) of the TEU reads as follows: 'The Union shall establish an internal market. It shall work for the sustainable development of Europe based on balanced economic growth and price stability, a highly competitive social market economy, aiming at full employment and social progress, and a high level of protection and improvement of the quality of the environment. It shall promote scientific and technological advance. It shall combat social exclusion and discrimination, and shall promote social justice and protection, equality between women and men, solidarity between generations and protection of the rights of the child. It shall promote economic, social and territorial cohesion, and solidarity among Member States. It shall respect its rich cultural and linguistic diversity, and shall ensure that Europe's cultural heritage is safeguarded and enhanced'. For a commentary, see e.g. Jean-Claude Piris, *The Lisbon Treaty: A Legal and Political Analysis* (Cambridge: CUP, 2010), pp. 72–73.

12 Amplius, see e.g. François-Xavier Priollaud, David Siritzky, *Le Traité de Lisbonne* (Paris: La Documentation Française, 2008), p. 281; Charles Twigg-Flesner, *A Cross–Border Only Regulation for Consumer Transaction in the EU: A Fresh Approach to EU Consumer Law* (New York: Springer, 2012), p. 90 ff; Francesco Seatzu, 'Politica dei consumatori nell'Unione europea' (2014) *Digesto delle Discipline Privatistiche-Sezione Commerciale*, pp. 444–45; M. Combet, 'Le renouvellement des sources du droit processuel de la consommation par le droit de l'Union européenne' (2013) 402 *Les Petites Affiches*, pp. 186–187.

13 Amplius, see Peter J. Oliver, *Oliver on Free Movement of Goods in the European Union* (Oxford: OUP, 2010), p. 2292.

14 See Lisa Waddington, 'Vulnerable and confused: the protection of "vulnerable" consumers under EU Law' (2013) 6 *European Law Review*, pp. 757–782.

15 See, apart from the authors quoted above, in note 9, M. Jagielska, M. Jagielski, 'Are consumer rights human rights?', in J. Devenney, M. Kenn (eds.), *European Consumer Protection: Theory and Practice* (Cambridge: CUP, 2012), pp. 336–353; Jarmila Lazikova, 'The consumer policy in the EU Law' (2016) V *EU Agrarian Law*,

integration clause itself is a source of neither additional integration powers nor goals conferred to it. This, ultimately, is the conclusion that could be inferred from a systematic reading of the TFEU and TEU that collocate common integration objectives into the TEU as common provisions and specify EU competences in the social and economic context in the TFEU. Provisions possessing general application pertain to the introductory part of the TFEU named 'Principles', which not only encompasses rules of a generally operative character like 'categories' (Articles 2 to 6) but even provisions which rules must be taken into consideration in all EU actions and policies and which also comprise the consumer integration clause.

The insertion under the 'Principles' immediately leads to the crucial query of whether EU general principles that possess direct exclusionary effect might be involved.[16] Far from being purely academic, this query has significant practical importance, given that the answer depends on, for instance, if and to what extent 'EU integration' clauses might be used in a dispute to hinder the application of a conflicting normative act. The provisions of Article 10 of the TFEU on non-discrimination on the grounds of racial and ethnic origin, sex, belief, age, disability or sexual orientation faithfully mirror such general principles as developed by the CJEU in a well-established case-law.[17] The same conclusion applies to Article 8 of the TFEU on equality between women and men. Non-discrimination and equality, nevertheless, are indicated in other TFEU Articles so that the acknowledgment as general principles cannot be desumed from their insertion in the introductory Title of the TFEU which the EU institutions and organs must aim to. The aim, overall recognition and normative content of these legal principles are so unconditional that they may be referred to within the EU legal order as possessing a horizontal direct effect.

In sharp contrast, the provisions of Article 12 of the TFEU, promotion of a high level of consumer protection, are legally indeterminate, as can be inferred in particular from the circumstance that, similarly to the provisions of Article 169 of the TFEU, such provisions encompass neither specific objectives, nor well

available at: https://www.degruyter.com/downloadpdf/j/eual.2016.5.issue-1/eual-2016-0003/eual-2016-0003.pdf

16 The literature on the subject of EU general principles is immense. See among others Koenraad Lenaerts, José Antonio Gutiérrez-Fons, 'The constitutional allocation of powers and general principles of EU law' (2010) 47 *Common Market Law Review*, pp. 1629–1669; Constanze Semmelmann, 'General principles in EU law between a compensatory role and an intrinsic value' (2013) 19 *European Law Journal*, pp. 457–487; Takis Tridimas, *The General Principles of EU Law* (Oxford: OUP, 2006).

17 See e.g. Mónica Martínez López-Sáez, 'The Principle of Non-Discrimination on The Grounds of Age: Recent Developments in European Law in Relation to the Rights of the Elderly', available at: https://s3.amazonaws.com/academia.edu.documents/39518409/NON_DISCRIM_AGE._MonicaMartinez.UniValencia.Spain..pdf?AWSAccessKeyId=AKIAIWOWYYGZ2Y53UL3A&Expires=1523447731&Signature=7CdjmZjxRmIlRsw9uuDIvb4QutM%3D&response-content-disposition=inline%3B%20filename%3DTHE_PRINCIPLE_OF_NON-DISCRIMINATION_ON_T.pdf

determined legal duties.[18] Moreover, and equally significantly, the equivalent of these provisions in the EUCFR has the nature not of subjective and actionable rights, but of general principles. Here, of course, the reference is to Article 38 of the EUCFR, which seeks to protect consumers, and that, like Article 37 of the EUCFR on environmental protection, has been drafted as one of the *parents pauvres* of the Charter,[19] e.g., more as a policy requirement rather than as an individual, subjective right.[20]

Article 12 therefore does not grant an actionable subjective right to EU citizens. In other words, it does not produce a direct effect on individuals or member countries. Altogether, the language used in the consumer horizontal clause is not precise enough to allow a classification of it as a general legal principle.[21] There is, thus, no point in entertaining rich hopes of the consumer horizontal clause legitimizing, for instance, the consumer or consumer representative organizations to derive any specific positive claims from the EU, member countries or directly from producers of goods or service providers. Thus, it is highly questionable that the horizontal consumer clause can function as 'trait d'union' between the economic and social sphere provided for in the TEU and the objectives of Article 3 of the TEU. The ultimate and most relevant consequence of this is that it is necessary to see more distinctly for which purpose and in which specific circumstances the consumer mainstreaming clause is referred to by the EU organs and institutions.

III The practical meaning of the horizontal consumer clause

The initial focus of this paragraph will be the European Economic and Social Committee (EESC) Report of the Single Market Observatory on the horizontal clause in consumer protection policy. Here, the EESC through its Rapporteur Bernardo Hernández Bataller formulated the belief that: 'The horizontal clause must be applied to the broad fields and overall architecture of the new Europe 2020 EU

18 For the interpretation of Article 169 of the TFEU as not having usually a direct effect, see e.g. *El Corte Inglés* v. *Riverro* (C–192/94, 20–23) relating to the omission of the transposition of a directive, where the Court states that a consumer is not entitled to base on the directive itself a right of action against a lender who is a private person following in the supply of goods or provision of services and assert that right before a national court.

19 We borrowed this expression from Nicolas de Sadeleer, *EU Environmental Law and the Internal Market* (Oxford: OUP, 2014), p. 109 ff.

20 Article 38 of the Charter reads as follows: 'Union policies shall ensure a high level of consumer protection'. For a commentary, see Steve Weatherill, 'Consumer Protection', in Steve Peers, Tamara Hervey, Jeff Kenner, Angela Ward (eds.), *The EU Charter of Fundamental Rights: A Commentary* (Oxford: Hart Publishing, 2014), p. 1005 ff, who also stresses, at p. 1025, that: 'the substance of Article 38 is already to be found in Articles 12, 114 (3) and 169 of the TFEU'. See also Yves Picod, *Droit de la consummation* (Paris: Dalloz, 2015), p. 100 ff.

21 See also D. Leczykiewicz, S. Weatherill, above n. 2, p. 416, stating that: 'the exact legal consequences of Article 12 of the TFEU … as there are too many linkages between horizontal and flanking policies, such as environmental, health and consumer policies as well as between these policies and the internal market, are rather unclear'.

socio-economic governance, so that the consumer is placed at the centre of EU policies in a more integrated, coordinated approach, supporting the proactive and preventive approach of the horizontal clause'.[22] Joaquín Almunia, formerly European Commissioner for Competition Policy, confirmed such a belief in his speech at the Spanish Competition Authority (CNC) of 15 March 2010, when he claimed that: 'Article 12 of the TFEU provides the EU Commission with the legal base to ensure that the provisions of Articles 81 and 82 of the TEC [Articles 101 and 102 of the TFEU] cover the interests of consumers'.[23] The study of Professor Diego Fernandez Arroyo *Consumer Protection in Private International Relationships* was even more straightforward: '*Article 12 of the TFEU constitutes* the basis for the extraordinary development of protective European regulation, which does not prevent Member States from being even more rigorous in their protective efforts'.[24]

Although not expressly stipulated in the EESC Report, it is fairly clear that the horizontal consumer clause encapsulated in Article 12 imposes not only an obligation on EU institutions (particularly the Commission, the Council and European Parliament for their legislative functions), but also on Member States to integrate consumer protection objectives when implementing existing EU acts and measures. Incidentally, this is so notwithstanding that the opposite conclusion might be inferred from the explicit and exclusive reference to the 'Union policies and activities' in Article 12. The obligation on Member States derives from the more general legal duty explicitly recalled in the text of Article 12 to integrate consumer protection objectives in the EU as a whole. This obligation entails the transposition into national law of EU secondary legislation reflecting or implementing the consumer protection's integration requirement. Moreover, if interpreted in combination with the duty of sincere cooperation, it also entails for Member States to refrain from actions that could frustrate the future achievement and observance of the EU consumer protection principles and aims, even outside concrete EU secondary legislation. In this case, omission to abide by the above-named obligation should, in principle, legitimize any claim against infringement. Moreover, such an action might prove difficult in several circumstances. The major challenge might lie in the difficulty of reviewing an omission, in violation of the duty in Article 12, to reconcile and integrate the consumer protection aims identified at EU level.

IV The EU Commission's approach to the horizontal consumer clause

It has been widely claimed that in the post-Lisbon era the EU Commission has focused time and energy on the pursuit of consumer protection objectives.[25] The

22 See Bernardo Hernández Bataller, above n. 4.

23 Available at: http://ec.europa.eu/competition/speeches/index_speeches_by_the_commissioner.html

24 See Diego Fernandez Arroyo, 'Consumer Protection in Private International Relationships', in Karen B. Brown, David V. Snyder (eds.), *General Reports of the XVIIIth Congress of the International Academy of Comparative Law* (Amsterdam: Springer, 2011), p. 145.

25 See e.g. Geraint Howells, Christian Twigg-Flesner, Thomas Wilhelmsson, *Rethinking EU Consumer Law* (Oxford: Routledge, 2017), ch. 1.

reason behind this claim is generally the following: the publishing of the so called 'European consumer agenda' of 2012 (the 'Agenda of 2012') that identifies the priority measures indispensable to empower consumers and to increase their participation.[26] The Agenda outlines the strategic vision on consumer policy with more than sixty action points grouped around four pillars: enhancing knowledge of consumer rights; enhancing consumer safety; strengthening the enforcement of consumer rules and integrating consumer interests into key sectoral policies.[27]

Yet, although this is overall quite correct, it is also true that the pursuit of these priorities did not lead the EU Commission to the withdrawal of its traditional market-oriented approach but to an adjustment of the pursuit of the consumer protection objectives with the purpose of competitiveness and macroeconomic balance.[28] In this respect, one can recall that the EU Commission has continued its consumer protection agenda in its own and long established manner (e.g. as envisaged and carried out in the Consumer Policy Strategy of the Commission for the years 2002–2006).[29] According to the Consumer Policy Strategy, 'the development of consumer policy at EU level *constitutes an essential requirement for* the progressive establishment of the internal market'.[30] The EU Commission's recent report on the results of its review of EU consumer law, the 'Fitness Check'[31] confirms, though indirectly, the above-recalled approach when it indicates the introduction of a number of targeted legislative amendments for reducing divergences in implementation and to ensure a better knowledge of all fundamental rights and obligations under EU consumer law as priority strands for future action.

Therefore, it cannot be claimed that the measures indicated above do not aim at a high level of consumer protection, as requested by the HCC. In order to better understand this, one can refer, in particular, to the above mentioned suggestion of extending the level of protection under the Consumer Rights Directive and to that of expanding and strengthening remedies for consumers, including by developing EU-wide rights to individual remedies, improving injunction procedures

26 See Miriam Hartlapp, Julia Metz, Christian Rauh, *Which Policy for Europe?: Power and Conflict Inside the European Commission* (Oxford: OUP, 2014), ch. 7.

27 See above n. 8.

28 Amplius, see Steve Weatherill, 'Consumer protection under EU law "is not absolute": yes, but be careful!' (2012) 8 *European Review of Contract Law*, pp. 221–233.

29 *Consumer Policy Strategy 2002–2006* COM (2002) 208 final6.

30 Ibid.

31 The 'Fitness Check' covered the following consumer law Directives (the 'Directives'): Directive 93/13/EEC of 5 April 1993 on unfair terms in consumer contracts; Directive 98/6/EC of 16 February 1998 on consumer protection in the indication of the prices of the products offered to consumers; Directive 1999/44/EC of 25 May 1999 on certain aspects of the sale of consumer goods and associated guarantees (the 'Sales and Guarantees Directive'); Directive 2005/29/EC of 11 May 2005 concerning unfair business-to-consumer commercial practices in the internal market (the 'Unfair Commercial Practices Directive'); Directive 2006/114/EC of 12 December 2006 concerning misleading and comparative advertising; and Directive 2009/22/EC of 23 April 2009 on injunctions for the protection of consumers' interests. The Commission also published a separate report evaluating Directive 2011/83/EC of 25 October 2011 on consumer rights (the 'Consumer Rights Directive').

and analysing ongoing assessments of collective redress across the EU. However, it remains doubtful whether these and analogous measures can be considered as bringing change against the existing consumer rights. In fact instead of stressing that consumers are not commodities and should never be considered as such and, furthermore, that fundamental consumer rights cannot make concession to the interest in economic growth, the large majority of afore-indicated measures aim at better adaptation of consumer protection to single market priorities, namely at giving a positive contribution to competitiveness and economic growth.

Analogously, a hypothetical assumption that the EU Commission would, in an alternative manner, with greater emphasis on consumer protection, conduct an impact assessment of the suggested legislation seems to neglect the circumstance that the Commission had already, in the early 2000s, enacted the method of integrated impact assessment that, additionally to economic impacts, also supervised social impact of prospective legislation.[32] And still before the entry into force of the Treaty of Lisbon with its Article 12 of the TFEU, the EU Commission had delivered updated 'Impact Assessment Guidelines', imposing the examination of the impact of the suggested measures explicitly on consumers' health, consumers' information and consumers' ability to benefit from the single market, i.e. essentially those principles that, either implicitly or explicitly, are indicated in the horizontal consumer clause.[33] Thus, it is not difficult to conclude that the potential for transformation represented by the horizontal consumer clause has so far endured intact.

V The horizontal consumer clause in the CJEU's case law and EU's legislative practice

The CJEU, too, has failed to contribute to the horizontal consumer clause becoming an instrument for balancing fundamental consumer rights and EU single market priorities. Yet, this is at the least what emerges from the fact that the CJEU only worked directly with the horizontal consumer clause in its case-law on one occasion. In the Case T 224/10 *Association Belge de Consommateurs test-achats* v. *Commission*, where Article 12 of the TFUE was exceptionally referred to, it did so in relation to a merger control affecting consumer interests with respect to price and to service as follows: 'under Article 153(2) of the EC, which essentially has the same wording as Article 12 of the TFEU, consumer-protection requirements must be taken into account in defining and implementing other EU policies and activities'.[34] Incidentally, a similar approach to the horizontal consumer clause of Article 12 is also found in the Advocate General Wahl's most recent Opinion of 21 March 2018 on the Case C-109/17 *Bankia SA* v. *Juan*

32 On this issue, see Miriam Hartlapp, Julia Metz, Christian Rauh, note 20, ch. 7.

33 For further references see the EU Commission's official webpage at: https://ec.europa.eu/info/law/law-making-process/planning-and-proposing-law/impact-assessments_en

34 *Association belge des consommateurs test-achats ASBL* v *Commission* (Case T-224/10) [2011] ECR II-7177, para. 43.

Carlos Marí Merino, Juan Pérez Gavilán, María de la Concepción Marí Merin. [35] Once more, this is a proof that the CJEU has never been consumer-insensitive, but also (and more importantly here) that it has not altered its approach due to the insertion of the consumer horizontal clause into the TFEU.

Albeit indirectly, such a conclusion is confirmed, respectively, by the reference of the CJEU to 'consumer welfare' as a goal of EU competition law and policy in various judicial decisions,[36] and by the lack of any use of Article 12 of the TFEU in the CJEU's prevailing case-law on competition law as a possible tool for clarifying the meaning of the notion of 'consumer welfare', which is far from being clear, as correctly pointed out by several authors including Pieter Kalbfleisch[37] and Victoria Daskalova.[38]

To conclude, a survey of the EU's legislative practice easily reveals that the EU legislator, after the insertion of Art 12 of the TFEU, has never mentioned the horizontal consumer clause. Indeed, this is true with the exception of the Proposal for a Regulation of the European Parliament and of the Council on a consumer programme 2014–2020 that refers to Article 12 only *en passant* by stating that: 'Integrating consumer interests into all Union policies, in accordance with Article 12 TFEU, should be given high priority',[39] and also, and more recently, of the European Parliament resolution of 11 June 2013 on a new agenda for European Consumer Policy, which stipulates generically that: 'consumer protection requirements shall be taken into account in defining and implementing other Union policies and activities'.[40] This all being said, the omitted reference to the HCC should, nevertheless, not lead to the conclusion that the EU legislator has deliberately excluded consumer protection considerations in the definition and

35 The text of the Advocate General's Opinion is available at: https://eur-lex.europa.eu/legal-content/EN/TXT/?qid=1524136158416&uri=CELEX:62017CC0109#Footref7

36 See e.g. Case C-95/04 *P British Airways v Commission* [2007] ECR I-2331, para. 106 (where the CJEU however rejected the exclusive consumer welfare approach); Joined Cases C-501, C-513, C-515 & C-519/06 *P GlaxoSmithKline Services v Commission* [2009] ECR I-9291, para. 63; Case C-52/09 *Konkurrenverket v. TeliaSonera Sverige AB* [2011] ECR 527, paras. 21–24; Case T-321/05 *AstraZeneca AB and AstraZeneca plc v European Commission* [2010] ECR II-2805, para. 804; Case C-468/06–478/01 *Sot Lelos Kai Sia EE v GlaxoSmithKline AEVE* [2008] ECR I-7139, paras. 56–57. On the subject, see *ex multis* B. van der Esch, 'The Principles of Interpretation Applied by the Court of Justice of the European Communities and their Relevance for the Scope of the EEC Competition Rules' (2001) *Fordham International Law Journal*, p. 366 ff.

37 See P. Kalbfleisch, 'Aiming For Alliance: Competition Law & Consumer Welfare' (2011) *Journal of European Competition Law & Practice*, p. 108, stressing that the TEU contains no explicit reference to consumer welfare as such.

38 See V. Daskalova, 'Consumer welfare in EU competition law: what is it (not) about?' (2015) 11 *The Competition Law Review*, pp 131–160.

39 Proposal for a Regulation of the European Parliament and of the Council on a consumer programme 2014–2020, COM (2011) 707 final, p. 9.

40 European Parliament resolution of 11 June 2013 on a new agenda for European Consumer Policy (2012/2133(INI)).

enforcement of its activities and policies. More likely, and straightforward, it should lead to conclude that the EU legislator did so only prompted by a lack of confidence in the possibilities offered in this sense by Article 12 as a result of its substantially non justiciable character.

VI The potential utility of the horizontal consumer clause for building a space in Europe for consumers

The discussion above makes it sufficiently evident that the horizontal consumer clause in Article 12 of the TFEU has so far had very little impact on the development of a consumer protection system in the EU; in fact it has not contributed in any way to the evolution of the concept of the consumer agenda as one of the factors of an equitable functioning of the EU single market. The widely celebrated Consumer Agenda of 2012, too, has its main focus on the EU's economic growth strategy. Thus, the necessity for introducing a comprehensive normative framework for consumer protection is not just a social must, it is also an indispensable requirement for the EU economy. Therefore, it does not come as a surprise that this Agenda does not substantially mention Article 12 of the TFEU or the HCC, even though it indicates the reinforcement of consumer safety and the improvement of enforcement and securing redresses for consumers as primary *raisons d'être* for why such a programming document was adopted by the EU Commission.

More in general, it can be observed that the recognition of the HCC as a driving force of change demands that there must be absolute parity of economic and consumer protection policy on the EU plane. Clearly, all this implies a far more prominent role of the issues of consumer welfare, enhancing consumer information, etc. than just possible exceptions to the four fundamental EU market freedoms in case they may justify themselves as the object of general interest.

To accomplish this parity of consumer protection and market growth imperatives of the EU is by all means a much more ambitious and wider issue than that of a more efficient enforcement of the HCC. However, more active employ of the horizontal consumer clause can challenge the CJEU's case-law and the EU Commission's programming documents and normative proposals, in particular if the principles of the HCC are employed as interpretative tools of the EU normative acts and in the ruling on their validity. Nevertheless, in order to stimulate EU institutions and organs to relinquish their long-standing pre-Treaty of Lisbon approaches, namely to lead them to full use of the intrinsic potential of the HCC, the policy-framing character of Article 12 of the TFEU, that makes it inapt as a basis for judicial review of the substance of measures,[41] has to be modified, otherwise it is hard to envisage a reason why they would act differently.

The enhanced language of the horizontal consumer clause should not necessarily entail its complete revision. Any modification of EU treaty rules imposes ratification by all member countries that clearly might be hard to obtain if the

41 For this expression, see Steve Weatherill, *EU Consumer Law and Policy* (Cheltenham: Edward Elgar publishing, 2013), p. 16.

rephrasing of the horizontal consumer clause is too extreme. Therefore, it would seem desirable for the advocates of consumers rights and freedoms to rephrase the HCC in order to ensure the interests of EU vulnerable consumers always prevail over business interests driven by the single market's four fundamental freedoms. Such a modification would not appear achievable in practice and also seems to sit in contrast with the balancing approach of the consumer sustainable economy. As already indicated above, the final objective is the parity between consumer protection and the market's economic imperatives, not a radical *revirement* of the market oriented consumer policy to consumer oriented market policy.

A possible solution could be inferred from the horizontal environmental clause contained in Article 11 of the TFEU for the following reasons: 1) only the horizontal environmental clause is 'clothed in highly imperative words'[42] *alias* demands that environmental requirements 'must' be integrated while the other mainstream clauses of the TFEU (including the horizontal consumer clause of Article 12) only demand that non-market requirements 'shall' be integrated. Incidentally, far from being of little importance, this implies that Article 11 of the TFUE does not merely require the deployment of best efforts or the consideration of certain matters, it requires the integration of environmental requirements in all EU policies and activities[43]; 2) a second reason is that Article 11 of the TFEU explicitly indicates sustainable development as an overarching objective; 3) a third, but no less important, reason is that Article 11 of the TFEU gives priority to environmental protection over other TFEU goals[44]; 4) a fourth reason is that Article 11 is crucial to the interpretation of EU law as a whole. This point has been well captured by Gracia Marín Durán and Elisa Morgera who also highlight the main consequence that arises from it, namely the existence of a duty on the ECJEU to opt for an interpretation of EU (primary and secondary) law that is either neutral or positive on the environmental interests involved; a fifth reason is that the horizontal environmental clause has led to practical changes in the EU institutions' decision-making processes. Our reference here is in particular to the European Commission's recent undertaking to carry out environmental impact assessments when making proposals that may have significant environmental

42 We borrowed this expression from Thomas Schumacher, 'The environmental integration clause in Article 6 of the EU Treaty: prioritising environmental protection' (2001) *Environmental Law Review*, pp. 29–43.

43 See Julian Nowag, 'Genesis, Purpose and Overarching Significance of Article 11 TFUE', in Beate Sjåfjell, Anja Wiesbrock (eds.), *The Greening of European Business Under EU Law: Taking Article 11 TFEU Seriously* (Abingdon: Routledge, 2014), p. 27. See also E. Psychogiopoulou, *The Integration of Cultural Considerations in the EU Law and Policies* (Boston: Martinus Nijhoff, 2017), pp. 68–73 and Gracia Marín Durán, Elisa Morgera, *Environmental Integration in the EU's External Relations: Beyond* (Oxford: Hart, 2012), p. 29, who go even further and stress that: 'As to legal strength, Article 11 TFEU is clearly framed in mandatory terms ("must be integrated"), and ECJ case law also points to an interpretation of this provision as imposing a legal obligation'.

44 See Thomas Schumacher, above n. 35, pp. 29–43.

implications and to the European Commission's introduction of a green star to label actions with potential environmental impacts.[45]

Of course, the above-indicated solution, per se, cannot guarantee a fully equivalent treatment of consumer goals and rights on the one hand and EU single market freedoms on the other hand in all the EU Commission's and CJEU's activities. It is, nevertheless, almost sure that if it is not sufficient to produce the required accommodation, then the European Union would have to accept that it is not adjustable in any easy manner and a much more extensive rearrangement, for instance a drastic reduction of the integration principles that have been proliferated under the Treaty of Lisbon,[46] would be indispensable to realize the change.

45 Ibidem.

46 Amplius, see Jan H. Jans, 'Stop the Integration Principle?' (2010) 33 *Fordham International Law Journal*, p. 1547, stressing that: 'the proliferation of integration principles brought about by the Lisbon Treaty has resulted in the weakening of the current environmental integration principle and could, ultimately, even act as a "Trojan horse" and lead to a weakening, or even a downgrading, of environmental standards'.

8 Animal welfare

Julinda Beqiraj[1]

Introduction

Promotion of animal welfare has progressively made its way into European Union (EU) policy and law and, as a result of the Treaty of Lisbon amendments, is now an EU stated value enshrined within the Treaty itself. Before the Treaty of Lisbon, in the absence of an express recognition of the relevance of animal welfare, concerns about animal wellbeing were occasionally addressed under a number of explicit treaty objectives, such as the common agriculture policy (CAP), the internal market, the common commercial policy, etc. Now, Article 13 of the Treaty on the Functioning of the European Union (TFEU) recognizes that animals are sentient beings and affirms that the Union and the Member States *shall pay full regard* to the welfare requirements of animals '*in formulating and implementing* the Union's agriculture, fisheries, transport, internal market, research and technological development and space policies' (emphasis added). However, this should be pursued while respecting the legislative or administrative provisions and customs of the Member States relating to, in particular, religious rites, cultural traditions and regional heritage.

After outlining the evolution of EU law and policy on animal welfare, this chapter addresses the question of the significance and impact of the mainstreaming provision in Article 13 TFEU. From a legislation-making perspective, the chapter will analyse and discuss the scope of the powers of the Commission to set out policy directions and develop secondary legislation on animal welfare, whether by mainstreaming animal welfare considerations in pre-legislation impact assessments, or by carefully drafting the rationales for new proposed legislation to accommodate animal welfare concerns. From the Member States' perspective, the chapter will also discuss their scope of action in promoting and protecting animal welfare through measures resulting in restrictions to trade, in light of the new Article 13 TFEU. From a judicial review perspective, the chapter will consider the role and powers of the Court of Justice of the EU (CJEU) in establishing the validity of EU secondary legislation related, directly or indirectly, to the promotion and protection of animal welfare, as well as in interpreting and applying EU law.

1 Dr Julinda Beqiraj is Associate Senior Research Fellow at the Bingham Centre for the Rule of Law, British Institute of International and Comparative Law (BIICL).

Finally, the chapter will consider possible external implications relating to compliance with international trade obligations in the WTO framework. It will conclude with some general considerations on the significance of the protection of animal welfare within the overall architecture of the Treaty of Lisbon.

1 Evolution of EC/EU animal welfare protection before Lisbon

1.1 Normative evolution – primary law

The Treaty of Amsterdam annexed a Protocol on Animal Welfare to the European Community Treaty,[2] which introduced for the first time, with effect from 1 May 1999, legal obligations on both institutions and the Member States to have regard to animal welfare in key areas of European law and policy. Prior to the introduction of the Protocol, there had been unsuccessful attempts to include a treaty provision on animal protection and welfare.[3] The only other relevant document had been the Declaration on the Welfare of Animals, included as an annex to the Treaty on European Union in 1992, which contained a statement of the political intent to give full consideration to animal welfare when formulating and implementing legislation in specific areas of EU activity.

Apart from these, the formal legal status of animals under European Community (EC) law was equivalent to that of goods or agricultural products. The only significant language relating to animal welfare in the EC Treaty was incorporated in Article 30 (now Article 36 TFEU). This allows Member States to introduce prohibitions or restrictions on imports or exports on the grounds of protecting (among other non-trade concerns) the health and life of animals, provided that this is not used as a means of arbitrary discrimination or a disguised restriction on trade. However, in practice, this enabling provision has proved of limited application because it has been interpreted restrictively to cover mainly measures related to the conservation of species rather than welfare-related measures motivated by the desire to mitigate unnecessary suffering of animals.[4]

2 Treaty establishing the European Community (consolidated version) – Protocol (No 33) on protection and welfare of animals [2006] OJ C 321 E. Analogously to Article 13 TFEU, it establishes that 'the High Contracting Parties desiring to ensure improved protection and respect for the welfare of animals as sentient beings' have agreed that 'In formulating and implementing the Community's agriculture, transport, internal market and research policies, the Community and the Member States shall pay full regard to the welfare requirements of animals, while respecting the legislative or administrative provisions and customs of the Member States relating in particular to religious rites, cultural traditions and regional heritage.' See Tara Camm and David Bowles, 'Animal welfare and the Treaty of Rome – a legal analysis of the protocol on animal welfare and welfare standards in the European Union' (2000) *Journal of Environmental Law* 197.

3 Diane Ryland and Angus Nurse, 'Mainstreaming after Lisbon: advancing animal welfare in the EU internal market' (2013) *European Energy and Environmental Law Review* 101.

4 Case C-1/96 *The Queen v Minister of Agriculture, Fisheries and Food, ex parte Compassion in World Farming Ltd* ECLI:EU:C:1998:113.

1.2 Normative evolution: secondary legislation

Despite this very limited legal basis, a considerable amount of animal welfare legislation has been adopted at the EC/EU level prior to the Treaty of Lisbon. The relevant legislation has emerged via other objectives within the EC Treaty, such as the articles concerning the common agricultural policy, the internal market, the common commercial policy, health and consumer protection and the environment.[5] Three main groups of legislation currently in force concerning or related to animal welfare can be discerned.

Firstly, a core group of legislation concerns the wellbeing of farm animals, whether when kept on the farm, during transport or at the time of killing. Legislation in this respect was introduced prior to the Lisbon Treaty despite some aspects taking effect more recently – such as prohibition of battery cage use for hens, or barren individual cages for pregnant sows. The Council Directive 98/58/EC on the protection of animals kept for farming purposes provides the general minimum horizontal legal framework for the protection of all farm animals kept for the production of food, wool, skin or fur, and for other farming purposes – particularly animals in intensive stock-farming systems. The Directive is informed by the Council of Europe (CoE) European Convention for the Protection of Animals kept for Farming Purposes, which was made part of EU law through Council Decision 78/923/EEC. Specific legislation adopted thereafter addresses standards for the keeping of calves,[6] pigs,[7] laying hens[8] and broilers,[9] as well as the protection of animals during transport[10] and rules on slaughtering.[11] The legal basis for the adoption of such legislation hinges mainly upon the provisions on the

5 See on the environmental protection Beate Sjåfjell, 'The environmental integration principle: a necessary step towards policy coherence for sustainability' in this Volume.

6 Council Directive 2008/119/EC of 18 December 2008 laying down minimum standards for the protection of calves, repealing Directive 91/629/EEC [2008] OJ L 10/7.

7 Council Directive 2008/120/EC of 18 December 2008 laying down minimum standards for the protection of pigs [2008] OJ L 47/5; Commission Recommendation (EU) 2016/336 of 8 March 2016 on the application of Council Directive 2008/120/EC laying down minimum standards for the protection of pigs as regards measures to reduce the need for tail-docking [2016] OJ L 62/20.

8 Council Directive 1999/74/EC of 19 July 1999 laying down minimum standards for the protection of laying hens [1999] OJ L 203/53.

9 Council Directive 2007/43/EC of 28 June 2007 laying down minimum rules for the protection of chickens kept for meat production [2007] OJ L 182/19.

10 Council Directive 91/628/EEC of 19 November 1991 on the protection of animals during transport and amending Directives 90/425/EEC and 91/496/EEC [1991] OJ L 340/17; Council Regulation (EC) 1/2005 of 22 December 2004 on the protection of animals during transport and related operations and amending Directives 64/432/EEC and 93/119/EC and Regulation (EC) 1255/97 [2005] OJ L 3/1.

11 Council Directive 93/119/EC of 22 December 1993 on the protection of animals at the time of slaughter or killing [1993] OJ L 340/21; more recently replaced by Council Regulation (EC) 1099/2009 of 24 September 2009 on the protection of animals at the time of killing [2009] OJ L 303/1, in force since 1 January 2013.

common agriculture policy and the establishment of the internal market through ensuring a level playing field for all business operators concerned.

Secondly, EU standards have been developed in relation to animals used for testing and scientific purposes. In these regards, the Cosmetics Directive 76/768/EEC modified by Directive 2003/15/EC provides the regulatory framework for the phasing out of animal testing in the cosmetics industry (for both finished cosmetic products and cosmetic ingredients) and introduces a marketing ban, irrespective of the availability of alternative non-animal tests. The provisions of the two Directives have been incorporated in the Cosmetics Regulation EC 1223/2009 with the purpose of clarifying EU law in this field.[12] Animal tested finished cosmetic products and cosmetic ingredients were banned, respectively, in 2004 and 2009, and since March 2013 no cosmetics tested on animals can be marketed in the EU. As concerns studies conducted on animals, whether for the development or production of new medicines, for physiological studies, for studying environmental effects or for the testing of chemicals or new food additives, the main EU legislative instrument is Directive 2010/63/EU which updated and replaced Directive 86/609/EEC on the protection of animals used for scientific purposes. The new Directive aims to establish the so-called principle of the 'Three Rs', to 'Replace, Reduce and Refine' the use of animals, in EU legislation.

Thirdly, a limited number of EU instruments concerns wild animals, more specifically rules relating to the trade of wild fauna (and flora), and animals kept in zoos.[13] These harmonised standards have emerged via the Treaty articles concerning the realization of a common commercial policy and environmental policy. There is also legislation related to the welfare of wild animals ensuring that hunting or trapping methods are as humane as possible within the European Union and in compliance with international standards. Examples include the Leghold Trap Regulation,[14] which prohibits the use of leghold traps within the EU and the importation of goods and products made from specific animal species originating from countries that use trapping methods that do not meet international standards,[15] and the legislation on trade in seal products. In this latter regard, the first

12 Regulation (EC) 1223/2009 of the European Parliament and of the Council of 30 November 2009 on cosmetic products [2009] OJ L 342/59.

13 Council Regulation (EC) 338/97 of 9 December 1996 on the protection of species of wild fauna and flora by regulating trade therein [1996] OJ L 61/1; Council Directive 1999/22/EC of 29 March 1999 relating to the keeping of wild animals in zoos [1999] OJ L 94/24.

14 Council Regulation (EEC) 3254/91 of 4 November 1991 prohibiting the use of leghold traps in the Community and the introduction into the Community of pelts and manufactured goods of certain wild animal species originating in countries which catch them by means of leghold traps or trapping methods which do not meet international humane trapping standards [1991] OJ L 308/1. The Regulation is complemented by Commission Decision 98/596/EC of 14 October 1998 listing those countries from which specific animal pelts and manufactured goods can be accepted [1998] OJ L 286/56.

15 A proposal for a Directive of the European Parliament and of the Council introducing humane trapping standards other than leghold traps for certain animal species (COM/

piece of legislation is the Seal Pup Directive 83/129/EEC,[16] later extended for an indefinite period by two subsequent directives, which prohibits the importation of products derived from certain seal pups (e.g. fur skins) into the European Union.[17] More recently, Regulation EC 1007/2009 by the European Parliament and the Council on trade in seal products prohibits the importation and marketing of all seal products, with some limited exemptions and derogations.

Legislative achievements for the benefit of animal welfare, whilst welcome, however, have been fragmentary and limited in scope – with a predominant focus on farm animals – and largely uncoordinated, with a lack of coherence in the existing legal and political approach. Very different legal bases have been employed, as already noted, and different objectives have been pursued – common organization of the market (e.g. CAP), harmonization, etc.[18] Accordingly, the EU Animal Action plan 2006–2010 and especially the strategic plan for 2012–2015, adopted under the framework of the Treaty of Lisbon, contemplate the possibility of moving away from a sector based approach (mainly farm sector) towards a crosscutting horizontal approach to animal welfare.

1.3 The Court of Justice case law

How has the Court of Justice construed the role and weight of animal welfare interests – prior to the entry into force of the Treaty of Lisbon – when interpreting and applying EU law or when deciding on the validity of secondary legislation?

1.3.1 Questioning the limits of national legislation on protection of animal welfare

In several cases brought before it, the Court has dealt with the issue of the compatibility between domestic restrictive trade measures aimed at promoting and protecting the welfare of animals and EU legislation in the field of the realization of the common agriculture policy or the establishment of the internal market.

In this regard, the Court has confirmed and applied the principle of preemption, meaning that where community harmonising legislation has completely 'occupied' a certain area, this preempts the possibility for Member States to introduce stricter national standards. The implicit assumption is that the level of

2004/0532 final – COD 2004/0183), was later withdrawn with legal effect on 2 June 2012.

16 Council Directive 83/129/EEC of 28 March 1983 concerning the importation into Member States of skins of certain seal pups and products derived therefrom [1983] OJ L 91/30.

17 Council Directive 85/444/EEC of 27 September 1985 amending Council Directive 83/129/EEC concerning the importation into Member States of skins of certain seal pups and products derived therefrom [1985] OJ L 259/70; Council Directive 89/370/EEC of 8 June 1989 amending Directive 83/129/EEC concerning the importation into Member States of skins of certain seal pups and products derived therefrom [1989] OJ L 163/37.

18 Camm and Bowles (n 2) 199.

protection of animal welfare established through the harmonization legislation sets a balance between animal welfare as an EU interest and the Treaty objective of free trade, which cannot be changed unilaterally through national measures aimed at introducing higher standards of protection of animals. It has been noted that such narrow interpretation, which equates minimum EU legislative standards of animal welfare with total harmonisation, has in practice slowed down the advancement of animal welfare in the EU.[19]

In earlier cases, such as the *Holdijk* case, the Court discussed the possibility for a Member State (the Netherlands) to introduce and maintain unilateral rules on enclosure for fatting calves aimed at protecting animals. It established that in the absence of specific community law on the protection of animals kept for farming purposes, compatibility had to be determined on the basis of general Treaty rules on the free movement of goods and on the common organization of the markets in the agricultural sector.[20] Reference had to be made to the articles on the prohibition of import and export measures amounting to quantitative restrictions on trade or having equivalent effect, and to the derogation provision (incorporated now in Article 36 TFEU) that allows restrictions on free movement of goods aimed at protecting specific legitimate public interests, including the health and life of animals. The Court ignored the argument raised by one of the defendants in the original proceedings that the public interest mentioned in the derogation provision is the 'health' of animals and not their 'wellbeing' – implicitly assuming a broad interpretation of 'health' as including 'welfare'. Instead, it focused only on the fact that the measures at issue did not establish a distinction between domestic trade and export trade such as to provide an advantage for national production. It concluded that 'as it stands at present, Community law does not prevent a Member State from maintaining or introducing unilateral rules concerning the standards which must be observed in the installation of enclosures for fatting calves with a view to protecting the animals' and which apply in a non-discriminatory manner.[21]

With the expansion of EU animal welfare law under the CAP or the internal market rules, the Court has progressively reduced the possibility to maintain restrictions on the free movement of goods by single Member States justified on grounds of the protection of health and life of animals (under Article 36), where European legislation has harmonised the sector. In the *Hedley Lomas* case, the Ministry of Agriculture for England and Wales had refused to issue a license for the export of live sheep to Spain requested by Hedley Lomas on the ground that the treatment of sheep in Spanish slaughterhouses was contrary to the Council Directive on stunning of animals before slaughtering (74/577/EEC).[22] The

19 Ludwig Rasso and Roderic O'Gorman, 'A cock and bull story? Problems with the protection of animal welfare in EU law and some proposed solutions' (2008) *Journal of Environmental Law* 363.

20 Joined Cases C-141/81 to C-143/81 *Gerrit Holdijk and others* ECLI:EU:C:1982:122 para 9.

21 Ibid para 14, 1314.

22 Case C-5/94 *The Queen v Ministry of Agriculture, Fisheries and Food, ex parte Hedley Lomas (Ireland) Ltd.* ECLI:EU:C:1996:205.

Court concluded that the existence of harmonising legislation at the European level prevents a Member State (UK) from relying on Article 36 to justify restrictive measures on exports to secure the results required by that legislation, where a public interest specified in Article 36 (i.e. animal health) is threatened by the failure of another Member State (Spain).[23] According to the Court, this is also the case where the harmonising European legislation, as in *Hedley Lomas*, does not lay down a procedure for monitoring compliance, or any penalties in case of breach of its provisions.[24] On this point, the opinion of Advocate General (AG) Léger differed substantially from the approach of the Court; he considered that there had not been full harmonization in the area of protection of animals regarding their export to other Member States and, therefore, Member States could adopt, in principle, the necessary protection measures under Article 36.[25] However, the AG still questioned the legitimacy of UK's refusal to issue export licenses in the light of Article 36, on the basis of its discretionary character and the extraterritorial purpose. It had not been established that Spain was in breach of its obligations under the Directive and 'a Member State can rely on Article 36 only in order to ensure protection of an interest safeguarded by that article *within its own territory*' (emphasis added).[26] In any case, where recourse to Article 36 is still possible, the relevant measures are only justified provided that they are proportionate to the aim pursued and that the protection objective cannot be achieved as effectively by less restrictive measures – this is often left to national authorities to determine.[27]

The Court has continued to apply the principle of preemption and the corollary inapplicability of Article 36 in subsequent jurisprudence – save when Member States are conferred specific powers to adopt additional restrictions under the harmonization legislation. The *Monsees* case, for instance, concerned the application of Community legislation on maximum journey times and distances for the transport of live animals for slaughter and whether Austria could maintain in place a stricter domestic regime that limited intra-community trade in order to protect the animals.[28] The Court found that the Austrian rules constituted a measure having an equivalent effect to a quantitative restriction on both imports and exports.[29] It reiterated the approach adopted in *Hedley Lomas* that 'While Article 36 allows the maintenance of restrictions on the free movement of goods, justified on grounds of the protection of the health and life of animals, which constitutes a fundamental requirement recognised by Community law, recourse to Article 36 is no longer possible where Community directives provide for harmonisation of the

23 Ibid para 18.
24 Ibid para 19.
25 Case C-5/94 (n 22) Opinion of AG Léger paras 17–21.
26 Ibid paras 24, 31.
27 Ibid para 41. See also Case C-219/07 *Nationale Raad van Dierenkwekers en Liefhebbers VZW, Andibel VZW v Belgische Staat* ECLI:EU:C:2008:353 para 44.
28 Case C-350/97 *Wilfried Monsees v Unabhängiger Verwaltungssenat für Kärnten* ECLI:EU:C:1999:242.
29 Ibid para 23.

measures necessary to achieve the specific objective which would be furthered by reliance upon this provision', i.e. protection of the health and life of animals.[30]

The arguments raised by the parties in the original proceedings and the reasoning of the AG in the case *Compassion in World Farming*, shed some new light on the possible uses of Article 36 for the protection of animals.[31] Although the Court dealt summarily with these arguments, it is worth mentioning them here as they have gained additional weight after the entry into force of the Lisbon Treaty and in light of recent CJEU jurisprudence.[32]

In *Compassion in World Farming*, one of the issues addressed by the Court was whether a Member State may restrict the export of live calves to prevent them from being reared in the veal crate systems used in other Member States that are detrimental to their health and welfare, relying on Article 36 – in particular, on the grounds of 'public morality, public policy or the protection of the health or life of animals'.[33] Interestingly, the applicants raised these justification grounds as distinct from one another (see below section 2.4). AG Léger recalled the case law of the Court regarding the preemption principle and exclusion of recourse to Article 36 resulting therefrom. However, in his view, that exclusion would apply where the harmonised area concerns 'animal welfare' but the 'public morality' and the 'public policy' justifications could still be relied on. In his words, 'a directive might exhaustively harmonize a field concerning the protection of animals but still not pacify pressure groups, which, judging the level of protection adopted to be insufficient, would still be likely to disturb public order.'[34] Accordingly, the presence of the harmonising directive would not be sufficient to rule out completely a defense under Article 36. Moreover, the use of 'public morality' or 'public policy' as a justificatory ground allows overcoming the obstacle of the extraterritorial nature of the restrictive measure, which is not covered by Article 36.[35] While the 'animal health and life' defense aims to ensure protection or avoid mistreatment that takes place in the territory of another Member State (i.e. *Hedley Lomas* case) the offence against 'public morality' or 'public policy' occurs within the State of exportation that adopts the restrictive measure. Such approach creates serious risks of fragmentation and multiplication of obstacles to trade, considering that public morality varies from one Member State to another and that it is primarily for national authorities to determine and define the scope of public morality.[36] Accordingly, in the view of the AG, Article 36 should be strictly interpreted[37]; the mere risk of a reaction in national public opinion against methods that are considered to be cruel towards animals 'cannot constitute measures for meeting a public policy objective within the meaning of Article 36'.[38]

30 Ibid para 24.
31 Case C-1/96 (n 4).
32 See infra jurisprudence related to the Seals case.
33 Case C-1/96 (n 4) para 38.
34 Case C-1/96 (n 4) Opinion of AG Léger delivered on 15 July 1997, para 72.
35 Ibid para 87.
36 Ibid para 102.
37 Ibid para 99.
38 Ibid para 112.

The Court omitted to address in detail the scope of Article 36 and its possible uses to justify measures related to the protection of animals. It summarily ruled out recourse to the public morality and public policy justifications on the basis that national derogation measures 'cannot rely on the views or the behavior of a section of national public opinion'.[39] As it will be discussed later, the public morality argument, however, has been raised successfully, more recently, in relation to (but separate from) animal welfare.

1.3.2 Questioning the validity of EU legislation

In addition to the jurisprudence that determines the limits of national legislation on animal welfare, where such legislation interferes with the Treaty objective of the free movement of goods, the Court has addressed animal welfare issues also form another viewpoint. It has dealt with the question of the status of 'animal welfare' under the Treaty– i.e. whether it is 'a principle', 'an interest', 'an objective', or 'a requirement' – and the extent to which lack of consideration thereof can undermine the validity of secondary legislation. The approach of the CJEU in this regard has been very restrictive.

In the *Jippes* case, the validity of Community legislation on measures for the control of foot-and-mouth disease in animals was questioned for being contrary to animal welfare.[40] Such Community legislation[41] introduced a general ban on the use of foot-and-mouth disease vaccines and provided for limited exceptions. These included emergency vaccination when the disease has been confirmed and threatens to become extensive, provided that it extends in limited geographical areas, and suppressive vaccination of animals in identified holdings situated in a defined area, which is carried out in conjunction with pre-emptive killing. Exceptions are intended to bring about an urgent reduction of the amount of virus circulating and the risk of virus spreading beyond the perimeters of the area. The logic of such legislation is that a non-vaccination policy accompanied by sanitary slaughter, where an outbreak occurs, better serves the purpose of circumventing the spread of the disease considering that vaccination is not effective in all cases and may facilitate the spread of the disease. Moreover, the available scientific tests at the

39 Case C-1/96 (n 4) para 67.

40 Case C-189/01 *H. Jippes, Afdeling Groningen van de Nederlandse Vereniging tot Bescherming van Dieren and Afdeling Assen en omstreken van de Nederlandse Vereniging tot Bescherming van Dieren v Minister van Landbouw, Natuurbeheer en Visserij* ECLI:EU:C:2001:420.

41 Article 13 of Council Directive 85/511/EEC of 18 November 1985 introducing Community measures for the control of foot-and-mouth disease [1985] OJ L 315/11 (as amended by Council Directive 90/423/EEC of 26 June 1990 [1990] OJ L 224/13), and of Commission Decision 2001/246/EC of 27 March 2001 laying down the conditions for the control and eradication of foot-and-mouth disease in the Netherlands in application of Article 13 of Directive 85/511/EEC [2001] OJ L 88/21, (as amended by Commission Decision 2001/279/EC of 5 April 2001 [2001] OJ L 96/19).

time would have not allowed infected animals to be distinguished from vaccinated animals, making it impossible to detect and control the disease.

The appellants in the proceedings brought before the Court of Justice for preliminary ruling asserted that the vaccination ban was contrary to a 'general principle of law' guaranteeing animal welfare and requiring that animals be not unnecessarily exposed to pain or suffering.[42] They also claimed that 'the fact that animal welfare is not listed amongst the objectives of the Community and of the common agricultural policy does not affect the existence of a principle aimed at ensuring such welfare'[43] and that such principle was not taken into account in the relevant legislation, which 'was aimed solely at promoting the profitability of stockfarming'. In its assessment, the Court recalled preliminarily that ensuring animal welfare does not form part of the *objectives* of the Treaty and is not mentioned among the objectives of the CAP.[44] It considered that neither the introduction of the (CoE) European Convention for the Protection of Animals kept for Farming Purposes into EU law through Council Decision 78/923/EEC nor the Animal Welfare Protocol annexed to the Treaty of Amsterdam 'lay down any well-*defined general principle of Community law* which is binding on the Community institutions' (emphasis added).[45] It also stated that the provision in Article 36 'refers to the "life of ... animals" only by way of exception to the prohibition of measures having equivalent effect, and there is nothing in the Court's case-law to indicate that the Court has accepted any plea of justification based on that provision'.[46]

While excluding the qualification of animal welfare as a 'general principle' of EU law, the Court in *Jippes* recognised that 'the health and protection of animals' is part of 'requirements of public interest' which the Community institutions must take into account in exercising their powers.[47] Accordingly, the fulfilment of such obligation depended on an examination of the proportionality of the measure; more precisely, considering the wide margin of discretion of European institutions in the context of the CAP, the legality of the measure would be affected only if this is 'manifestly inappropriate'.[48] The Court found that the EU legislation at issue did not exceed the limits of what is 'appropriate and necessary'.[49]

As regards the relevance of animal welfare in the framework of EU law, also in *Compassion in World Farming* the Court stated that neither the (CoE) European Convention for the Protection of Animals kept for Farming Purposes nor a related Recommendation created obligations the non-observance of which would affect the validity of the Directive at issue.[50]

42 Case C-189/01 (n 40) para 36.
43 Ibid para 50.
44 Ibid para 71.
45 Ibid para 73.
46 Ibid para 75.
47 Ibid para 78.
48 Ibid para 82.
49 Ibid para 100.
50 Case C-1/96 (n 4) para 33.

In more recent cases, the Court has continued to maintain the *Jippes* approach and has failed to recognize a general principle of European law on animal welfare protection. It has recalled that 'the protection of animal welfare is *a legitimate objective in the public interest*' as shown by the adoption of the Protocol on the protection and welfare of animals, annexed to the Treaty and that its own case law has recognised that 'the *interests* of the Community include the health and protection of animals' (emphasis added).[51]

In summary, before the Lisbon Treaty, successfully challenging the validity of EU legislation on the basis of lack of consideration of animal welfare has been very difficult because of the wide discretion of EU institutions in the main areas affecting animal welfare (i.e. CAP and the internal market) and because of the non-recognition of animal welfare as a general principle of EU law by the Court. A more viable solution aimed at protecting animal welfare interests (although strictly interpreted as well) has been recourse to Article 36 in relation to the introduction or maintenance in place of national measures establishing higher protection standards compared to the European ones, as a derogation to free movement.

2 Animal welfare in the post Lisbon context

As earlier noted, Article 13 of the TFEU brings with it a solid recognition of animal welfare concerns and places the issue on a firmer legal footing. It embeds a fundamental 'competence to protect'[52] animal welfare; animals are recognised in law as sentient beings and this should inform the formulation of EU policies, including the internal market and the agricultural policy. It would purportedly facilitate the emergence of a coordinated political and legal approach to animal welfare standards that is motivated by a direct moral concern for the welfare of individual animals rather than one indirectly related to a commercial or conservationist interest in the health of species or of farm stocks. How and to what extent is the potential of Article 13 TFEU translated in practice?

2.1 Animal welfare in the context of legislation making

2.1.1 The new animal welfare strategy

At the policy level, already in 2006, the Commission adopted for the first time a Community Action Plan on the Protection and Welfare of Animals 2006–2010 to

51 Joined Cases C-37/06 and C-58/06 *Viamex Agrar Handels GmbH (C-37/06) and Zuchtvieh-Kontor GmbH (ZVK) (C-58/06) v Hauptzollamt Hamburg-Jonas* ECLI:EU:C:2008:18 paras 22, 23; Case C-219/07 *Nationale Raad van Dierenkwekers en Liefhebbers VZW, Andibel VZW v Belgische Staat* ECLI:EU:C:2008:353 para 27.

52 Bruno De Witte, 'A competence to protect. The pursuit of non-market aims through internal market legislation' in Phil Syrpis (ed), *The Judiciary, the Legislature and the EU Internal Market* (Cambridge University Press, 2010) 25.

guide EU action in this field,[53] but this has been criticised for its narrow focus on specific policy fields and overemphasis on farm animals.[54] The new Strategy 2012–2015 builds on the lessons learned from the previous years and proposes a two-pronged approach.[55]

First, it acknowledges that a holistic horizontal approach is necessary to tackle some common problems. There is a need to go beyond ad hoc legislation addressing specific problems, by establishing general horizontal principles in a consolidated revised EU legislative framework, with a view to simplifying the animal welfare *acquis* and ultimately facilitating its enforcement.[56] This may be achieved, among others, through adoption of framework legislation that should establish a common minimum threshold for animal welfare throughout the European Union. Secondly, the Commission has noted that there are actions that it already performs which need 'to be reinforced or better used', including implementing plans to strengthen Member States' compliance, and providing consumers and the public with appropriate information.[57] At the same time, the Commission will assess the impact of actions undertaken in the context of the animal welfare strategy on fundamental rights, such as freedom of religion, and address possible contrasts, e.g. through labelling in the food sector.[58]

In a resolution that followed the launch of the Strategy, the European Parliament shared the Commission's view that there is often a lack of compliance with the existing legislation on animal welfare by the Member States, and called for effective and proportionate sanctions accompanied by ample information and guidance from the competent authorities.[59] Having been a strong supporter of good animal welfare standards in EU legislation, the Parliament particularly welcomed the inclusion in the Strategy of a European animal welfare framework legislation that would go beyond the current coverage of animals kept for farming purposes.[60] In the European Parliament's view the 'Framework Law should be a tool for the simplification and streamlining of existing animal welfare legislation'.[61] By establishing an EU common base level for animal welfare, the framework legislation would contribute to free and fair competition in the internal market;

53 European Commission, Community Action Plan on the Protection and Welfare of Animals 2006–2010, COM (2006) 13 final, 23 January 2006.
54 Resolution of the European Parliament on a Community Action Plan on the Protection and Welfare of Animals 2006–2010 (2006/2046(INI)), 12 October 2006, especially points 2, 6, and 9.
55 Communication from the Commission to the European Parliament, the Council and the European Economic and Social Committee on the European Union Strategy for the Protection and Welfare of Animals 2012–2015, 15.2.2012, COM/2012/06 final.
56 Ibid para 3.
57 Ibid.
58 Ibid. See Vasiliki Kosta, 'Fundamental rights mainstreaming in the EU' in this volume.
59 European Parliament resolution of 4 July 2012 on the European Union Strategy for the Protection and Welfare of Animals 2012–2015 (2012/2043(INI)), 4 July 2012, paras 30, 42.
60 Ibid para 61 ff.
61 Ibid para 62.

however, such legislation should allow Member States and/or individual producers or groups of producers to set up voluntary systems which go beyond EU rules, while avoiding competition distortions and protecting EU competitiveness in international markets.[62] Finally, the European Parliament has put emphasis on the external dimension of the inclusion of animal welfare standards in EU legislation. While welcoming the Commission's proposal to better integrate animal welfare in the framework of the European neighbourhood policy, the Parliament has urged the Commission 'to be more ambitious in including and prioritising reciprocity of animal welfare standards, as a non-trade concern in its trade policy and when negotiating multilateral and bilateral international trade agreements, and to promote animal welfare in third countries by requiring equivalent welfare standards for imported animals and products accompanied by strict controls'.[63] It has also called on the Commission to 'refrain from submitting free trade agreements to the European Parliament that fail to ensure that equivalent animal welfare regulations apply to imported products as to European products'.[64]

In summary, the significance of the EU animal strategy 2012–2015 rests with the anticipated adoption of a Framework Law that will address horizontally protection concerns, distortions of competition and monitoring of compliance. In view of the changed approach of the Commission, which favours a holistic approach, the Treaty internal market provisions rather than the narrower CAP will (predictably) be used increasingly as a legal basis when legislating on animal welfare issues.[65] As it is explained below, this has been successfully pursued in relation to two recent sector-specific secondary legislation instruments.

2.1.2 Beyond the CAP, a balance to be struck in the internal market framework

This section discusses the impact of Article 13 TFEU on the prospects for EU institutions to make use of internal market provisions to legislate on animal welfare. The limits within which EU institutions can pursue a non-trade objective using the legal basis on the approximation of laws in relation to the establishment or the functioning of the internal market are set out in the first Tobacco case.[66]

62 Ibid paras 66, 67.
63 Ibid para 12.
64 Ibid para 14.
65 In C-31/86 *United Kingdom of Great Britain and Northern Ireland v Council of the European Communities* ECLI:EU:C:1988:211, the Court dealt with the problem of the appropriate legal basis of Council Directive 86/113/EEC of 25 March 1986 laying down minimum standards for the protection of laying hens kept in battery cages [1988] OJ L 74/83. Assessing the relationship between CAP provisions and the Treaty provision on the harmonization of national legislation in the framework of the internal market (now article 114 TFEU), the Court affirmed that 'the Treaty gives precedence to specific provisions in the agricultural field over general provisions relating to the establishment of the common market.'
66 Case C-376/98 *Germany v Parliament and Council* ECLI:EU:C:2000:544. See Maria Eugenia Bartoloni, 'The horizontal social clause in a legal dimension' in this volume.

The case raised, firstly, issues of competence related to the choice of the right legal basis (i.e. compliance with the principle of conferral),[67] and secondly, the question whether the measure failed to respect the principles of proportionality or subsidiarity.[68] The Court concluded that the internal market measure at issue did not actually contribute to either 'eliminating obstacles to the free movement' or 'to removing distortions of competition', contrary to what is requested under Article 114 TFEU.[69] The Court has consistently applied such test thereafter, and in its own words:

> According to consistent case-law the object of measures adopted on the basis of Article [114(1) TFEU] must genuinely be to improve the conditions for the establishment and functioning of the internal market … . While a mere finding of disparities between national rules and the abstract risk of infringements of fundamental freedoms or distortion of competition is not sufficient to justify the choice of Article [114 TFEU] as a legal basis, the Community [Union] legislature may have recourse to it in particular where there are differences between national rules which are such as to obstruct the fundamental freedoms and thus have a direct effect on the functioning of the internal market … . Recourse to that provision is also possible if the aim is to prevent the emergence of such obstacles to trade resulting from the divergent development of national laws.
>
> However, the emergence of such obstacles must be likely and the measure in question must be designed to prevent them … .[70]

Accordingly, internal market legislature that pursues animal welfare goals will be valid if it genuinely improves the conditions for the establishment and functioning of the internal market – even if animal welfare concerns are overriding factors in the adoption of the legislative measure. Legislation where animal welfare issues have been mainstreamed using the internal market legal basis has been adopted both before and after the entry into force of the Lisbon Treaty. Two recent examples include the Regulations concerning trade in seal products in the EU and the Directive on animals used for scientific purposes.

The seals Regulation is explicitly the result of 'concerns by members of the public and governments sensitive to animal welfare considerations due to the pain, distress, fear and other forms of suffering which the killing and skinning of seals … cause to those animals.'[71] In response to such concerns, several Member States adopted or intended to adopt legislation regulating trade in seal products by prohibiting the import and marketing of such products, as these would have adversely

67 For a discussion on the principle of conferral of powers see Nic Shuibhne, 'Deconstructing and reconstructing Article 7 TFEU' in this volume.

68 Ibid., Opinion of A.G. Fennelly.

69 Case C-376/98 (n 66) paras 95, 105, 112.

70 Case C-58/08 *Vodafone, O2 et al v. Secretary of State* ECLI:EU:C:2010:321 paras 32-33.

71 Regulation (EC) 1007/2009 of the European Parliament and of the Council on trade in seal products [2009] OJ L 286/36, recitals 4–8.

affected the operation of the internal market. Accordingly, the Regulation was aimed at harmonising the rules in this sector across the EU 'and thereby prevent the disturbance of the internal market in the products concerned'.[72] The Preamble to the Regulation stated that 'In accordance with the Protocol on protection and welfare of animals annexed to the Treaty, the Community is to pay full regard to the welfare requirements of animals when formulating and implementing, inter alia, its internal market policy. The harmonised rules provided for in this Regulation should accordingly take fully into account considerations of the welfare of animals.'[73] The legality of the Regulation was challenged before the Court of Justice – among other grounds – on the basis that its primary objective was clearly the protection of animal welfare and not the functioning of the internal market.[74] The Court however, relied on the Regulation's Recitals and the observations of the Commission, and found that the conditions for recurring to Article 114 (then Article 95 TEC) had been met.[75]

The Directive on animals used for scientific purposes builds on similar premises.[76] It refers to disparities between laws and implementing measures of the Member States regarding the protection of animals used for experimental and other scientific purposes which are liable to constitute barriers to trade. Accordingly, the Directive aims to reduce such disparities by approximating the relevant rules, and to ensure a proper functioning of the internal market. The second Recital in the Preamble states that 'animal welfare is a value of the Union' enshrined in Article 13 TFEU. The Preamble also refers to the available scientific knowledge regarding factors influencing animal welfare as well as to the capacity of animals to sense and express pain, suffering, distress and lasting harm: 'It is therefore necessary to improve the welfare of animals used in scientific procedures by raising the minimum standards for their protection in line with the latest scientific developments.'[77] The intrinsic value of animals as sentient creatures and the ethical concerns of the general public are also acknowledged.

As regards the correct use of the internal market legal basis (Article 114) in relation to such legislation, which is openly directed at the protection and promotion of animal welfare, it has been noted that the limits set forth in the case law (Tobacco case) 'are easily met by intelligent drafting'.[78] The text of EU legislation

72 Ibid recital 8.

73 Ibid recital 9.

74 Case T-526/10 *Inuit Tapiriit Kanatami and Others v European Commission* ECLI:EU:C:2013:215 para 26.

75 Ibid paras, 48, 58. See also Case C-398/13 P *Inuit Tapiriit Kanatami and Others v European Commission* ECLI:EU:C:2015:535 paras 25, 69. See Bartoloni (n 66) for a discussion on the correct use of the internal market legal basis (Article 114) in relation to human health.

76 Directive 2010/63/EU of the European Parliament and of the Council on the protection of animals used for scientific purposes OJ L 276/33, recitals 1, 2, 6, and 12.

77 Ibid para 6.

78 Stephen Weatherill, 'The limits of legislative harmonization ten years after tobacco advertising: how the court's case law has become a "drafting guide"' (2011) *German Law Journal* 843.

frequently draws on such case law as a guide, although quite often there is assertion of compliance rather than demonstration thereof.[79] For example, Recital 56 of the Directive on animals used for scientific purposes (Recital 21 of the seals Regulation contains an identical formula) provides that:

> Since the objective of this Directive, namely the harmonisation of legislation concerning the use of animals for scientific purposes, cannot be sufficiently achieved by the Member States and can therefore, by reason of its scale and effects, be better achieved at Union level, the Union may adopt measures, in accordance with the principle of subsidiarity as set out in Article 5 of the Treaty on European Union. In accordance with the principle of proportionality, as set out in that Article, this Directive does not go beyond what is necessary in order to achieve that objective.

The scope for judicial review of the competence of EU institutions to legislate on animal welfare issues using the internal market as a legal basis has been quite narrow, and the incorporation of Article 13 in the Treaty reinforces this approach. In other words, it can be expected that it will be easier for EU institutions to legislate on animal welfare issues using as a legal basis the provision on approximation of laws in the context of the internal market (Article 114 TFEU, ex Article 95 TEC), even when this amounts to important restrictions on trade. As Weatherhill concludes 'one would have little expectation of success in persuading the Court to intervene in the name of proportionality once competence to legislate in the first place is successfully established'.[80] Also, successful use of Article 114 (for the time being) has diverted attention from the flexibility clause in Article 352 TFEU (ex Article 308 TEC), which assigns residual law-making powers to EU institutions but sets very high procedural standards to meet.

2.2 Case law concerning animal welfare after Lisbon

Recent case law sheds some light on the broader significance of the provision in Article 13 TFEU, in particular, on whether omission to act or failure to take into consideration animal welfare concerns on the part of EU institutions can be successfully challenged before the Court; and on the use of Article 13 as an interpretation tool to determine the scope of application of secondary legislation.[81]

In *HB v Commission*, the applicants had submitted a citizens' initiative entitled 'Ethics for Animals and Kids' on the subject of the adoption of legislation concerning criminalization of ill treatment and physical punishment of stray animals and the implementation of sensitization programmes for children in this respect.[82]

79 Ibid.

80 Ibid 838.

81 For a discussion on the judicial review of the 'provisions having general application' articulated in Articles 7–13 TFEU, see Nic Shuibhne (n 67), in particular Section III A.

82 Case T-361/14 *HB and Others v European Commission* [2017] OJ C 161/21. The appeal case was dismissed by the Court of Justice as manifestly unfounded (Case C-336/17 P).

The Commission rejected the registration of the request on the grounds that 'it falls manifestly outside the framework of the Commission's powers to submit a proposal for a legal act of the Union for the purpose of implementing the Treaties'.[83] The applicants brought an annulment claim (of the decision to reject the proposal) submitting that the Commission had failed to observe the limits of its competence to legislate and had infringed, among others, its duty to protect animals as required under Article 13 TFEU. Interestingly, the reasons provided by the Commission for the rejection of the proposal expand on the status of animal welfare in EU law after the introduction of Article 13 TFEU and on how the Commission defines the scope of its competences in these regards.

The Commission noted that the proposal to use Article 13 TFEU as a legal basis for measures aimed at ensuring welfare and protection of stray animals in the EU could not be accepted because 'there is no legal basis in the Treaties for a legal act of the Union which would cover [that] subject matter'.[84] Referring to the *Jippes* jurisprudence, which established that protection of animal welfare does not form part of the objectives of the Treaty, the Commission also clarified that although the Court's interpretation in that case was given against the background of the Protocol on protection and welfare of animals, annexed to the TEC by the Treaty of Amsterdam '[i]t remains valid under the current Treaties, since the Protocol was in substance taken over as the current Article 13 TFEU'. The Commission recalled that EU legislation on animal welfare has been adopted but this has taken place in the context of the CAP (now Article 43(2) TFEU), the internal market (Article 114 TFEU) and the protection of the environment (Article 192 TFEU) as the adopted legislation contributed to the advancement of the specific objectives of these respective policies. Instead, in the Commission's view, the proposed citizens' initiative did not come under any of those objectives.

In the case brought before the General Court, the latter fully backed the position of the Commission. Any legislative act on the protection of animal welfare needs to be adopted in the context of one of the policies mentioned in Article 13 TFEU, i.e. agriculture, fisheries, transport, internal market, research and technological development and space.[85] The applicants' submission that the different regulations existing in the Member States had a distortion impact on competition between veterinaries in the EU, was not considered solid evidence by the Court so as to justify coverage by one of the policies listed in Article 13 TFEU.[86]

The case at issue represents an interesting example of the use of judicial review to address omission to act to protect animal welfare on the part of EU institutions. While building on previous case law which establishes that animal welfare cannot, on its own, provide the legal basis for legislation in this area, the Court seems to

83 The Commission's reply stating the reasons for refusal of registration is available at: http://ec.europa.eu/citizens-initiative/public/initiatives/non-registered/details/1856
84 For this line of reasoning see Bartoloni (n 66).
85 Case T-361/14 (n 82) para 37.
86 Ibid para 41.

shift the burden of proof on the applicants. From the reasoning of the Court, it appears that, had the applicants' evidence been stronger and more structured, regarding the impact that the lack of legislation on stray animals has on competition and the internal market, the annulment request might have been successful.

Two other examples of case law post Lisbon highlight the use of Article 13 TFEU as an interpretation tool to determine the scope of application of secondary legislation. In *Brouwer* [87] the Court was asked to define the substantive scope of application of Council Directive 91/629/EEC laying down minimum standards for the protection of calves confined for rearing and fattening. The question was whether the prohibition of tethering established in the Directive also applied to calves kept for milking. Agreeing with the Commission, the Court relied on Article 13 TFEU to establish that a narrow definition of the substantive coverage of the Directive – limited to rearing and fattening of claves – would have been contrary to the principle set out in Article 13 TFEU to pay full regard to the welfare requirements of animals as sentient beings while implementing the agricultural policy.[88]

In *Zuchtvieh-Export GmbH* [89] the Court relied on Article 13 TFEU to determine the geographical scope of application of Council Regulation (EC) 1/2005 on the protection of animals during transport and related operations. Contrary to the Opinion of General Advocate Bot, the Court recognised that the obligations deriving from the Regulation apply to the transport of animals with a point of departure within the territory of the European Union and a destination in a third country in the same way as they apply to transport within the European Union.[90] The Court took this decision in light of the general purpose of the Regulation, based on the principle that animals must not be transported in a way likely to cause injury or undue suffering to them, and Article 13 TFEU, which has incorporated the substance of Protocol 33 and is a provision of general application of the Treaty.[91]

2.3 Mainstreaming animal welfare in other policies through pre-legislation impact assessment

In addition to policy making (Section 2.1) and judicial review (Section 2.2), the significance of Article 13 TFEU can also be assessed in relation to pre-legislation impact assessment studies or reports. Impact assessments (IAs) are generally carried out during the preparation phase of legislation, before the Commission finalises a proposal for a new instrument. IAs examine the possible economic, social or environmental impacts of available solutions, to inform and support the decision-making process. To what extent does the Commission consider the welfare of

87 Case C-355/11 *G. Brouwer v Staatssecretaris van Economische Zaken, Landbouw en Innovatie* ECLI:EU:C:2012:353.
88 Ibid para 43.
89 Case C-424/13 *Zuchtvieh-Export GmbH v Stadt Kempten* [2015] OJ C 205/5.
90 Ibid para 47.
91 Ibid para 35.

animals among the impact scenarios of proposed legislation? The question can be answered at various levels.[92]

From a methodological perspective, with a view to improving the law making process, IAs form a key part of the Commission's 'better regulation' agenda, and in that regard, a set of Guidelines provides guidance on how to conduct impact assessments.[93] The accompanying Toolbox,[94] which contains complementary advice, does not include animal welfare in the list of possible impacts that may be identified in assessments and evaluations,[95] but mentions it among the key environmental impacts.[96] The Toolbox suggests a number of questions that should be asked for the purpose of identification of significant environmental impacts, such as: whether the option has an impact on the health of animals (including a risk assessment on animal health); whether the option affects animal welfare (i.e. humane treatment of animals); and whether the option affects the safety of food and feed.

From a practical viewpoint, on a general note, impact on animals has been addressed more frequently in the reports between 2011 and 2015, and less in the last two years. In very few cases the Commission has omitted to refer to animal welfare issues, despite an anticipated impact of the proposed legislation in that regard – such as in relation to legislation on risks from exposure to carcinogens or mutagens at work, which rests on evidence obtained from animal testing of these substances.[97]

The Commission often considers the impact on animal welfare alongside the impact on animal health and on safety of animal feed. By way of example, when drafting secondary legislation laying down the authorised levels of substances that have endocrine disrupting properties, the Commission considered potential interference with the hormone systems in animals and humans as part of health and food safety.[98] Another example is the IA accompanying the proposal of a Regulation on appliances burning gaseous fuels - under the category industry and entrepreneurship - which considers at various points how the new legislation will affect the life and health of domestic animals.[99]

92 For a discussion on this topic see Francesca Ippolito, 'Mainstreaming equality in the EU legal order: more than a Cinderella provision?' in this volume.

93 Better regulation guidelines on impact assessment are available here: http://ec.europa.eu/smart-regulation/guidelines/ug_chap3_en.htm

94 Better regulation 'Toolbox' is available here: http://ec.europa.eu/smart-regulation/guidelines/docs/br_toolbox_en.pdf

95 Ibid Chapter 3.

96 Ibid 108.

97 Commission staff working document, Impact Assessment accompanying the document proposal for a Directive of the European Parliament and of the Council amending Directive 2004/37/EC on the protection of workers from the risks related to exposure to carcinogens or mutagens at work, SWD(2017)7; SWD(2016) 152.

98 Communication on endocrine disruptors and the draft Commission acts setting out scientific criteria for their determination in the context of the EU legislation on plant protection products and biocidal products, 15 June 2016, SWD(2016)211.

99 Commission staff working document, Impact Assessment accompanying the document Proposal for a Regulation of the European Parliament and of the Council on appliances burning gaseous fuels, 12 May 2014, SWD(2014)151.

Instead, specific impact on animal welfare has been assessed in relation to: the proposals for a Regulation on the manufacture, placing on the market and use of medicated feed[100] and a Regulation on veterinary medicinal products[101]; the implementing Regulation on the indication of the country of origin for fresh, chilled and frozen meat[102]; the EU guidelines for state aid in the agricultural and forestry sectors and in rural areas 2014 to 2020[103]; or a Directive on the placing on the market of food from animal clones.[104] Quite importantly, the proposal for amendments to the Directive on the assessment of the effects of public and private projects on the environment, reports relevant examples in which the impact of big infrastructure works on animals has been assessed and measures have been taken.[105] The impact on animal welfare is also examined in the context of the external commercial policy, cooperation and development, in particular, as regards different standards of animal welfare protection existing in the EU and in third countries.[106]

100 Commission staff working document, Impact Assessment accompanying the document Proposal for a Regulation of the European Parliament and of the Council on the manufacture, placing on the market and use of medicated feed and repealing Council Directive 90/167/EEC, 10 September 2014, SWD(2014)271.

101 Commission staff working document, Impact Assessment accompanying the document Proposal for a Regulation of the European Parliament and of the Council on veterinary medicinal products, 10 September 2014, SWD(2014)273.

102 Impact Assessment on Commission implementing Regulation laying down rules for the application of Regulation (EU) 1169/2011 of the European Parliament and of the Council as regards the indication of the country of origin or place of provenance for fresh, chilled and frozen meat of swine, sheep, goats and poultry [2011] OJ L 304/18, 13 December 2013, http://ec.europa.eu/smart-regulation/impact/ia_carried_out/docs/ia_2013/ia_meat_origin_labelling.pdf

103 Commission staff working document, Impact Assessment accompanying the document European Union Guidelines for State aid in the agricultural and forestry sectors and in rural areas 2014 to 2020, Commission Regulation declaring certain categories of aid in the agriculture and forestry sector and in rural areas compatible with the internal market in application of Articles 107 and 108 TFEU and repealing Commission Regulation (EC) 1857/2006, 25 June 2014, SWD(2014)196.

104 Commission staff working document, Impact Assessment accompanying the proposal for a Directive of the Parliament and of the Council on the cloning of animals of the bovine, porcine, ovine, caprine and equine species bred and kept for farming purposes, and proposal for a Council Directive on the placing on the market of food derived from animal clones, 19 December 2013, SWD(2013)519.

105 Commission staff working paper, Impact Assessment accompanying the document proposal for a Directive of the European Parliament and of the Council amending Directive 2011/92/EU on the assessment of the effects of certain public and private projects on the environment [2011] OJ L 26/1, 26 October 2012, SWD(2012)355 final.

106 Commission staff working document, Impact Assessment accompanying the document Proposal for a Regulation on information provision and promotion measures for agricultural products on the internal market and in third countries, 21 November 2013, SWD(2013)470; Commission staff working document, Impact Assessment accompanying the document Recommendation for a Council Decision authorising the European Commission and the High Representative of the Union for Foreign Affairs and Security Policy to open negotiations and negotiate with Mexico a modernised

2.4 Animal welfare as part of public morals: internal and external dimensions

While the Union is trying to simplify and consolidate the animal welfare acquis, there has been at the international level an important recognition of animal welfare as a relevant justification for restrictive trade measures (intra and extra EU) aimed at protecting public morality. The accent is therefore placed on consumer and public concerns, to which animal welfare is instrumental. The attitude of the EU (the Commission in particular) vis a vis animal welfare protection is very clearly framed in these terms and is discussed in the disputes concerning the seals legislation, which were brought before the ECJ as well as the WTO dispute settlement organs.

As earlier mentioned, the seals disputes arose following the enactment of EU legislation[107] that introduced a ban on the importation and marketing of seal products (because of the cruel methods employed in seal hunting) with the exception of products obtained from the traditional hunt of the Inuit indigenous community. The adoption of the Regulations triggered a strong reaction that was voiced before the EU judicial organs by individuals and organisations representative of the Inuit community, and before the WTO dispute settlement organs by two non-EU states in which such communities live and carry out trade in seal products for commercial purposes, namely Canada and Norway. Two important issues were raised in such proceedings that offer an insight on the significance of animal welfare in the post-Lisbon framework.

First, on the substance, in the cases before the WTO, the panel and the Appellate Body had to assess whether animal welfare constitutes a solid policy justification for trade restrictions (the ban) under Article XX of the GATT.[108] The European Union emphasised that moral concern with regard to the protection of animals is regarded as a value of high importance in the European Union, which is now expressly enshrined in its constitutional treaties. Regarding the restrictive effects on trade, the EU admitted that the Seal Regime aims at being very trade-restrictive, consistently

Global Agreement, 16 December 2015, SWD(2015)289; Commission staff working document, Impact Assessment accompanying the document Recommendation for a Council Decision authorising the opening of negotiations with Turkey on an Agreement on the extension of the scope of the bilateral preferential trade relationship and on the modernisation of the Customs Union, 21 December 2016, SWD(2016)475; Commission staff working document, Impact Assessment accompanying the document Joint Communication to the European Parliament and the Council: A renewed partnership with the countries of Africa, the Caribbean and the Pacific, 22 November 2016, SWD(2016)380.

107 Council Regulation (EC) 1007/2009 of 16 September 2009 on Trade in Seal Products [2009] OJ L 286/36; Commission regulation 737/2010 of 10 August 2010 laying down detailed Rules for the Implementation of Regulation (EC) 1007/2009 of the European Parliament and of the Council on Trade in Seal Products [2010] OJ L 216/1 (EU). For a discussion on mainstreaming equality at the Eu external level see Ippolito (n 91.)

108 European Communities – Measures Prohibiting the Importation and Marketing of Seal Products, WT/DS400/R, WT/DS401/R, WT/DS400/AB/R and WT/DS401/AB/R.

with the desired high level of fulfilment of the underlying policy objective. The Panel observed that the term 'public morals' in Article XX(a) of the GATT 1994 denotes 'standards of right and wrong conduct maintained by or on behalf of a community or a nation' and added that the content of the concept of public morals 'can vary in time and space, depending upon a range of factors, including prevailing social, cultural, ethical and religious values'. This suggests a certain degree of discretion for WTO members in defining the scope of 'public morals' with respect to various values prevailing in their societies at a given time.

After analysing the legislative history of the regulation, the panel concluded that the EU had provided sufficient evidence that the public concerns about seal welfare constitutes a moral issue for EU citizens. The panel established that the objective of the EU Seal Regime is 'to address the moral concerns of the EU public with regard to the welfare of seals'. Specifically, these concerns have two aspects, as claimed by the European Union: (a) 'the incidence of inhumane killing of seals'; and, (b) EU citizens' 'individual and collective participation as consumers in, and exposure to ("abetting"), the economic activity which sustains the market for' seal products derived from inhumane hunts. Such link between animal welfare and consumer concerns should be emphasised. It is worth noting that EU's defence strategy did not rest on animal welfare as part of the protection of animal life or health as such – i.e. an extensive interpretation of the concept of health – but rather on the safeguard of public morals of EU citizens, which is damaged by the inhumane killing of seals.

It should be noted that Article XX of the GATT/WTO – on which the EU based its defence – is very similar to and pursues the same objectives of Article 36 TFEU; the arguments raised by the EU could thus potentially be used in the EU context as well, to support national restrictive trade measures that protect animal welfare. As earlier mentioned, such approach was pursued unsuccessfully by the applicants in the *Compassion in World Farming* case, but the WTO seals case opens new scenarios in these regards.

Secondly, from a procedural perspective, the cases filed before the EU judicial organs raise the issue of the locus standi of private individuals, groups or companies to challenge the validity of EU legislation. Traditionally, the ECJ has interpreted restrictively the possibility for these actors to challenge the legality of measures of general application (such as a regulation) that are of 'direct and individual concern' for them. The 'individual concern' component requires proof that the act in question affects the applicants 'by reason of certain attributes which are peculiar to them or by reason of circumstances in which they are differentiated from all other persons' (the *Plaumann* formula).[109] Such approach maintains in place important gaps in judicial remedies because private parties are left, in practice, only with the option of challenging general measures indirectly, i.e. via the preliminary review procedure.[110] Moreover, whether this is pursued in practice

109 Case 25/62 *Plaumann &Co. v Commission* ECLI:EU:C:1963:17.
110 Case C-50/00 P *Unión de Pequeños Agricultores v Council* ECLI:EU:C:2002:462, Opinion AG Léger, para 35.

and the precise content of the issue that is referred to the European judges are upon the discretion of domestic courts.

The Lisbon Treaty corrects, but only in part, such shortcomings by adding a third limb in Article 263(4); this stipulates that with respect to 'regulatory acts' that do not entail implementing measures, private parties need only establish 'direct concern' but not 'individual concern'. In the context of the seals litigation at the EU level – the first to address the scope of application of Article 263(4) – the Court, however, confirmed that the concept of regulatory acts does not encompass legislative acts.[111] This conclusion is problematic because it maintains in place some of the deficiencies in respect of access to an effective remedy, which is now established in Article 47 of the Charter of Fundamental Rights and bears the same value as other Treaty provisions. It is also difficult to reconcile the approach to animal welfare as relevant to the public morals of EU citizens – which was put forward by the EU in the context of the WTO dispute – with such limited scope for judicial remedies for individuals in the EU system. This calls for a possible recast and/or relaxation of the *Plaumann* test, at least on certain issues, including animal welfare protection where there is a direct link with consumer concerns as part of EU public morals.

3 Concluding remarks

This chapter has carried out an assessment of the impact of the new provision in the Lisbon Treaty concerning the streamlining of animal welfare in the main EU policies, from the perspective of legislation-making, judicial interpretation and law enforcement. Analysis has shown some positive steps in advancing animal welfare at the EU level but has also exposed the underlying tension in EU law and its enforcement, between the free movement objectives embodied in the internal market policy and the protection of non-trade interests, including animal welfare. The approach of the institutions reflects such tension: analysis of the case law and practice of the CJEU and the Commission, in particular, shows a selective and partial use of the potential of the new provision on animal welfare in Article 13 TFEU.

First, the Commission and the Court have framed the competence to legislate on animal welfare issues under the internal market legal basis, which allows the Commission to be selective in its approach to regulate in this area, while reducing the scope for judicial review – as regards both enacted legislation and failure to legislate on certain issues. Challenging the validity of EU legislation on the basis of lack of consideration of animal welfare has been and still is very difficult because of the wide discretion of EU institutions in the main areas affecting animal welfare (i.e. the internal market and CAP) and because of the failure to recognise animal

111 Case T-18/10 *Inuit Tapiriit Kanatami and Others v European Parliament and Council of the European Union* ECLI:EU:T:2011:419 para 56; Case C-583/11 P *Inuit Tapiriit Kanatami and Others v European Parliament and Council of the European Union* ECLI:EU:C:2013:625 paras 58–62.

welfare as a general principle of EU law. Loopholes in the EU system of judicial remedies for individuals and groups support this scheme. On a positive note, the Commission tends to take into account systematically the possible impact of the proposed legislation on animal welfare, and the CJEU has recently used Article 13 TFEU as an interpretation tool to expand the substantive and geographical scope of application of secondary legislation.

Secondly, as regards action undertaken at the national level, the CJEU has established that the room for manoeuvre under the general exception provision, which allows Member States to adopt or maintain restrictive trade measures aimed at protecting legitimate public interests, is significantly reduced once the EU has regulated the area and set out its own protection standards. This is expected to narrow down even more in the light of the EU animal welfare strategy that aims to bring coherence in EU legislation.

Thirdly, the EU attitude in the seals case, where the protection of animal welfare is not promoted as a value per se, but as instrumental to the protection of public morals, denotes a preference for a flexible concept and leaves broader room for discretion in the decision to discard or maintain trade restrictive measures. Externally, the EU was able to justify successfully a trade restrictive measure aimed at protecting the public morals of EU citizens threatened by the cruel killing of animals. However, internally – while available in principle – the same defence would be of lesser use to validate domestic trade restrictive measures and proof of a particular relevance of such public policy objective would be required. This raises issues of coherence, effectiveness and coordination at the EU and international levels.

From an overall perspective and looking forward, at the policy level, the mainstreaming clause has prompted a closer attention on animal welfare issues, as indicated by the adoption of the second animal welfare strategy, notwithstanding the absence of an express legal basis. This calls for and provides opportunities for an increased role by the CJEU to promote enhanced animal welfare standards, through judicial interpretation, implementation and enforcement, at the EU and national levels.

9 Deconstructing and reconstructing Article 7 TFEU

Niamh Nic Shuibhne

I. Introduction

Article 7 TFEU states that '[t]he Union shall ensure consistency between its policies and activities, taking all of its objectives into account and in accordance with the principle of conferral of powers'. Noting the reach of the other 'provisions having general application' that it frames, Article 7 is considered to speak to the Union in a broad and inclusive sense i.e. addressing its various institutions, bodies, offices and agencies.[1] But what does – or what should – it require these actors to do? After all, the range of policies, activities and objectives spread across the EU Treaties is now immense.

This chapter first traces the Treaty history of the three distinct parts now bound together in Article 7, demonstrating that the commitments to consistency, to taking all Union objectives into account, and to doing both in accordance with the principle of conferral have independent primary law origins. It will be seen that the obligation to ensure consistency between Union policies and activities is the most developed part of Article 7, which is not surprising having regard to its established function in the shaping and practice of EU competence in external relations. The commitments to taking all Union objectives into account and to respecting the conferral of powers could, in that light, be described as flanking responsibilities.

The chapter then asks if Article 7 generates a 'fourth element' i.e. does it contribute or require something, in terms of legal capacity or legal obligation, as the sum of its three parts? Here, it will be seen that the compound energy created by Article 7 seems to date to be pushing more in the direction of *expanding* the available space for Union activity – an outcome that is perhaps contrary to the impression created by looking at its three parts in isolation or by reflecting on the wider context of the Lisbon Treaty that introduced the provision in the first place. The terms of Article 7 are also linked to the current context of EU law making,

1 See e.g. C.N.K. Franklin, 'The burgeoning principle of consistency in EU law' (2011) 30 *Yearbook of European Law* 42, 59; confirming that this includes the Court of Justice, see Thomas Horsley, 'Reflections on the role of the Court of Justice as the "motor" of European integration: legal limits to judicial lawmaking' (2013) 50 *Common Market Law Review* 931, 949–950.

coalescing around one basic query: is this provision just intended to express a set of nice ideas, or should it be engaged more substantively beyond that? In particular, in seeking to resolve freshly acute concerns about uniformity and differentiation in the Union's structure and functioning, it is suggested that Article 7 may yet have something more to contribute.

II. Three parts: the Treaty path(s) to Article 7 TFEU

Article 7 TFEU – first drafted in this form for the Treaty establishing a Constitution for Europe[2] – collects together a set of principles with distinct Treaty origins. Tracking these different Treaty paths reveals characteristics that could still influence the current provision's impact, as well as highlight its limitations.

A 'to ensure consistency between its policies and activities'

The obligation on the Union to ensure consistency between its policies and activities imparts Article 7 TFEU's centre of gravity. That view aligns with the fact that consistency has the longest and most developed Treaty history of the provision's three parts. What the introduction to this volume refers to as a '*universal* requirement of policy consistency' emerged over time from three inter-connected lineages: first, to manage the disjointed structure of the post-Maastricht Union; second, to establish a specific guiding objective in the field of external relations; and, third, to allocate institutional responsibility for oversight of these goals.

A Treaty-rooted role for consistency can be traced back to the Single European Act i.e. the first revision of the founding Treaty of Rome. At a general level, the preamble to the SEA conveyed:

> aware[ness] of the responsibility incumbent upon Europe to aim at speaking ever increasingly with one voice and *to act with consistency and solidarity* in order more effectively to protect its common interests and independence, in particular to display the principles of democracy and compliance with the law and with human rights to which they are attached, so that together they may make their own contribution to the preservation of international peace and security in accordance with the undertaking entered into by them within the framework of the United Nations Charter.

The outward-facing aspect of this objective was mapped onto the substantive reference to consistency in Article 30(5) of the Treaty, which stated that '[t]he external policies of the European Community and the policies agreed in European Political Co-operation[3] must be consistent'. That requirement was also addressed

2 See Article III-115 of the adopted version (2004 OJ C310/1); like Article 7 TFEU, the provision was the first of those 'of general application' in Part III of this Treaty (i.e. covering 'the policies and functioning of the Union').

3 The predecessor to the EU's Common Foreign and Security Policy.

from an institutional angle, with the provision continuing that '[t]he Presidency and the Commission, each within its own sphere of competence, shall have special responsibility for ensuring that such consistency is sought and maintained'.

In the next stage of Treaty development, the Maastricht reforms fundamentally changed the very structure of the polity, as well as the nature, scope and functioning of its competence in external relations. These amendments in turn shaped an enhanced role for consistency in the altered EU system. On the first point, acknowledging the splintering of the European Economic Community's unitary framework into three distinctive pillars, and picking up elements of the SEA's preamble, Article A TEU provided that '[t]he Union shall be founded on the European Communities, supplemented by the policies and forms of cooperation established by this Treaty. Its task shall be to organise, *in a manner demonstrating consistency and solidarity*, relations between the Member States and their peoples'. Reflecting that idea and continuing with the allocation of specific institutional responsibility seen in Article 30(5), but progressing further the particularly important role of consistency in external relations, Article C then established:

> The Union shall be served by *a single institutional framework which shall ensure the consistency and the continuity of the activities carried out* in order to attain its objectives while respecting and building upon the acquis communautaire. The Union shall *in particular ensure the consistency of its external activities as a whole in the context of external relations, security, economic and development policies.* The *Council and the Commission shall be responsible for ensuring such consistency.* They shall ensure the implementation of these policies, each in accordance with its respective powers.[4]

In that provision, we can see also early shades of the requirement to take the Union's objectives into account as well as indications of respect for the allocation (if not yet expressed in the language of conferral) of powers.

The Nice Treaty attached an objective of consistency to two further instances, responding again to the increased complexity of the Union's governance framework. First, while the Amsterdam Treaty had introduced provisions on enhanced cooperation, the post-Nice Article 27a TEU provided that the practice of it 'shall respect the principles, objectives, general guidelines and consistency of the common foreign and security policy and decisions taken within the framework of that policy'. More generally, Article 45 TEU confirmed the responsibility of the Council and Commission to 'ensure the consistency of activities undertaken on the basis of [enhanced cooperation] and the consistency of such activities with the policies of the Union and the Community, and shall cooperate to that end'.

4 See further, Article J.8(2) TEU (on the role of the Council). The Amsterdam Treaty added that the Council and Commission 'shall cooperate to this end' in light of their shared responsibility for ensuring consistency. Article I-19(1) of the Treaty establishing a Constitution for Europe would have added ensuring of the 'consistency, effectiveness and continuity of [the Union's] policies and actions' as one of the tasks of its 'institutional framework'.

Second, Article 225 EC established the appellate jurisdiction of the (then) Court of First Instance vis-à-vis judicial panels and also provided in principle for that Court's jurisdiction to hear and determine questions referred for a preliminary ruling. However, a 'serious risk of the unity or consistency of Community law being affected' would enable exceptional review by the Court of Justice in both situations.

Bringing these steps together, and looking beyond Article 7 TFEU's 'universal' requirement, references to consistency are found across the current versions of the TEU and TFEU in five main contexts, all clearly traceable from the evolutionary path outlined above: (1) as one of the overarching tasks of the Union's institutional framework, remembering that while the Union's structure is formally 'de-pillared' following the coming into force of the Lisbon Treaty, some structural asymmetries remain operationally in place[5]; (2) conferring specific institutional and post-holder responsibilities[6]; (3) as an obligation within substantive policy areas, especially for policies that engage with the world beyond the Union[7]; (4) as a

5 See Article 13(1) TEU: 'The Union shall have an institutional framework which shall aim to promote its values, advance its objectives, serve its interests, those of its citizens and those of the Member States, and ensure the consistency, effectiveness and continuity of its policies and actions'. I am grateful to Panos Koutrakos for pointing out that there are also persisting *substantive* asymmetries, recalling Article 24(1) TEU's statement that '[t]he common foreign and security policy is subject to specific rules and procedures'.

6 E.g. Article 16(6) TEU: 'The General Affairs Council shall ensure consistency in the work of the different Council configurations. It shall prepare and ensure the follow-up to meetings of the European Council, in liaison with the President of the European Council and the Commission. The Foreign Affairs Council shall elaborate the Union's external action on the basis of strategic guidelines laid down by the European Council and ensure that the Union's action is consistent'. See further, Articles 17(6) (the President of the Commission must ensure that that institution 'acts consistently, efficiently and as a collegiate body') and 18(4) TEU (the High Representative of the Union for Foreign Affairs and Security Policy 'shall ensure the consistency of the Union's external action').

7 See especially, Articles 21(3) ('The Union shall ensure consistency between the different areas of its external action and between these and its other policies. The Council and the Commission, assisted by the High Representative of the Union for Foreign Affairs and Security Policy, shall ensure that consistency and shall cooperate to that effect') and 26(2) TEU ('The Council and the High Representative of the Union for Foreign Affairs and Security Policy shall ensure the unity, consistency and effectiveness of action by the Union'). See further, Article 121 TFEU (on coordination of the Member States' economic policies, cross-referenced in Article 146 TFEU on Member State employment policies); Article 181(1) TFEU ('The Union and the Member States shall coordinate their research and technological development activities so as to ensure that national policies and Union policy are mutually consistent'); Article 196(1) TFEU ('Union action shall aim to: … promote consistency in international civil-protection work'); Article 21(7) TFEU ('The Union shall ensure that its humanitarian aid operations are coordinated and consistent with those of international organisations and bodies, in particular those forming part of the United Nations system'); and Article 42(7) TEU (requiring that 'commitments and cooperation' to aid and assist a Member State that is 'the victim of armed aggression on its territory … shall be

factor triggering exceptional appellate review within the Court of Justice of the European Union[8]; and (5) as a procedural tool for managing approved variation within the Union system or its procedures.[9]

However, while all of these instances tell us something about *why* consistency is resorted to as well as *who* needs to apply it – and that it is mainly styled as a functional or procedural *objective* in pursuit of *coordination* – few insights can be found on the question of *what* it actually entails or requires. The role of consistency within the appellate system of the Court of Justice of the European Union could offer a legally tangible instruction, but the degree or extent of the obligation of consistency that might actually trigger such an appeal is not yet obvious. At the time of writing, it has been successfully invoked in only three cases, all of which concerned the review of appeal decisions of the General Court in staff cases[10] – from which it is, by their very individual nature, difficult to draw more general or systemic insights.

B 'taking all of its objectives into account'

Since its inception at Maastricht, the preamble to the TEU has observed that the signatories are 'determined to promote economic and social progress for their peoples, *taking into account* the principle of sustainable development *and within the context of* the accomplishment of the internal market and of reinforced cohesion and environmental protection, and to implement policies ensuring that advances in economic integration are accompanied *by parallel progress in other fields*'. This recital reflects, though still at a relatively pared down level, the fact that the Union and its founding legal instruments pursue a range of different objectives at once – as any polity does. Additionally, the accompanying EC Treaty included a very specific requirement stipulating the taking of 'cultural aspects into account in [Community] action under other provisions of [the EC] Treaty' (Article 128(4) EC). These examples introduce two different types – general and particular – of what are now widely known as policy integration clauses. Both have since multiplied quite spectacularly.

consistent with commitments under [NATO]'. We could also add Articles 52(3) (corresponding of Charter and ECHR rights) and 52(4) (interpretation of Charter rights 'in harmony' with the common constitutional traditions of the Member States) of the Charter of Fundamental Rights.

8 See Article 256(2) TFEU, on exceptional jurisdiction up *to* and up *from* the General Court.

9 See Article 329(2) TFEU on enhanced cooperation within the framework of the common foreign and security policy; see more generally, Article 334 TFEU ('The Council and the Commission shall ensure the consistency of activities undertaken in the context of enhanced cooperation and the consistency of such activities with the policies of the Union, and shall cooperate to that end').

10 Case C-197/09 RX *Réexamen M v EMEA* EU:C:2009:391; Case C-579/12 RX-II *Réexamen Commission v Strack* (11 December 2012); Case C-417/14 RX *Réexamen Missir Mamachi di Lusignano v Commission* EU:C:2014:2219. For a negative decision, see Case C-141/18 RX *Réexamen FV v Council* EU:C-2018:218.

Looking, first, at the more specific version, the SEA introduced the idea that '[e]nvironmental protection requirements shall be a component of the Community's other policies' (Article 130r(2) EEC)[11]; this was rephrased as 'must be integrated into the definition and implementation of other Community policies' at Maastricht. It was then relocated to the front of the Treaty at Amsterdam (to Article 6 EC, and later Article 3c). The Amsterdam Treaty further introduced (in Article 129a) the requirement that '[c]onsumer protection requirements shall be taken into account in defining and implementing other Community policies and activities'. Additionally, Article 3(2) EC provided that 'the Community shall aim to eliminate inequalities, and to promote equality, between men and women' in the carrying out of the activities listed in Article 3(1). Following the Lisbon Treaty, these and other policy integration instructions now constitute the 'provisions having general application' articulated in Articles 7–13 TFEU.

Second, however, more general expressions of the Union's objectives had also expanded with each Treaty amendment process. Comparing the Maastricht and Lisbon iterations of what began life as Article 2 EC demonstrates this point:

> Article 2 EC (Maastricht)
>
> The Community shall have as its task, by establishing a common market and an economic and monetary union and by implementing the common policies or activities referred to in Articles 3 and 3a, to promote throughout the Community a harmonious and balanced development of economic activities, sustainable and non-inflationary growth respecting the environment, a high degree of convergence of economic performance, a high level of employment and of social protection, the raising of the standard of living and quality of life, and economic and social cohesion and solidarity among Member States.
>
> Article 3(3) TEU (Lisbon)
>
> The Union shall establish an internal market. It shall work for the sustainable development[12] of Europe based on balanced economic growth and price stability, a highly competitive social market economy, aiming at full employment and social progress, and a high level of protection and improvement of the quality of the environment. It shall promote scientific and technological advance. It shall combat social exclusion and discrimination, and shall promote social justice and protection, equality between women and men, solidarity between generations and protection of the rights of the child. It shall promote economic, social and territorial cohesion, and solidarity among Member States. It shall respect its rich cultural and linguistic diversity, and shall ensure that Europe's cultural heritage is safeguarded and enhanced.

11 See, on the environmental protection principle, Beate Sjåfjell, 'The environmental integration principle: a necessary step towards policy coherence for sustainability' in this volume.

12 See section 2 of the chapter referenced in footnote 11

It can be noticed that many of these objectives are then reiterated in the more specific policy integration clauses of the TFEU.

Looking across these amendments, from Maastricht to Lisbon, three main points can be observed: first, the incremental expansion of policy integration objectives; second, the gradual positioning of these requirements at the beginning of the Treaty texts, communicating the sense that these interests should frame Union activity more generally as well as more prominently; however, third, the non-prioritised or horizontal nature of any relationship between them.

In other words, while Article 7 TFEU asks that *all* Union objectives should be taken into account, the Treaties do not provide explicit guidance about how this could actually be achieved in practice. No clue is offered either about the intended significance – or not – of the objectives further singled out as having 'general application' in the provisions immediately following Article 7. These points are returned to in Section III.B below.

C *'in accordance with the principle of conferral of powers'*

The Maastricht-generated Article 3b EC stated that '[t]he Community shall act within the limits of the powers conferred upon it by this Treaty and of the objectives assigned to it therein'. The core standards of subsidiarity and proportionality were also expressed in this provision. These obligations have been developed considerably over the intervening years and are now spread primarily across Articles 3(6),[13] 4,[14] and 5 TEU[15]; and complemented by the express delineation of Union competences

13 'The Union shall pursue its objectives by appropriate means commensurate with the competences which are conferred upon it in the Treaties'.

14 '1. In accordance with Article 5, competences not conferred upon the Union in the Treaties remain with the Member States. 2. The Union shall respect the equality of Member States before the Treaties as well as their national identities, inherent in their fundamental structures, political and constitutional, inclusive of regional and local self-government. It shall respect their essential State functions, including ensuring the territorial integrity of the State, maintaining law and order and safeguarding national security. In particular, national security remains the sole responsibility of each Member State. 3. Pursuant to the principle of sincere cooperation, the Union and the Member States shall, in full mutual respect, assist each other in carrying out tasks which flow from the Treaties. The Member States shall take any appropriate measure, general or particular, to ensure fulfilment of the obligations arising out of the Treaties or resulting from the acts of the institutions of the Union. The Member States shall facilitate the achievement of the Union's tasks and refrain from any measure which could jeopardise the attainment of the Union's objectives'.

15 '1. The limits of Union competences are governed by the principle of conferral. The use of Union competences is governed by the principles of subsidiarity and proportionality. 2. Under the principle of conferral, the Union shall act only within the limits of the competences conferred upon it by the Member States in the Treaties to attain the objectives set out therein. Competences not conferred upon the Union in the Treaties remain with the Member States. 3. Under the principle of subsidiarity, in areas which do not fall within its exclusive competence, the Union shall act only if and in so far as the objectives of the proposed action cannot be sufficiently achieved by the Member States, either at central level or at regional and local level, but can rather, by

in Articles 3–6 TFEU as well as by Protocols on the application of the principles of subsidiarity and proportionality, and on the role of national parliaments. As a provision rooted in that environment, Article 7 TFEU seems to provide another reminder of the limits imposed on Union action through its reference to the principle of conferral of powers – limits that the drafters felt compelled to restate but also to enhance and elaborate through each process of Treaty amendment and certainly for the Lisbon Treaty, as outlined in more detail in Section III.C below.

However, Article 7 does not necessarily produce the expected 'back off' signal that a conferral reminder might reasonably be expected to manifest, an observation also returned to in Section III.C below.

III. The nature and capacity of Article 7: three questions

Knowing more about how each of Article 7 TFEU's three parts originated does not reveal much about what kind of provision it was intended to be, or what kind of contribution it might reasonably be expected to make to realising the Union's policies, activities and objectives. In this Section, three crosscutting questions are examined with the aim of shedding further light on the nature and capacity of the provision, examining in turn: first, its legal character; second, how the multiplicity of Union activities, policies and objectives was intended to be managed, including whether any sense of hierarchy among them can be discerned from within the Treaties; and, third, whether the sum of the three parts of Article 7 TFEU in fact creates a substantive 'fourth' responsibility or obligation.

A Legal character

It was noted in Section II that consistency is the most developed element of Article 7 TFEU, owing to its embedded role in EU external relations in particular.[16] Nevertheless, even in that field, there is an unresolved definitional question about whether the English language references to 'consistency' in the Treaties mirror the meaning of *cohérence* used in French – a difference in terminology also found in other language versions. Underpinning this discussion in EU external relations law is a view that consistency is essentially a static objective whereas coherence – which includes but is broader than consistency – conveys a more active or dynamic responsibility.[17]

reason of the scale or effects of the proposed action, be better achieved at Union level. … 4. Under the principle of proportionality, the content and form of Union action shall not exceed what is necessary to achieve the objectives of the Treaties'.

16 See generally, Marise Cremona, 'Coherence in foreign policy – the legal dimension' in Panos Koutrakos (ed.), *European Foreign Policy: Legal and Political Perspectives* (Edward Elgar 2011) 55; Christophe Hillion, '*Tous pour un, un pour tous!* Coherence in the external relations of the European Union' in Marise Cremona (ed.), *Developments in EU External Relations Law* (OUP 2008) 10.

17 E.g. the French Treaty text provides: 'L'Union veille à la cohérence entre ses différentes politiques et actions, en tenant compte de l'ensemble de ses objectifs et en se

The coherence/consistency distinction seems to raise questions about the extent and nature rather than existence of consistency-related obligations (the term used throughout this chapter in order to align with the English version of Article 7 TFEU). For example, Bertea considers coherence as a criterion of the rule of law, pointing out that 'coherence should be considered a fundamental … value in every legal system, for it relates to the idea that the system has to make sense as a whole. And making sense as a whole is a precondition of intelligibility, which in turn is a requirement essential to law'.[18] Nevertheless, there is broad agreement that even the more narrowly drawn concept of consistency has evolved beyond a mere guideline or abstract objective even if perceptions of the intensity of resulting obligations and of whether or not it qualifies as a general principle of Union law still vary.[19]

Classification as a general principle of Union law is especially important from the perspective of attaching to Article 7 both capacity for review of its application and the nature of the consequences that can be drawn through that process. Reflecting the definition of general principles applied by Tridimas – i.e. 'fundamental propositions of law which underlie a legal system and from which concrete rules or outcomes may be derived'[20] – and drawing from Court of Justice case law that constructed EU standards of judicial protection, many commentators expressly characterise the judicially conceived obligation of consistency as a general principle of EU law.[21] In the field of external relations law pre-Lisbon, the decision in *ECOWAS* is typically pointed to as the classic exposition of the Court's understanding of and approach to consistency.[22] Aspects of this case law are

conformant au principe d'attribution des competences'. Discussing the implications of the distinction, see Christian Tietje, 'The concept of coherence in the Treaty on European Union and the Common Foreign and Security Policy' (1997) 2 *European Foreign Affairs Review* 211, 212–213; Leonhard den Hertog and Simon Stroß, 'Coherence in EU external relations: concepts and legal rooting of an ambiguous term' (2013) 18 *European Foreign Affairs Review* 373, 375–377; Marise Cremona, 'Coherence through law: what difference will the Treaty of Lisbon make?' (2008) 3 *Hamburg Review of Social Sciences* 11, 13–14; Ester Herlin-Karnell and Theodore Konstadinides, 'The rise and expectations of consistency in EU law: legal and strategic implications for European integration' (2013) 15 *Cambridge Yearbook of European Legal Studies* 139, 141–143.

18 Stefano Bertea, 'Looking for coherence within the European Community' (2005) 11 *European Law Journal* 154, 170.

19 E.g. 'the nature and different dimensions of coherence as a principle are still difficult to pin down' (Cremona (n 17) 13); 'a free-standing formal legal imperative which governs the EU legal integration process' (Herlin-Karnell and Konstadinides (n 17) 140); 'the notion of coherence is one of the main constitutional values of the EU' (Tietje (n 17) 211).

20 Takis Tridimas, *General Princples of EU Law*, 2nd ed. (OUP 2007) 1.

21 E.g. Franklin (n 1) 52 and Tietje (n 17) 214; referring to e.g. Case 314/85 *Foto-Frost* EU:C:1987:452, Case C-221/88 *Busseni* EU:C:1990:84, and Case C-143/88 *Zuckerfabrik* EU:C:1991:65. Herlin-Karnell and Konstadinides emphasise a particular role for consistency as a general principle in the context of issues beyond the reach of the TFEU, such as Treaty opt-outs (n 17) 158–161 and 165.

22 Case C-91/05 *Commission v Council (ECOWAS)* EU:C:2008:288.

returned to in Section IV below. But critique of the *ECOWAS* judgment should also be acknowledged here, since it projects caution about how we might apply consistency as a legally consequential principle in an attempt to evaluate policy decisions.[23] At a descriptive level, however, we can note that the evolution of consistency as a general principle reflects three different phases: initial development as part of the construction of EU constitutional governance; then somewhat narrowed by early Treaty expressions that linked consistency to specific fields or policies as well as serving more specific tasks and functions; but then broadened outwards again – re-generalised, in a sense – through Article 7 TFEU and the Lisbon Treaty.

If consistency does qualify as a general principle of EU law, then it is important to consider not just how it can or should be applied; but also, as noted above, to examine how its application can be reviewed and what consequences might flow from assessments made in that respect. Before the adoption of the Lisbon Treaty, these questions had been discussed in terms of the extent to which the different elements now joined together in Article 7 TFEU were justiciable.[24] For example, addressing the extent of a 'taking into account' obligation, Jans observed that judicial review of compliance with the environmental policy integration clause had been 'limited to the question of whether the Union legislator committed "a manifest error of appraisal"', having regard to the fact that 'the Union's institutions have wide discretionary powers as to how they shape their environmental policy'.[25] That approach could logically be mapped onto judicial evaluations undertaken on the basis of Article 7 more generally.

But for now, we do not know – since the Lisbon Treaty took effect and up to the time of writing, Article 7 TFEU has not yet been engaged with in a judgment of the Court of Justice. However, in line with the cautious future anticipated by Jans, Franklin offers a compatible premonition by recalling the Court's largely hands-off approach to the scrutiny of institutional choices made on the basis of subsidiarity, just two Treaty steps away in Article 5 TFEU.[26] It is similarly well established that judicial review of the proportionality of EU legislation is considerably more temperate than review of national measures undertaken on the same premise. All of this would suggest that only the most blatant failures of responsibility under the Article 7 criteria could derail an EU measure.

Nevertheless, judicial review materialises both exceptionally and at the end of a much bigger process. Conceiving of Article 7 as a positive and substantive coordinate of the wider EU law-making matrix, there remains general agreement that its terms should be understood as operating not just to *inspire* but also to *deliver* harmonious policy outcomes. For example, discussing the role of consistency in the context of legal drafting, Herlin-Karnell and Konstadinides suggest that this

23 E.g. Panos Koutrakos, 'EU law: external relations' (2010) 59 *International and Comparative Law Quarterly* 481, 483–484.

24 E.g. on consistency, see Franklin (n 17) 60.

25 Jan Jans, 'Stop the integration principle?' (2011) 33 *Fordham International Law Journal* 1533, 1543; referring to Case C-341/95 *Bettati* EU:C:1998:353.

26 Franklin (n 17) 84–85.

would entail 'not only … consistency of content (i.e. coordination and avoidance of contradiction) but also … consistency of logic (consolidation) and goals'[27] – an ambition underscored when Article 7's requirement also to take different objectives into account is recalled.

Thinking then about how such goals could be realised in practice, Cremona develops a useful typology based on three 'levels of analysis' for consistency, which in turn suggest its key functions. Her approach involves rules of hierarchy; rules of delimitation, which link also to Article 7's third part (respect for the conferral of powers); and principles of 'cooperation and complementarity'.[28] However, she acknowledges that there can be operational tensions between these different levels; as well as potential complications caused by the conferring of responsibility on a range of different institutional actors: '[n]ot only will there be a number of different actors to coordinate, a number of different actors will have responsibility for that coordination'.[29] In other words, there is no one consistency 'controller' prior to the endgame of judicial review through litigation in the Court of Justice – an event itself unlikely to lead to intensive scrutiny of policy decisions in any event, for the reasons noted above.

Den Hertog and Stroß propose a fourth category to add to Cremona's framework i.e. 'rules of substantive guidance', which concern the actual content of policies.[30] Leaning more into the active demands of coherence than the passive construct of consistency, to recall the distinction applied in EU external relations scholarship, they specifically identify a function of *stimulation* for rules of substantive guidance as a function of coherent policy-making: i.e. 'not "merely" imply [ing] a negative connotation of *absence of* contradiction but would, ideally, require a substantive (re)orientation of policies around common principles and objectives'.[31] Den Hertog and Stroß constitute these rules at a general level by reference to Articles 2 and 3 TEU. From a normative perspective, they suggest that the values articulated in that part of the Treaty 'should inform policy-makers about the outer boundaries of policy formulation and implementation', since 'even if actors cooperate sincerely and respect the limits of their proper competences this does not automatically result in coherent policy outcomes'.[32] Bertea's observation that 'what is coherent forms a rational unit rather than a chaotic assemblage of possibly inconsistent normative statements' resonates here too[33]; though it should be remembered that chaos can stem from 'contradictions *and* overlapping'.[34] Thus while the idea of using Articles 2 and 3 TEU to cut through ambiguity regarding the values that should guide Union action is logical, the problem is that those provisions themselves express attachment to so many values as to render any

27 Herlin-Karnell and Konstadinides (n 17) 146.
28 Cremona (n 17) 14–16.
29 Ibid 34.
30 Den Hertog and Stroß (n 17) 379–383.
31 Ibid 381 (emphasis in original).
32 Den Hertog and Stroß (n 17) 379.
33 Bertea (n 18) 170.
34 Franklin (n 1) 43 (emphasis added).

formal sense of instruction that they could provide ultimately futile. That point leads then to the more biting prospect of hierarchy.

B Questions of hierarchy

Further refining the functional character of consistency, commentators tend to separate out its horizontal (i.e. 'inter-policy and inter-pillar coherence') and vertical (i.e. 'the relationship between Member State and Union action') application.[35] The broader Treaty scheme outlined in Section II above entails this distinction too, with vertical consistency 'reflected in the notions of loyalty and primacy' and horizontal consistency invoking 'the broader principles of good administration and good governance related to openness, transparency and accountability to democratic institutions'.[36] The former point is reinforced within Article 7 itself, through the reference to conferral of powers. Looking across all three parts of the provision more holistically, Cremona suggests that horizontal consistency places 'emphasis ... on policy coordination, complementarity and even integration, rather than hierarchy' and she points out that this understanding fits well with the policy integration clauses that follow on from Article 7.[37]

But it is also arguable that a scheme or system of hierarchy is sometimes necessary to facilitate the making of decisions that are both defensible and effective, providing an interesting point of tension with the ethos of horizontally driven policy integration that is clearly captured by Article 7's appeal to take *all* Union objectives into account.

The particular dimension of the problem for present purposes is the incremental multiplication of Treaty objectives that need to be taken into account combined with the absence of detailed guidance on how to negotiate through the resulting range of interests committed to in parallel – especially when it is remembered that values pursued under different headings can conflict with each other in reality.[38] The upshot of the Lisbon-intensified proliferation of principles that this project aims to investigate is therefore that 'everything has to be taken into account with everything!'[39]

Relatedly, and connecting to Section III.A's questions about justiciability, Jans states that owing to the coming into force of the Lisbon Treaty, '[t]he already difficult task of the European legislator to balance sometimes conflicting interests

35 E.g. Cremona (n 17) 19 and 16 respectively. See further, Den Hertog and Stroß (n 17) 377–378.

36 Herlin-Karnell and Konstadinides (n 17) 142.

37 Cremona (n 17) 19; as one of her three levels of analysis, she frames consistency in this sense as 'encompassing rules for conflict avoidance between potentially conflicting norms and for resolving conflicts when they arise' (ibid 14).

38 E.g. even focusing on the comparatively narrower task of environmental policy integration, Jans remarks that 'the manner in which potential and actual conflicts between protection of the environment and, for example, how the functioning of the internal market should be resolved cannot be inferred from the integration principle as such' (Jans (n 25) 1542).

39 Ibid 1545.

has become even more complex' and argues that the Court of Justice might in consequence 'show even more deference to the EU's political institutions than before ... and become even more reluctant to reach the conclusion that the European legislator committed a "manifest error of appraisal"'.[40] Moreover, joining that conclusion to the principle of conferral, he further asserts that '[t]he requirement to balance multiple objectives, according to the multiplicity of integration principles, makes it more difficult to draw a clear line between Union and Member State competences. The blurrier the objectives become, the blurrier the division of powers between the Union and Member States'.[41]

It is useful in that light to look not only at the policy integration clauses that follow on from Article 7, but also at the provisions that precede it. Here, similarly, we see further evidence of a Treaty that seeks to achieve everything at once while, at the same time, suggesting little reflection on how different commitments might end up in tension with each other. Article 4 TEU provides a good example for present purposes, noting that respect for the national identity of the Member States and the principle of sincere cooperation between the Union and the Member States are simultaneously articulated: which objective should yield where they tend towards different outcomes in a concrete situation? A related hierarchy – or better, absence of hierarchy – problem is noted by Jans where, addressing environmental policy integration specifically, he cautions:

> [D]ecision-making on the basis of multiple integration principles could result in measures where the component elements are still visible, but not as sharply and clearly as before. There is, therefore, an inherent danger that under the disguise of integration, certain environmental standards will be diluted or offset against other interests and policy considerations. As an ultimate consequence, it might result in what could be called "reversed integration," a process by which certain environmental standards, such as environmental quality standards or emission standards, are lowered as a consequence of the requirement that other than environmental interests are to be taken into account.[42]

However, Franklin is less concerned about the likely impact of this danger in reality, emphasising that '[c]ertain objectives may naturally be considered in policy-making activities only to be subsequently left out in the actual policy formulation that takes place, without thereby falling foul of [Article 7] requirements'.[43] Seen in that perspective, we are perhaps reminded once again of the limited role and capacity of a legal principle within the complexities of the policymaking process.

40 Ibid 1545, drawing an analogy with judicial review in the area of the common agricultural policy as demonstrating 'the reluctance of the Court to intervene in matters where the Union legislator has to weigh various objectives against each other'.

41 Ibid 1546.

42 Jans (n 25) 1547.

43 Franklin (n 1) 67.

There is therefore much appeal in Cremona's presentation of consistency as something in between; as 'provid[ing] a context and rationale for the operation of fundamental legal principles governing the relations between Member States and the EU institutions and between the institutions themselves, including the principle of primacy [and] the duty of cooperation'.[44] Applying that idea to Article 7 more generally, it could then be conceived of and applied not just as a locus of ideals bundled symbolically together but rather, and alongside the other provisions of general application, as containing tools that are needed to navigate between the Treaties' bundled ideals more generally.

However, while that understanding of Article 7 works well for thinking about the premises of consistency and conferred powers in particular, it remains less obviously useful for finding a way through the well-meaning but impractical commitment to taking all Union objectives into account as part of the wider task encoded in the provision.

C A fourth part?

As the sum of its parts, then, one view is that Article 7 can administer little more than a good governance reminder, reaffirming an administrative or process-based priority that resonates with, for example, the 'fair balance' logic applied in EU legal reasoning where several relevant interests fall to be reconciled.[45] But Franklin considers that since consistency is now 'made contingent upon two separate matters' in Article 7 TFEU, the provision in fact 'represents a … new legal reality to which the EU institutions and Member States will have to adjust'.[46] It is therefore worth examining in more detail whether the three parts of Article 7 fuse together to generate something autonomous, a 'fourth part' that somehow reflects or even defines the 'new legal reality'.

Turning from questions connected to the horizontal understanding of consistency to the often more fraught context of vertical governance relations, Herlin-Karnell and Konstadinides identify the 'promoting [of] clearer competence delimitation and conflict prevention/resolution between the EU and the Member States' legal orders' as a characteristic of the Lisbon emanation of consistency in particular.[47] This point is set within a more general argument about integration and uniformity, based in essence on the idea that 'consistency has over time become an anchoring point for extending EU law competences'.[48] Leaving the specific question of uniformity to the side, for now, the perspective outlined by

44 Cremona (n 17) 13; Sjåfjell (n 11).

45 E.g. Case C-283/11 *Sky Österreich* EU:C:2013:28 para 60 ('[w]here several rights and fundamental freedoms protected by the European Union legal order are at issue, the assessment of the possible disproportionate nature of a provision of European Union law must be carried out with a view to reconciling the requirements of the protection of those different rights and freedoms and a fair balance between them').

46 Franklin (n 1) 61.

47 Herlin-Karnell and Konstadinides (n 17) 140.

48 Ibid 143.

Herlin-Karnell and Konstadinides depicts consistency as going beyond a desire to make laws and policies fit together; acting (also) as a funnel that pulls competence towards Union level.

At first sight, it would seem that Article 7 would act as an antidote to precisely that kind of funnelling effect. As Cremona observes, 'the Treaty of Lisbon responds to the challenge of vertical coherence, not by giving more power to the Union but by emphasising the boundaries to Union power, the concurrent powers of the Member States and their role in furthering Union policy'.[49] Similarly, Franklin describes how EU policy-making choices can be 'inhibited' by the principle of conferred powers.[50] It is obvious, after all, that the messages permeating several aspects of the Lisbon Treaty connect very explicitly to articulating and protecting the division of powers between the Union and the Member States: to the principle of conferral, exemplified through express classification and delimitation of Union and Member State competences[51]; to the principle of subsidiarity, with a novel function for national parliaments in the EU law-making process[52]; to principles of and mechanisms for explaining and enhancing the role of both participatory and representative democracy in the composite Union system[53]; and to protecting fundamental rights as a priority of the EU legal order.[54] A unifying theme across these innovations evokes the objective of decentralisation, a (re-) prioritising of the authority and force of the *national* as an integral (and perhaps even superior?) actor in the composite system and structures of EU governance.

Interestingly, however, these expectations do not seem to be holding up in what little Article 7 practice we can look at to date. The particular lineage of the consistency obligation vis-à-vis EU external relations leaves a stubborn imprint here, especially noting the added impact of the principle of sincere cooperation in Article 4(1) TEU. In particular, the inherited starting point of 'loyalty has a "pre-emptive" effect upon the behaviour of Member States in that it pre-empts them from undertaking any action that could potentially undermine the objectives of the treaties'.[55] The resulting 'blocking effect of EU law' is well demonstrated by Tridimas in his analysis of judgments of the Court of Justice that develop its approach to international law. Overall, he concludes that 'in the field of external competence, oddly the presumption lies with exclusive rather than shared competence' and this 'reversing, in effect, the rule of priority of Article 4(2) TFEU'.[56]

49 Cremona (n 17) 29.
50 Franklin (n 1) 56.
51 Esp. Article 4 TEU and Articles 2–6 TFEU.
52 Esp. Article 5(3) TEU, Protocol on the Role of National Parliaments in the European Union, and Protocol on the Application of the Principles of Subsidiarity and Proportionality.
53 Esp. Article 10 TEU.
54 Esp. Articles 2 and 6 TEU.
55 Herlin-Karnell and Konstadinides (n 17) 151.
56 Takis Tridimas, 'Competence after Lisbon: the elusive search for bright lines' in Diamond Ashiagbor, Nicola Countouris and Ioannis Lianos (eds.), *Legal Issues of the Lisbon Treaty* (CUP 2012) 47, 63.

For example, in *Commission v Luxembourg*, which Tridimas characterises as reflecting a more 'intrusive' version of consistency than the traditional *ERTA* paradigm,[57] the Court ruled:

> The adoption of a decision authorising the Commission to negotiate a multilateral agreement on behalf of the Community marks the start of a concerted Community action at international level and requires, for that purpose, if not a duty of abstention on the part of the Member States, at the very least a duty of close cooperation between the latter and the Community institutions in order to facilitate the achievement of the Community tasks and to ensure the coherence and consistency of the action and its international representation.[58]

It is not clear what recourse to coherence and consistency adds here beyond longstanding case law on the duty of cooperation as affirming 'the requirement of unity in the international representation of the Community'.[59] Moreover, Cremona points out that, in this case, while 'the Member States' duty of cooperation is [expressly framed] in terms of coherence and consistency of EU external action [it] is cast in procedural terms ... affecting how the Member State's competence is exercised, and is to be distinguished from both exclusivity and pre-emption, where the Member State is prevented from acting at all'.[60] However, while she argues that 'the distinction is important', she also concedes that 'the line can be a thin one'.

It is important to note that the decision in *Commission v Luxembourg* was delivered pre-Lisbon. However, it is the atmosphere that the Court's approach generates that may be prove to be significant in trying to understand what the implications of Article 7 as a *compound* objective might be. If the scaffolding around that provision is drawn mainly from the requirements of primacy and sincere cooperation, and flavoured strongly by the continuing legacy of EU external relations law, then Article 7 does indeed support a bias in favour of EU competence – the 'blocking effect' identified by Tridimas.[61] If that proves correct, then it arguably transcends the message of Article 7's individual parts and of the wider Lisbon Treaty context too, demonstrating once again that what is written into the Treaties proves ultimately less definitive than how it is subsequently interpreted.

57 Ibid 62.

58 Case C-266/03 *Commission v Luxembourg* EU:C:2005:341 para 60. See also e.g. Case C-246/07 *Commission v Sweden* EU:C:2010:203 and Case C-263/14 *Parliament v Council* EU:C:2016:435. See further, Den Hertog and Stroß (n 17) 378 and 388. The seeds of this analysis can also be seen in Tietje (n 17) 230–231. Moreover, recalling the discussion on terminology in Section III.A, Hillion has argued that the Court's use of *both* consistency and coherence here mitigates against the concepts having the same meaning (n 16) 13.

59 E.g. Opinion 1/94 EU:C:1994:384 para 108; Opinion 2/91 EU:C:1993:106 para 36.

60 Cremona (n 16) 72.

61 See, on this topic, Maria Eugenia Bartoloni, 'The horizontal social clause in a legal dimension' in this volume, para VII.

However, it is not the Court of Justice that should attract particular criticism in this respect. Rather, when political actors design and/or agree to a Treaty text that embeds all kinds of policies, activities and objectives in an ostensibly horizontal manner, that in itself creates the necessary space for their selective balancing and blending in due course.

IV. Article 7 and the evolving Union

It was seen in Section II that before the generalisation of consistency through Article 7 TFEU, the principle was understood and applied to ensure that the Union's legal order would function across different rules and structures, especially in the specific domain of the CFSP and external relations. In those policy fields, the challenge now is to relocate consistency in a legal context where measures still adopted under different sets of rules are, post-Lisbon, governed by a single set of objectives.[62] This partial legal fusion may make the functioning of the legal order even more difficult to monitor in practice. Beyond that specific – still special – policy domain, and with several years now passed since Article 7 acquired legal effect, it remains the case that the provision has made hardly any detectible legal imprint.[63]

Could the provision be somehow invigorated to play a more visible role in the current context of Union governance questions, drawing from its legacy in external relations law as a prescription for creating order across the potential chaos of disparity and diversity? Consider, for example, the following extract from Herlin-Karnell and Konstadinides, which picks up on the role of consistency in the sphere of enhanced cooperation:

> [C]onsistency manifests itself within the area of enhanced cooperation as a means of aligning diversity with the wider policies of the EU. However, differentiation also includes a number of modalities which do not expressly require consistency in order to operate. For instance, there is no reference to consistency in the relevant treaty provisions regulating the so-called 'opt-outs'.

62 See here, Article 21 TEU.

63 Or any kind of imprint; one of the few references to Article 7 TFEU more generally is in the European Parliament's Committee on Legal Affairs 2011 Report on guaranteeing independent impact assessments (A7–0159/2011; available at http://ec.europa.eu/smart-regulation/refit/admin_burden/docs/111020_niebler_report_en.pdf); see para 15 ('Calls for impact assessments to not focus exclusively on cost/benefit-analysis but to take a large number of criteria into account, in accordance with the principle of an integrated approach, in order to provide the legislator with as comprehensive a picture as possible; draws attention in this context to the economic, social and environmental aspects referred to in the interinstitutional agreement of 16 December 2003 and the common approach of 2005, which are to be combined in a single evaluation; underlines, in this respect, the need to ensure consistency between policies and activities of the EU by taking all of its objectives into account and in accordance with the principle of conferral of powers as laid down in Article 7 TFEU').

> This is despite the dangers that such 'differentiation' carries for European integration from the perspective of uniformity.[64]

Later, they explain their perspective on the synergy between consistency and uniformity in more detail, observing that, in pursuit of European integration through case law in particular, 'the notions of effectiveness and uniformity formed part of the broader constitutional understanding of consistency in EU law'.[65]

We can find precisely this linkage in Opinion 2/13 on accession by the EU to the ECHR. Here, as part of its potent presentation of 'the specific characteristics and the autonomy of [the EU] legal order', the Court of Justice stated that 'the Treaties have established a judicial system intended to ensure *consistency and uniformity* in the interpretation of EU law'.[66] It expanded on that point through the context of the preliminary ruling procedure, the object of which is to 'secur[e] uniform interpretation of EU law … thereby serving to ensure its consistency, its full effect and its autonomy as well as, ultimately, the particular nature of the law established by the Treaties'.[67] On one view, the reasoning applied in Opinion 2/13 is simply a natural evolution of the idea of systemic coherence enunciated in classic judgments such as *ERTA*.[68] Examining that decision through a coherence lens, Bertea, for example, notes that 'the correct interpretation of Community norms is dictated by global coherence considerations: the Court of Justice is asking us to interpret certain norms as not to undermine the system's overall coherence … . The idea of coherence is thereby understood as a device for uniformly developing a system of laws'.[69] The collapsing together of coherence and uniformity fits well also with the funnelling effect that can be attributed to Article 7, discussed above.

However, the consistency/uniformity linkage arguably raises a different order of challenge at the present time. This is because the varieties and versions of differentiation operating – legitimately – as part of the persistently complex structure of the Union reflect a reality where differentiation is more explicitly an inherent than exceptional feature of integration; a manifestation of rather than risk to integration. If differentiation is accepted as an inherent and enduring feature of integration, it might indeed be necessary to ring-fence at least some hard manifestations of consistency in tandem with uniformity – such as, for example, the core Union value of equal treatment – from a still legally demanding but potentially softer understanding of 'Article 7 consistency', the latter constituting a less rigid principle of governance that would frame but not funnel more disparate and diverse EU rules and structures. It is not the overlap but the *differences* between consistency and uniformity that should, in other words, be animated.

64 Herlin-Karnell and Konstadinides (n 17) 140.
65 Ibid 143; see also, 148.
66 Opinion 2/13 EU:C:2014:2454 para 174 (emphasis added).
67 Ibid para 176, referring to Opinion 1/09 EU:C:2011:123 paras 67 and 83.
68 Case 22/70 *Commission v Council (ERTA)* EU:C:1971:32.
69 Bertea (n 18) 167 and 169.

The fact that the February 2016 Decision, addressing the relationship between the EU and the United Kingdom before the latter's June 2016 Brexit referendum, committed to Treaty recognition of distinctions between Member States whose currency is and is not the euro (as part of the 'new settlement' for the UK) provides an interesting example of where Article 7's obligations would have needed to feature.[70] In particular, in Section A ('Economic Governance'), and having noted that not all Member States participate 'in the further deepening of the economic and monetary union', it was stated that '[t]he Union institutions, together with the Member States, will facilitate the coexistence between different perspectives within the single institutional framework *ensuring consistency*, the effective operability of Union mechanisms and the equality of Member States before the Treaties, as well as the level-playing field and the integrity of the internal market'.[71] Thus, whereas Herlin-Karnell and Konstadinides distinguish between a 'value-driven' approach to consistency and 'a "constitutional diktat" based on the methodical application of coercive constitutional principles to justify EU competence and ensure the maximum effectiveness of EU law',[72] perhaps the current phase of Union adaptation means that we have to move towards understanding the latter function as 'value-driven' too; conversely, we would also recognise more the constitutional value of consistency.

The UK's Brexit decision rendered the February 2016 Decision void. But the Commission's March 2017 White Paper on the future of Europe sustains the broader questions that informed those proposals, demonstrating in its sketching of five scenarios for the Union's evolution in the years ahead that more enduring accommodation of difference remains a realistic direction of travel for the remaining 27 EU Member States as they reflect on and steer the next phase of the Union's life.[73] Although making the point to address the post-Lisbon relationship between the CFSP and other Union policies specifically, Cremona captures the nuanced potential of Article 7 more generally in this sense too when she argues that consistency 'does not necessarily imply removal of differences between policies and institutional structures; rather it is about recognising the differences and ensuring that they can live together harmoniously'.[74]

Then, if the accommodation and practice of difference are admitted as more central and sustainable than peripheral and temporary features of European Union integration, the role of consistency in the more complicated frameworks and structures that inevitably result becomes critical. It should still set obligations, but perhaps more nuanced obligations on the basis of altered expectations. Its role

70 Decision of the Heads of State or Government, meeting within the European Council, concerning a new settlement for the United Kingdom within the European Union, 2016 OJ C691/1.

71 Ibid 12 (emphasis added).

72 Herlin-Karnell and Konstadinides (n 17) 152.

73 European Commission, White paper on the future of Europe: reflections and scenarios for the EU27 by 2025, 1 March 2017, available at https://ec.europa.eu/commission/sites/beta-political/files/white_paper_on_the_future_of_europe_en.pdf

74 Cremona (n 17) 31.

would also become more complex; not purely to facilitate the pursuit of integration conceived more straightforwardly through a funnel of uniformity, but instead to manage integration pursued at once in a range of ways, through a range of means, and across a range of levels – an integration perhaps focused more on systemic unity than uniformity, reflecting how European integration actually manifests in practice – the varieties and contours of which have, somewhat ironically, become even clearer through Brexit-influenced analysis[75] – and how it might be sustained beyond one particular vision of its supposed ideal form. This notion of unity borrows from language in other strands of the Court's recent case law.[76] But what might seem like slender linguistic distinctions could acquire substantive legal significance if we are forced to rethink established and entrenched conventions or preferences about integration, which current events and challenges would suggest is indeed the case.[77]

V. Conclusion

This chapter examined the legal profile of Article 7 TFEU. The centre of gravity of the provision confers an obligation of consistency; shaped by the history of that principle in EU external relations law, in particular, but now generalised or universalised across the span of Union activity. Article 7 also confers flanking obligations around the balancing of Union objectives and respect for the conferral of powers.

It was shown that consistency does qualify as a general principle of Union law, but that the implications that flow from this are quite limited in terms of legal consequences, especially for any expectations that might be held around intensity of judicial review on the basis of Article 7. It was also seen that notwithstanding developed and imaginative academic thinking on how the principle might be given life, Article 7 has not yet made a conspicuous imprint on Union governance practice.

Is it worth trying to change that? The analysis and limited impact associated with Article 7 to date suggest a provision much more about *message* and *process* than *means* or *outcome*. But even then, many questions remain open. For example,

75 See generally, Bruno de Witte, 'An undivided Union? Differentiated integration in post-Brexit times' (2018) 55 *Common Market Law Review* 227.

76 See in particular, Case C-399/11 *Melloni* EU:C:2013:107 para 60 ('It is true that Article 53 of the Charter confirms that, where an EU legal act calls for national implementing measures, national authorities and courts remain free to apply national standards of protection of fundamental rights, provided that the level of protection provided for by the Charter, as interpreted by the Court, and the primacy, unity and effectiveness of EU law are not thereby compromised').

77 The Eurozone crisis provides another example of fertile ground for events-driven reconceptions of EU constitutional premises. See e.g. Claire Kilpatrick 'On the rule of law and economic emergency: the degradation of basic legal values in Europe's bailouts' (2015) 35 *Oxford Journal of Legal Studies* 325; Mark Dawson and Floris de Witte 'Constitutional balance in the EU after the euro-crisis' (2013) 76 *Modern Law Review* 817; Edoardo Chiti and PG Texeira 'The constitutional implications of the European responses to the financial and public debt crisis' (2013) 50 *Common Market Law Review* 683.

how does Article 7 relate to the more general principles that precede it in the Treaty and to the more specific policy integration clauses that follow on from it? Are the latter clauses intended to be where the real policy shaping work is done? If so, the chapters in this volume examining these provisions suggest a similarly slow route to substantive progress.

Does Article 7 add anything beyond the sum of its three parts? Consistency, taking all objectives into account and a commitment to respect for the conferral of powers were shown not to be straightforwardly harmonious ambitions to bring together. In that light, tensions were evident between the horizontal impetus of the provision and the gaps in practice on the resolution of more vertical questions – about the respective competences of the Union and the Member States, for example; but also concerning the multiplicity of policies, activities and objectives in simultaneous play in many situations. Where consistency obligations have been considered in legal settings post-Lisbon, it would seem that conventional expectations about uniformity, primacy and loyalty – which tend to resolve in favour of Union competence – still manifest more obviously than more novel reflections on either the nature or consequences of the different responsibilities articulated together in Article 7.

However, in trying to think about and develop a more active purpose for the provision into the future, it was argued that we might need to think more creatively – as well as more concretely – about how Article 7 could prove central to the current wave of events-driven work that seeks to reconceive some entrenched premises of EU legal understanding. A dominant purpose of the Lisbon Treaty process concerned the bringing together of disparate and diverse facets of the Union's legal order, seen most obviously in the formal, at least, demolition of its three Maastricht pillars. However, recent challenges such as the Eurozone crisis and Brexit ramifications have perhaps unmasked the enduring complexity of the Union, and of its rules and structures. Into the future, the messages captured in Article 7 TFEU may yet, then, gain more appreciation. Indeed, that may be more necessary than ever.

10 Conclusions

Integration clauses – a comparative epilogue

Bruno De Witte

1. Introduction

This concluding chapter will look at the various integration clauses in a comparative way, using the insights that are presented in the preceding chapters. The ambitions of this comparison are limited: the aim is not to produce an exhaustive taxonomy of the different legal and political characteristics of each of those integration clauses, but rather to highlight some key features of this relatively novel field of EU law. In section 2, we will underline the eclectic nature of the integration clauses, some of them being grouped together at the start of the TFEU, and others spread around in other parts of primary EU law; and we will reflect on why we have seen such a proliferation of integration clauses in EU constitutional law. In section 3, we will present an overall impression of the (modest) way in which the integration clauses have affected the activity of the EU's political institutions and in the concluding section 4, we will survey the even more modest role that the integration clauses play in the activity of the European judicial branch.

2. An eclectic collection of integration clauses

The core group of integration clauses was conveniently grouped together, by the Treaty of Lisbon, in the Articles 8 to 13 TFEU: these articles cover the equality of men and women, social protection, non-discrimination, environmental protection, consumer protection and animal welfare. These six integration clauses are at the heart of this book, but they are not the only ones contained in primary EU law. Two other integration clauses are 'hidden' in other parts of the TFEU. Article 167, dealing with culture, states in paragraph 4 that the Union shall 'take cultural aspects into account in its action under other provisions of the Treaties', and Article 173(3) TFEU states more or less the same thing for industrial policy.

These are all what one could call 'active' integration clauses, in that they are intended to affect the nature of EU action in the various policy domains of the Union. They were preceded, and are still complemented, by a 'passive' integration clause: a specific legal basis that contains a duty to integrate the policy objectives of other domains of EU law. That clause is in Article 114(3) TFEU which, since its original formulation by the Single European Act in 1986, instructs the EU institutions to pursue a high level of health, safety, environmental protection and consumer protection when adopting internal market legislation. The insertion of this clause in Article 114 (or, rather, in its predecessor Article 100A EC Treaty) reflected what was already a well-established practice at the time, namely the adoption of internal market legislation that did not just aimed at facilitating the functioning of the internal market but also pursued other policy objectives, including (but not limited to) the ones that were included in Article 100A. In fact, the functional nature of the internal market competence makes it into a natural locus for the combination of economic and non-economic policy objectives, and therefore a place of mainstreaming *avant la lettre.* [1]

In addition to these specific integration clauses, the text of the Treaties insists, in various places, on the need for coherence among EU policies. Article 7 TFEU, the provision that immediately precedes the six mainstreaming clauses within the TFEU, states that 'the Union shall ensure consistency between its policies and objectives, taking all of its objectives into account and in accordance with the principle of conferral of powers.' This statement is so general that it may appear entirely redundant, and Nic Shuibhne, in her contribution to this volume, explores whether the provision is 'just intended to express a set of nice ideas' or whether it is politically and legally consequential. She notes that 'the provision has made hardly any detectible legal impact' so far, but this may change in the future. The general consistency clause of Article 7 TFEU is echoed, for the domain of the EU's foreign relations, by various provisions in the TEU, in particular its Article 21(3) TEU.

The Charter of Fundamental Rights, being part of primary EU law since the Treaty of Lisbon's entry into force, has its own mainstreaming clause in Article 51(1) which states that the Union's institutions, and the Member States when implementing Union law, shall 'promote the application' of Charter rights 'in accordance with their respective powers'. As the Charter itself does not create new competences for the Union (this is emphatically stated in its Article 51(2)), the phrase of Article 51(1) can only mean that, in the exercise of the *other* competences of the Union, the EU institutions must promote the application of the fundamental rights of the Charter. In other words, fundamental rights must be integrated in all domains of EU law. As Kosta notes in her chapter, 'to the extent that mainstreaming is understood to mean a public sector duty to promote compliance with fundamental rights obligations as derived from the Charter, this is a duty that expressly results from the Charter.' In substance, the mainstreaming duties resulting from the Charter overlap largely with the integration clauses of Articles 8 to 13 TFEU.

After having made this inventory of integration clauses, let us now briefly reflect on why the EU's primary law contains so many of those clauses. In our view, this is not a necessary consequence of the fact that, with each treaty revision, the

1 For further elaboration of this point, see Bruno De Witte, 'A Competence to Protect: The Pursuit of Non-Market Aims through Internal Market Legislation', in P. Syrpis (ed), *The Judiciary, the Legislator and the Internal Market* (Cambridge University Press 2012) 25–46.

competences of the Union have been extended to new policy domains.[2] In fact, States are faced with the same problem of how to coordinate their policy measures across the many areas of governmental activity, but their constitutions do not contain the same amount of mainstreaming clauses: national parliaments and governments 'integrate' diverse policy objectives all the time, but they do not seem to need a constitutional basis for doing so. What makes the European Union special in this respect?

A partial explanation may be found in the limited scope of EU competences. Indeed, some of the mainstreaming clauses contain policy objectives for the pursuit of which the EU does not possess law-making competences. The clearest example is the animal welfare clause of Article 13 TFEU: no competence has been conferred on the European Union to pursue a policy for the protection of animal welfare *per se*, and therefore this policy objective must necessarily be achieved in the framework of other policies; the integration clause serves, in this case, as a reminder to the EU institutions that they should indeed consider the animal welfare implications of their laws and policies.[3] The integration clause for culture can be explained in a similar way. In the field of culture, the EU institutions are merely given a supplementary competence to support EU policies by means of incentives and recommendations; as a partial counterpart to these weak cultural policy tools, Article 167(4) TFEU calls on the EU to take culture into account when it takes more robust action under other competence headings, for example when adopting internal market legislation.

However, this kind of explanation does not hold for other integration clauses. For environmental and consumer protection, and for non-discrimination, the Treaty provides law-making competences that can be used to pursue those policy objectives directly. In these cases, the inclusion of a mainstreaming clause may seem somewhat superfluous. And yet, this proliferation of integration clauses complementing specific law-making powers can, maybe, also be explained by the EU's special system of competences. As any piece of EU legislation must have a legal basis in the Treaties, and as these legal bases often define a limited set of objectives, it may appear doubtful whether the EU legislator may pursue other objectives beyond those defined in the legal basis. The integration clauses help to remove such doubts; they clarify, beyond discussion, that it is perfectly legitimate for agricultural policy measures to include an environmental dimension, or for migration policy measures to have a gender equality dimension. This is what Jans has called the 'enabling function' of the integration clauses.[4]

2 For an argument in this sense, see Valérie Michel, 'Les objectifs à caractère transversal', in E. Neframi (ed), *Objectifs et compétences dans l'Union européenne* (Bruylant 2012) 177–209, at 183: 'c'est cet accroissement des domaines d'action de l'Union, par adjonction continue et progressive de politiques sectorielles, qui appelle inéluctablement la mise en exergue d'objectifs à caractère transversal'.

3 The fact that there is no dedicated competence for animal welfare led the Commission to reject a Ctitizen's Initiative 'Ethics for Animals and Kids', and the General Court backed the Commission's position in case T-361/14; see Beqiraj's chapter.

4 Jan H. Jans, 'Stop the Integration Principle?', 33 *Fordham International Law Journal* (2011) 1533–1547, at 1540.

However, in my view, as long as an EU measure sufficiently contributes to the achievement of the objectives formulated in the legal basis, there is no impediment for the EU legislator to *also* pursue other objectives laid down elsewhere in the Treaties, and in particular the general objectives of the Union laid down in Article 3 TEU which are very broad and apply to *all* EU activity. Take the following example: the stability of the euro area is not one of the objectives of the EU's competition and state aid policies as defined in the Treaties, but the European Commission could, during the recent economic crisis, rightfully take into account the objectives of Economic and Monetary Union when recalibrating its policy on state aid to banks. In other words, the integration clauses are not strictly needed to allow for cross-cutting policies that pursue a set of different objectives. In fact, as we will see in the next sections, the integration clauses have been largely treated, in the practice of the EU institutions, including the Court of Justice, as superfluous and redundant; by this, I do not mean to say that the EU institutions have been insensitive to the values and objectives contained in the integration clauses, but rather that these institutions have pursued those objectives in an inconsistent way and without bothering to refer to the integration clauses.

3. The integration clauses in the practice of the EU institutions

One common characteristic of the integration clauses is that they appear more often in policy documents of the EU institutions than in actual EU legislation. Moreover, when mainstreaming occurs, the integration clauses are not always mentioned. Internal market law continues to be, because of its functional nature, the most common domain for such *implicit* mainstreaming. Beqiraj documents this practice in relation to animal welfare, but internal market legislation may also pursue cultural policy objectives (thereby meeting the integration requirement of Article 167 TFEU) or social policy objectives (thereby implementing the horizontal social clause of Article 9 TFEU).

The domain of the EU's external relations offers an interesting example of strong mainstreaming that does not go under the mainstreaming flag, namely the system of special trade preferences for developing countries that comply with a set of human rights and good governance obligations. This so-called GSP+ scheme, which was originally adopted in 2005 and revised in 2012, currently applies to 10 countries, of which the largest by far, in trade terms, is Pakistan.[5] The Annex 9 of the GSP Regulation lists a number of core human rights treaties and other 'good governance' treaties which the beneficiary country is expected to ratify, implement and apply in return for the trade preferences. The Union created a special monitoring system in which it relies on the reports and findings of international monitoring bodies. One concrete instance where the EU's action under the GSP scheme may have helped to advance the application of a human rights instrument

5 Regulation 978/2012 of the European Parliament and of the Council of 25 October 2012 applying a scheme of generalised tariff preferences, OJ 2012, L 303/1, Articles 9–12.

concerned El Salvador. After the Commission had, in 2009, opened an investigation into that country's failure to ratify the ILO Convention no. 87 on freedom of association, the country's constitution was amended so as to permit ratification.[6] What is happening here is the mainstreaming of fundamental rights (in accordance with Article 51 of the Charter), of the horizontal social clause of Article 9 and of the environmental protection clause of Article 11, but none of those provisions of primary EU law is mentioned in the GSP+ regulation.

Integration clauses may not frequently appear in EU legislative acts, but they are mentioned more often in the impact assessments that precede the adoption of legislative proposals by the Commission. Several contributions to this volume discuss legislative impact assessments as a tool allowing for consideration of the integration clauses.[7] Whereas social and environmental impacts are explicitly mentioned as core elements of the impact assessment mechanisms, fundamental rights have also been added as a horizontal consideration, animal welfare is included within the environmental impacts and the other integration clauses have also, gradually and less prominently, found their way into the impact assessment regime. From a purely quantitative perspective, the results may seem impressive. In their empirical analysis covering 35 impact assessments adopted between 2011 and 2014, Smismans and Minto counted no less than 1.444 references to one of the integration clauses, with the horizontal social clause of Article 9 TFEU accounting for 53% of that number.[8] It is far from certain, though, whether the clauses have also played a meaningful role in qualitative terms.

Also, the practice is rather uneven, as can be seen from a recent example (not covered in the study of Smismans and Minto), namely the impact assessment accompanying the controversial Commission proposal for amending the posted workers directive. The impact assessment of that proposal was published, together with the proposal itself, on 8 March 2016. It is a careful 50-page study devoting, naturally, some attention to the social impact of the proposal, namely the impact it may have on the salaries and employment opportunities of workers in both sets of countries, those sending and receiving the posted workers.[9] Yet, the impact assessment report does not at all mention the Treaty's social integration clause, despite the fact that we have here a typical example of policy integration. Indeed, the original posted workers directive was an internal market directive with the dual objective of, on the one hand, contributing to the smooth functioning of the

6 The example is reported by S. Velluti, 'The Promotion and Integration of Human Rights in EU External Trade Relations', 32 *Utrecht Journal of International and European Law* (2016) 41, at 51.

7 This role has also been examined, in a more systematic way, in a recent publication by Stijn Smismans and Rachel Minto, 'Are integrated impact assessments the way forward for mainstreaming in the European Union?', *Regulation & Governance* (2017) 231–251.

8 Smismans and Minto (note 7 above), at 241.

9 Commission Staff Working Document SWD (2016) of 8 March 2016, *Impact assessment on the proposal for a Directive amending Directive 96/71 concerning the posting of workers.*

internal market for services, and, on the other hand, offering some social protection to posted workers. The revised directive is similarly based on an internal market legal basis and similarly has the dual aim of contributing to the operation of the internal market whilst increasing further the social protection of posted workers. The proposal for the Directive itself does mention Article 9 TFEU in its preamble, but did the existence of Article 9 make any difference to the substantive choices made by the Commission when proposing its new directive? It seems rather unlikely.

A final element of institutional practice that distinguishes some integration clauses from the others is that the EU institutional landscape contains a number of independent agencies with a special mainstreaming mandate and activity. Thus, Kosta notes, in her contribution, how both the Fundamental Rights Agency and the European Data Protection Supervisor see it as part of their mandate to promote the mainstreaming of fundamental rights and data protection throughout all EU policies. Similarly, the European Institute for Gender Equality, based in Vilnius, has made of gender mainstreaming one of its prominent fields of interest, including through the creation of a special Gender Mainstreaming Team within the agency. Finally, although the European Ombudsman has a more general role to monitor maladministration, Ippolito notes, in her chapter, the special interest taken by that body in non-discrimination issues.

4. Absence of the integration clauses from the judicial practice

In principle, as the integration clauses are laid down in Treaty articles, they are legally binding and therefore capable of being used by the Court of Justice as a standard for assessing the validity of EU measures or the compatibility of national implementing measures with the Treaties. However, the formulation of some of those clauses tends to weaken that formal legal status: for example, Article 12 TFEU states that consumer protection 'shall be taken into account' when defining Union policies, which does not imply that consumer protection standards should necessarily be maximised in any given piece of EU legislation. As Seatzu notes in his chapter, such a tentative formulation makes it difficult for the Court to Justice to use the consumer integration clause as a benchmark for the review of specific policy measures. But even those integration clauses that are more strongly formulated (such as the environmental one) have not made a noticeable imprint on the Court's case law.

Some of the clearest examples of judicial use of the integration clauses can be found in two Opinions of Advocates General that were, however, not echoed by subsequent judgments of the Court of Justice.[10] The first example is a pre-Lisbon one. In the case of *Austria v European Parliament and Council*, the applicant

10 See also a third, and more recent, case, mentioned in Ippolito's chapter: the Opinion of Advocate General Tanchev in Case C-414/16, *Egenberger*, EU:C:2017:851, paragraph 93 (using the non-discrimination clause of Article 10 TFEU).

government had argued that EU Regulation 2327/2003[11] violated the environmental integration clause which was laid down, at the time, in Article 6 EC Treaty. The Advocate General considered that Article 6 laid down 'an obligation on the part of the Community institutions to take due account of ecological interests in policy areas outside that of environmental protection stricto sensu', but recommended a very cautious role for judicial review of that obligation: 'It is only where ecological interests manifestly have not been taken into account or where they have been completely disregarded that Article 6 EC may serve as the standard for reviewing the validity of Community legislation.'[12] And this, according to Advocate General Geelhoed, was not the case with Regulation 2327/2003. It would have been interesting to see how the Court of Justice would have addressed this plea of the Austrian government, but the application was withdrawn before the Court could give judgment in this case.

In the *Santos Palhota* case, discussed in Bartoloni's contribution, Advocate General Cruz Villalón argued that the mainstreaming clauses of the Treaty should modify the normal standard for assessing restrictions of common market freedoms by the Member States. The case dealt with the control powers of labour inspectorates on workers posted by companies established in other EU states. This was analysed by the Advocate General (and then by the Court) as a restriction of the freedom to provide services (namely, the provision by a company of a cross-border service by using posted workers). In assessing the proportionality of such a restrictive measure, the Advocate General argued that account should be taken of the social integration clause, which, just some months before, had been inserted in the text of the TFEU. In his view, 'as a result of the entry into force of the Treaty of Lisbon, when working conditions constitute an overriding reason relating to the public interest justifying a derogation from the freedom to provide services, they must no longer be interpreted strictly.'[13] The standard of proportionality should thus be lowered in cases in which the national authorities pursue a policy objective recognised in one of the Treaty's integration clauses. More broadly speaking, the integration clause is here used as a (flexible) barrier against the application of the market logic to public policy domains that are covered by that integration clause. However, the Court did not adopt the view of the Advocate General and decided the case without referring to the horizontal social clause.

Indeed, the Court of Justice has so far made very little use of the various integration clauses, and when it did so, it was mainly as a tool for the interpretation of

11 OJ 2003, L 345/30. This regulation established a temporary points system for heavy good vehicles travelling through Austria. This was a measure of transport policy based on Article 71 of the Treaty establishing the European Community (currently Article 91 TFEU). The Austrian government considered that the regulation allowed for an excessive number of lorries on the Alpine routes connecting Germany and Italy, thus causing an excessive burden for the environment of those Alpine valleys.

12 Case C-161/04, *Austria v European Parliament and Council*, Opinion of Advocate General Geelhoed, EU:C:2006:66 (both quotes are from paragraph 59).

13 Case C-515/08, *Santos Palhota*, Opinion of Advocate General Cruz Villalón, EU: C:2010:245, paragraph 53.

other norms of EU law, and not as a tool for reviewing the validity of EU law. Thus, Beqiraj mentions, in her chapter, the *Brouwer* judgment of 2012 and the *Zuchtvieh-export* judgment of 2015, in both of which the Court referred to Article 13 TFEU in order to give an animal-friendly construction to EU legislative acts. In other cases, the interpretative use of integration clauses serves as a support for the validity of EU law against challenges by a Member State or by an individual applicant. For example, in the *Deutsches Weintor* judgment, mentioned in Bartoloni's chapter, the Court upheld the validity of an EU regulation that restricted the possibility to make nutrition claims for alcoholic beverages by invoking, among other things, the health integration clause of Article 9 TFEU.[14] What the Court of Justice has definitely not done, so far, is to annul an EU measure for failing to implement a mainstreaming obligation; nor has it used the mainstreaming clauses to mitigate the deregulatory impact of the common market freedoms or the Commission's competition policy.

The apathy of the Court of Justice towards the integration clauses may be partly due to something we noted in section 2, namely the fact that the Charter of Fundamental Rights' own mainstreaming clause of Article 51(1) duplicates, in substance, most of the integration clauses of Articles 8 to 13 TFEU. The Charter calls on the EU and its Member States to respect *and promote* gender equality (Article 23), social rights (the whole of Chapter IV on Solidarity), non-discrimination (Article 21), environmental protection (Article 37) and consumer protection (Article 38). So, when the Court of Justice decides to interpret norms of secondary EU law in conformity with those values, it does not need to invoke the integration clauses of Articles 8 to 13 TFEU, but can refer to the corresponding Charter provisions – and, as we know, the Court of Justice decided to actively use the Charter of Rights ever since its incorporation into primary law by the Lisbon Treaty.

14 Case C-544/10, *Deutsches Weintor*, EU:C:2012:526, paragraph 49.

Index

academia 122
access to justice 18
accountability 40
advisory bodies with legislative role 43, 44; Committee of the Regions (CoR) *see separate entry*; European Economic and Social Committee (EESC) *see separate entry*
Africa, Caribbean and Pacific (ACP): Cotonou Agreement 63–4
Afrophobia 67
age discrimination 55–6, 58, 62, 70, 74, 127; Court of Justice 76–7, 82
agencies/expert bodies with advisory role 44; European Data Protection Supervisor (EDPS) 14, 36–43, 44; Fundamental Rights Agency (FRA) *see separate entry*
agriculture 46–7, 51, 146, 152, 153, 183; common agricultural policy (CAP) 4, 136, 138–9, 140, 141, 145, 146, 148, 152, 158; state aid 155; *see also* animal welfare
air travel 70
alcoholic beverages 95, 96, 188
Algeria 63, 64
Almunia, Joaquín 129
Amsterdam Treaty 2, 45, 47, 49, 55, 57, 137, 145, 152, 162, 165
animal feed 154; medicated 155
animal welfare 3, 11–12, 136–7, 146, 158–9, 183, 184, 185; case law after Lisbon 151–3, 188; citizens' initiative: 'Ethics for Animals and Kids' 151–3, 183n3; domestic animals 154; evolution before Lisbon 4, 137–46; leghold traps 139; legislation making 146–51; mainstreaming in other policies through pre-legislation impact assessment 153–5; as part of public morals: internal and external dimensions 156–8, 159; public interest 141, 142, 145, 146, 159; public morality 143–4, 156–8, 159; public policy 143–4, 159; religious rites, cultural traditions and regional heritage 3, 136, 147; seal products 139–40, 149–50, 151, 156–8, 159; slaughterhouses 141–2; stray animals 151–3; testing and scientific purposes 139, 149, 150–1, 154; third countries 153, 155; veal crate systems 143; wild animals 139–40
Anthropocene 107
anti-Semitism 67
appliances burning gaseous fuels 154
Area of Freedom, Security and Justice 69, 75, 81
Article 7 TFEU: deconstructing and reconstructing 1–2, 12, 160–1, 179–80, 182; coherence/consistency distinction 167–8, 170; consistency/uniformity linkage 176–7; difference, accommodation of 178; evolving Union and Art 7 176–9; fourth part 160–1, 167, 173–6; 'in accordance with the principle of conferral of powers' 160, 166–7; legal character 167–71; questions of hierarchy 167, 171–3; 'taking all of its objectives into account' 160, 164–6; 'to ensure consistency between its policies and activities' 160, 161–4
association agreements 63–4
association, freedom of 185
asylum 70, 75, 76
Austria 49

banks 184
Barcelona Declaration (1995) 63
biodiversity 106, 120

biogeochemical flows 108
biosphere integrity 108
blue card 70
Brexit 178, 180
business: and finance 122; models 122; *see also* competition; single market/internal market; trade

Canada 156
Charter compatibility assessments (CCAs) 23, 24, 44
Charter of Fundamental Rights 44, 46, 64, 66, 72, 84–5, 95, 188; Art 7: privacy 36, 42; Art 8: personal data 36, 42; Art 11: freedom of expression and information 96–7; Art 15: right to work 95; Art 16: conduct business 95, 96–7; Art 17: right to property 97; Art 22: pluralism 78; Art 34: social and housing assistance 71, 72, 79; Art 37: environmental protection 128, 188; Art 38: consumer protection 126, 128, 188; Art 47: effective remedy and fair trial 18, 78, 158; Art 51: field of application 18–20, 33, 44, 78, 182, 185, 188; Art 52(1): legitimate limitations 29; Art 52(5): principles 19; justiciability 19; mainstreaming 14, 16, 18; obligation to promote 19–22, 33–4; rights and principles 19–20
checklist/methodology/toolkit 22, 23–4, 29, 39–40, 44, 72, 121–2, 154
children 52–3; institutionalisation of 72; Ombudsman: integration in schools of children with disabilities 73–4
civil society 30, 34, 122; organisations 94
climate change 106, 108, 109, 110, 114, 119, 120, 121
collective bargaining 94
Commission *see* European Commission
Committee of the Regions (CoR) 14, 44; influence/impact of 32–4, 44; institutional mechanisms for taking Charter into account 31–2; legal framework 30–1; Opinions 30–1, 32, 33, 34; selectiveness 39
common agricultural policy (CAP) 4, 136, 138–9, 140, 141, 145, 146, 148, 152, 158
common commercial policy (CCP) 4, 136, 138, 139
Common Foreign and Security Policy (CFSP) 176, 178
comparison: integration clauses 13, 181–4; absence from judicial practice 186–8; 'enabling function' 183; practice of EU institutions 184–6
competences 5–6, 46, 170; EU 5–6, 59, 62, 71–2, 87, 89–90, 102–3, 104, 149, 151–3, 166–7, 172, 173–5, 180, 182, 183; Fundamental Rights Agency (FRA) 35–6, 44; Member States 5–6, 57, 59, 102–3, 104, 172, 173–5, 180; shared 59, 174
competition 45, 84–5, 86, 130, 131; animal welfare 147–8, 152–3; law and policy 132, 184, 188; merger control 131
Conciliation Committee 112
conferral principle 5, 89, 90, 104, 123, 149, 160, 166–7, 170, 171, 172, 173, 174, 179, 180
consistency *see* Article 7 TFEU: deconstructing and reconstructing
Constitution for Europe, Draft Treaty Establishing 4, 61–2, 124, 161
consumers 1, 165, 182, 183; animal welfare and 138, 156, 157, 158; consumer integration clause *see* horizontal consumer clause
cooperation/loyalty, principle of sincere 117, 118, 129, 172, 173, 174, 175
cosmetics 139
cost-benefit analysis 75
Cotonou Agreement 63–4
Council of Europe: gender equality 15, 49
Council of the European Union 85, 162; animal welfare 159; checklist 29, 40; EDPS 40, 41; environmental integration 110–13; equality mainstreaming 65–6, 75–6, 78–9; evaluation of application of Charter at Council level 29–30; fundamental rights mainstreaming 14, 27–30, 31, 34, 35, 40, 41, 44; Guidelines 28–9; High Level Group on Non-Discrimination, Equality and Diversity (HLG) 75; horizontal consumer clause 129, 132–3; impact assessments 66, 75–6; Legal Service 28, 29, 44; Member State expertise 28, 29; Multiannual Framework (MAF) 34, 35
counter-terrorism policies 67
Court of Justice of European Union 3, 4, 8, 163, 164, 168–9, 170, 171–2, 173, 174–6; absence of integration clauses from judicial practice 184, 186–8; animal welfare 136, 140–6, 148–9, 150, 151–3, 156, 157–9, 188; consistency and uniformity in interpretation of EU

law 177; direct and indirect discrimination 45; dynamic, contextual and teleological method 113; EDPS 37; environmental integration 3, 109, 111, 113–15, 116–17, 118, 119–20, 121, 134, 186–7; equality mainstreaming 76–80, 81–2, 127; horizontal consumer clause 3, 131–2, 133, 186; horizontal social clause 85, 86, 87, 88–9, 94–100, 101, 102, 103, 104, 188; locus standi 157–8; market interests and social protection 86
criminal law 111, 114
culture 181, 183, 184

data protection: European Data Protection Supervisor (EDPS) 14, 36–43, 44
decentralisation 174
democracy, participatory and representative 174
developing countries: GSP+ scheme 184–5
development 51, 110, 122; research and technological 152
disability/ies 53; discrimination 4–5, 55–6, 57, 58, 61, 62, 67, 69, 70, 71, 74, 79, 82, 127; institutionalisation of persons with 72; Ombudsman: staff members of Commission with 72–3
discretionary margin 98, 145, 169
discrimination: age 55–6, 58, 62, 70, 74, 76–7, 82, 127; direct 45, 60; disability 4–5, 55–6, 57, 58, 61, 62, 67, 69, 70, 71, 74, 79, 82, 127; evolution: from non-discrimination and positive actions to positive duties 55–60; indirect 45, 60, 67, 80; racial or ethnic origin 55, 57, 58, 61, 62–3, 67, 69, 70, 72, 74, 127; religion or belief 55, 58, 62, 67, 78, 82, 127; roots of non-discrimination mainstreaming before Lisbon Treaty 60–5; sex 55, 56, 57–8, 62, 76, 127; sexual orientation 55–6, 58, 62, 76, 82, 127
diversity 55, 58, 64–5; within and across groups 60

economic growth 63, 106, 131, 133
economic impact 24, 25, 131
Economic and Monetary Union (EMU) 93–4, 178, 184
education 56, 59, 62, 64; Ombudsman: integration of children with disabilities 73–4; right to 19, 70; *see also* horizontal social clause
effective remedy, right to 18, 78, 158
Egypt 63, 64
El Salvador 185
employment 51, 55–6, 62, 64, 100; guidelines for employment policies of Member States for 2015 92–3, 102; horizontal consumer clause 125; positive action 57–8; posted workers 99–101, 185–6, 187; risks from exposure to carcinogens or mutagens 154; third-country nationals: highly skilled (blue card) 70; *see also* horizontal social clause
energy 46–7, 51; security 110
enhanced cooperation 162, 176
enlargement 80
environment 1, 3, 164, 165, 182, 183; animal welfare and 138, 139, 152, 154, 155, 185; Environment Action Programme to 2020 108; horizontal consumer clause and 126
environmental integration 2, 11, 54, 105–6, 134–5, 169, 172, 183, 185, 186–7, 188; Art 11 TFEU and EU institutions 109–16, 134–5; Art 11 TFEU and Member States 116–21; goal of sustainable development and 106–9, 134; impact assessments (IAs) 25, 66, 113, 134–5; realising potential of Art 11 TFEU 121–2; sustainability potential of Art 11 TFEU 109–21
equality mainstreaming 3, 4–5, 10, 25, 80–2, 127, 183, 186, 188; EuroMed Association Agreements (EMAAs) 63, 64; evolution: from non-discrimination and positive actions to positive duties 55–60; impact assessment and relative impact of constitutionalisation of 65–8; Lisbon Treaty and broader mainstreaming horizontal 'institutional' permeation 68–80; proposed Multi-Ground Directive 56–7; REFIT platform 67, 81; Regulatory Scrutiny Board 67, 81; roots of non-discrimination mainstreaming before Lisbon Treaty 60–5
ethics 150
ethnic origin or racial discrimination 55, 58, 61, 62–3, 67, 69, 70, 74, 127; positive action 57; social housing 72
Eurobarometer on Discrimination 68
EuroMed Association Agreements (EMAAs) 63, 64
European Central Bank (ECB) 93
European Commission 2, 4–5, 7–8, 85, 162, 188; animal welfare 136, 146–7, 148, 151–2, 156, 158–9; Annual Report

on application of Charter 23, 70; Charter compatibility assessments (CCAs) 23, 24, 44; disabilities, staff members with 72–3; economic crisis 184; El Salvador 185; environmental integration 110–13, 115–16, 134–5; equality mainstreaming 60–1, 64, 65–6, 67, 68–73, 74, 78–9, 81; ex post evaluation 69, 71, 81; Explanatory Memoranda 23, 24; fundamental rights mainstreaming 7, 14, 16, 17, 22–5, 30, 31, 33, 34, 36, 38, 39, 40, 43, 44, 61; gender mainstreaming 15–16, 21, 48–9, 60–1, 64; horizontal consumer clause 3, 125–6, 129–31, 133; horizontal social clause 93, 94; impact assessments (IAs) 23, 24–5, 33, 43, 44, 65–6, 67, 69, 72, 75, 81, 88, 131, 134–5, 153–5, 185–6; infringement proceedings 71; Interservice Consultation (CIS) 23–4; Legal Service 24, 43, 44; non-discrimination clauses 69; personal data and EDPS 38, 39, 40; problem definition stage 25; White paper on the future of Europe (2017) 178

European Convention on Human Rights (ECHR) 29, 42

European Council: environmental integration 109–10

European Data Protection Supervisor (EDPS) 14, 36–43, 44, 186; advice on data protection vs advice on other fundamental rights 42–3; Court of Justice of EU 37, 38; expert advice of highest quality 39; explaining methodology and creating accountability 39–40; integrity 40; involvement all along legislative process 40–1, 43; legal framework 36–8; lessons from 38–41; pragmatism 41, 43; proactiveness 40; selectiveness 39; transparency 41, 43

European Economic and Social Committee (EESC) 14, 44; horizontal consumer clause 128–9; influence/impact of 32–4, 44; institutional mechanisms for taking Charter into account 31–2; legal framework 30–1; Opinions 30–1, 32, 33, 34; selectiveness 39

European Institute for Gender Equality 186

European neighbourhood policy 148

European Ombudsman 72–4, 81, 186

European Parliament 85; access for people with disabilities to EU institutions 73; animal welfare 147–8; association agreements 62–3; Directorate General for Impact Assessment and European Added Value 27; EDPS 37, 40, 41; environmental integration 110–13; equality mainstreaming 62–3, 66, 73, 74–5, 78–9, 81; fundamental rights mainstreaming 7, 14, 16, 26–7, 28, 30, 31, 32, 34, 37, 40, 41, 44; horizontal consumer clause 129, 132–3; impact assessments 66, 75, 81; Legal Service 26, 44; LIBE Committee (Committee on Civil Liberties, Justice and Home Affairs) 26; Rule 36 26; trialogues 26–7, 28

European Pillar of Social Rights 46, 47–8, 53, 85

European Social Fund (ESF) 91–2, 101–2

Eurozone 93–4, 179n77, 180, 184

expert bodies/agencies with advisory role 44; European Data Protection Supervisor (EDPS) 14, 36–43, 44; Fundamental Rights Agency (FRA) *see separate entry*

expression and information, freedom of 96–7

external relations 59, 61, 160, 161, 162, 167, 168–9, 170, 174, 175, 176, 179, 182; Cotonou Agreement 63–4; EuroMed Association Agreements (EMAAs) 63, 64; European neighbourhood policy 148; free trade agreements 148; GSP+ scheme 184–5

fair trial 18

female genital mutilation 64

feminism 47–8, 50–1, 53

Finland 49

fishing/fisheries 120, 152

flexibility clause (Art 352 TFEU) 151

flexible working 53

food 155; labelling 147; safety 154

foot-and-mouth disease vaccines 144–5

free movement 114, 116, 118, 134, 135; animal welfare 141–4, 146, 149, 157, 158; of goods 141–4, 146; services 99–101, 187

free trade agreements 148

FREMP (Fundamental Rights, Citizenship and Free Movement of Persons) Working Party 29

Fundamental Rights Agency (FRA) 7, 14, 16–17, 34–6, 43, 44, 186; Committee of the Regions 34; Council of the European Union 28; European

Economic and Social Committee 34; European Parliament 27; legislative scrutiny competence 35–6, 44; Multiannual Framework (MAF) 34, 35; police and judicial cooperation 35; selectiveness 39; tasks 34; toolkits 40
fundamental rights mainstreaming 7, 9, 14, 44, 61, 182, 185, 186; 'classic obligations': respect, protect and fulfil 18–19, 20; mechanisms to implement 22–43; nature of 18–22; obligation to promote 19–22, 33–4; origins and meaning of 14–17; participation 17; proactive approach 17; rights and principles 19–20; systematic consideration 17; timing 17

GATT (General Agreement on Tariffs and Trade) 156–7
gender mainstreaming 2, 9–10, 15–16, 45–8, 53–4, 60–1, 69, 127, 183, 188; Art 8 TFEU 47, 49, 63, 77, 79; Art 10 TFEU 47, 49, 58–9, 60, 64, 77; concept 48–50, 53; Cotonou Agreement 63–4; Court of Justice 77–8; difficult process 50–3; direct and indirect discrimination 45; EuroMed Association Agreements (EMAAs) 64; European Institute for Gender Equality 186; feminist reading 47–8, 50–1, 53; funding 71; gender budgeting 50; impact assessments (IAs) 25, 50, 66, 68; LGBTI people 68; resistance 51, 53; snow clearing from roads 52; work-life balance 47, 51–3
general principles of EU law 127, 128, 145, 159, 160; consistency 168–9, 179; definition 168
GSP+ scheme 184–5

health/healthcare 56, 62, 63–4, 66, 74, 94–9, 101, 103–4, 182, 188; animal welfare 138, 141–3, 146, 154, 157; consumers 131; *see also* horizontal social clause
Hernández Bataller, Bernardo 128–9
HIV/AIDS 64
horizontal consumer clause 11, 123–4, 183, 188; adjectives, use of 126; in CJEU's case law and EU's legislative practice 131–3, 186; Commission's approach to 129–31; genesis, legal meaning and normative content of 124–8; impact assessments (IAs) 25, 66, 131; potential utility of 133–5; practical meaning of 128–9
horizontal social clause 3, 4, 10–11, 83–7, 101–4, 184, 185–6, 187, 188; constraints falling upon EU institutions and Member States 87–9; ECJ practice: clause and objectives of general interest 94–9; impact assessments (IAs) 25, 66; legal basis 89–90; overriding reasons 99–101; regulatory practice 90–4
housing 57, 71–2; ICESCR: right to adequate 18n25
human dignity 55, 84
humanitarian assistance 63

impact assessments (IAs) 23, 24–5, 33, 43, 44, 69, 72, 74, 75–6, 79, 81, 88, 185; animal welfare 153–5; consumer integration 25, 66, 131; environmental integration 25, 66, 113, 134–5; European Parliamentary Research Service (EPRS) 75; posted workers 185–6; and relative impact of constitutionalisation of equality mainstreaming 65–8; social clause 25, 66
indigenous community: Inuit 156
indirect discrimination 80; direct and 45
industrial policy 181
information: animal welfare 147; campaigns 54; CFR Art 11: freedom of expression and 96; consumers 131, 133, 147; sharing 34
infrastructure works and animal welfare 155
internal market *see* single market/internal market
international human rights law 20
International Monetary Fund (IMF) 93
intersecting inequalities 80, 82
Islamophobia 67
Italy 71–2

judicial cooperation 35

land-system integrity 108
legal aid 18
lesbian, gay, bisexual, transgender and intersex (LGBTI) people 68, 74, 75
liberalism 86
Lisbon Strategy 66
loyalty *see* cooperation/loyalty, principle of sincere

Maastricht Treaty 1, 162, 164, 165, 166
macroeconomic adjustment programs 93–4
margin of appreciation 115
margin, discretionary 98, 145, 169

maritime and inland waterways transport 70
market-correction 30
market-making 30
maternity leave 52
media 122
Member States 4, 171, 172; animal welfare 3, 136, 137, 140–1, 146, 147–8, 159; competences 5–6, 57, 59, 102–3, 104, 172, 173–5, 180; environmental integration 109, 115, 116–21, 122; equality mainstreaming 56, 57–8, 59, 63, 64, 65, 67, 70, 72, 75, 77–8; fundamental rights mainstreaming 14, 18, 19, 20, 28, 29, 34; horizontal consumer clause 129, 133–4; horizontal social clause 89, 92–4, 99–101, 102–3, 104; principle of sincere cooperation/ loyalty 117, 118, 129, 172, 173, 174, 175
merger control 131
methodology/checklist/toolkit 22, 23–4, 29, 39–40, 44, 72, 121–2, 154
migrants/migration 63, 67, 80, 183
minorities 65, 67
mobile apps 41
Morocco 63
Multiannual Framework (MAF) 34, 35
multiculturalism 65
multiple discrimination 57, 59, 74, 80
Muslims 67

national constitutional law 20
national parliaments 167, 174, 183
natural mineral waters 95, 96–7
Nice Treaty 4, 162–3
non-discrimination *see* discrimination
Norway 156

objectives of Union: Maastricht and Lisbon 165–6
Ombudsman 72–4, 81, 186
open market economy 84–5
opt-outs 176–7
ordinary legislative procedure 31, 76
ordoliberalism 84
overload, mainstreaming 54

Pakistan 184
participation: fundamental rights mainstreaming 17
paternity leave 52, 53
path dependency 113, 122
planetary boundaries 107–9, 110, 116, 120, 122
Plaumann formula 157, 158
police and judicial cooperation 35
posted workers 99–101, 185–6, 187
poverty 53, 92, 102
precautionary approach 108, 109
preemption principle 140–1, 142, 143, 175
pregnancy 52
privacy 36, 42
Prodi, Romano 22–3
proportionality 82, 95, 97, 100, 142, 145, 147, 149, 151, 166–7, 169, 187
public morality and animal welfare 143–4, 156–8, 159

racial or ethnic origin discrimination 55, 58, 61, 62–3, 67, 69, 70, 74, 127; positive action 57; social housing 72
radicalisation 67
regulatory burdens 25
religion or belief 65; animal welfare 3, 136, 147; discrimination 55, 58, 62, 67, 78, 82, 127
remedy, right to effective 18, 78, 158
renewables-based, circular and just economy 122
researchers 70
Roma 71–2
Romania 71–2

seal products 139–40, 149–50, 151, 156–8, 159
self-employment 56
sex discrimination 55, 56, 58, 62, 76, 127; positive action 57–8
sexual orientation discrimination 55–6, 58, 62, 127; Court of Justice 76, 82
Single European Act (SEA) 1, 161–2, 165, 181–2
single market/internal market 130, 131, 133, 134, 135, 164, 181–2; animal welfare 4, 136, 138–9, 140, 141, 146, 147, 148–51, 152–3, 158, 178, 184; culture 183, 184; posted workers 185–6
snow clearing from roads 52
social cohesion 4, 67
social exclusion/inclusion 3, 62, 72, 102, 165; *see also* horizontal social clause
social market economy 4, 84–5, 125
social protection 3, 18, 56, 62; *see also* horizontal social clause
social security 18, 56
socio-economic rights 18
socioeconomic status 74
soft law 4, 37, 50, 85

solidarism 86
special legislative procedure 31
standard of living, adequate 18
state aid 155, 184
stereotypes 76
structural funds 51, 61, 64, 71, 72; European Social Fund (ESF) 91–2, 101–2
students 70
subsidiarity 149, 151, 166–7, 169, 174
surrogacy 79
sustainable development 2, 53, 54, 105, 164; definition 107; environmental integration and goal of 106–9, 134; potential of Art 11 TFEU 109–21; realising potential of Art 11 TFEU 121–2
Sweden 49

terrorism 67
third-country nationals 70
tobacco 91, 95, 97–8, 103–4
toolkit/checklist/methodology 22, 23–4, 29, 39–40, 44, 72, 121–2, 154
trade 46–7, 51, 53; animal welfare 136, 137, 140–4, 148, 151, 156–7, 159; *see also* business; competition; single market/internal market
training 29, 43, 62, 64, 70; *see also* horizontal social clause
transparency 44, 125, 171; confidentiality 43; EDPS 41, 43
transport 70, 152; of animals from EU to destination in third country 153; of animals for slaughter 142–3
trialogues 26–7, 28
Tunisia 63

United Kingdom 178; Brexit 178, 180
United Nations: mainstreaming human rights 14–15, 16; Sustainable Development Goals (SDGs) 106, 122; World Conference on Women (Beijing, 1995) 2, 15, 48–9

values 46, 55, 83–5, 94, 170–1; accommodating diversity as meta-value 65
veterinary medicinal products 155
Vitorino, António 22–3
vulnerable consumers 134; use of adjective 126
vulnerable groups 67, 68

waterways transport, maritime and inland 70
work-life balance 47, 51–3
World Trade Organization (WTO) 137, 156–7

xenophobia 69

FSC
www.fsc.org
MIX
Papier | Fördert
gute Waldnutzung
FSC® C083411

Kolibri 360 GmbH
Ferdinand-Jühlke-Straße 7
99095 Erfurt, Deutschland
produktsicherheit@kolibri360.de